EYES

of an

ANGEL

To Elisa,

The truth is in your heart!

Paul Elder
05/06/07

PAUL ELDER

EYES

of an

ANGEL

Soul Travel, Spirit Guides, Soul Mates,
and the Reality of Love

HAMPTON ROADS
PUBLISHING COMPANY, INC.

Hampton Roads Publishing Company, Inc.
1125 Stoney Ridge Road
Charlottesville, VA 22902

434-296-2772
fax: 434-296-5096
e-mail: hrpc@hrpub.com
www.hrpub.com

If you are unable to order this book from your local
bookseller, you may order directly from the publisher.
Call 1-800-766-8009, toll-free.

Library of Congress Cataloging-in-Publication Data

Elder, Paul, 1951-
Eyes of an angel : soul travel, spirit guides, soul mates, and the reality
of love / Paul Elder.
    p. cm.
Summary: "A spiritual memoir by a former CTV news reporter, it explores
his personal near-death and psychic experiences, introduces the idea that
there is spiritual guidance available to everyone and we are never alone.
The book explores reunions with departed souls, the discovery of soulmates,
and past lives, as well as our purpose in the universe"--Provided by publisher.
    ISBN 1-57174-429-0 (5-1/2x8-1/2 tp : alk. paper)
    1. Astral projection. 2. Guides (Spiritualism) 3. Elder, Paul, 1951-
I. Title.
    BF1389.A7E43 2005
    133.9--dc22
                        2004028314

ISBN 1-57174-429-0
10 9 8 7 6 5 4 3 2
Printed on acid-free paper in the United States

Contents

Acknowledgments

There are many people who have contributed to the completion of this book to whom I am eternally grateful. To Robert Friedman, Frank DeMarco, Ginna Colburn, and the entire staff at Hampton Roads Publishing Company, I offer my sincerest appreciation. Sarah, Richard, Grace and all the rest—thank you for your dedication to excellence.

To an extraordinary agent and friend, Bill Gladstone of Waterside Productions in California, thank you for your enthusiasm and faith.

To my friend and colleague, Skip Atwater, author, former Operations Officer of U.S. Army Intelligence "Project Stargate," and current Research Director at The Monroe Institute, I offer my heartfelt gratitude and admiration.

To Dale Graff, author, and former civilian director of "Project Stargate," thank you, Dale, for your friendship and tutoring.

To my friend, Will Murray, prolific author and extraordinary writer, thank you so much for your assistance, advice and tutoring. I am forever grateful for your guidance and friendship.

To Laurie Monroe, Darlene Miller, and all my fellow facilitators and friends at The Monroe Institute, in Virginia, thank you for your years of friendship and support.

To Paul Bernstein, editor of the International Association for Near Death Studies magazine, *Vital Signs*, thank you for your encouragement. To the people of Swift Current, Saskatchewan, Canada: thank you for your trust and faith over these many years.

To my friends, Steve Garrison, Ron Reinhart, and my sister, Josie McGuire. Thank you for spending so much of your time reviewing my manuscripts, providing valuable feedback, and keeping me on track. And to the rest of my brothers and sisters, Dale, Joe, Marg, Evalina, Pauline, Eva, Anna, Elizabeth, and Lena, thank you for sharing your love.

I would also like to offer special thanks to numerous other dear friends for their reviews and encouragement: Margaret Whelan, Ariane de Bonvoisin, Duff Marshal, Carol Hansen, Donalee Campbell, David Hughes, Tom Coates, Winston Fuller, Ed Thrall, Tamera Knobel, Celeen Vizer, and Professor Buddy Wynn. Thank you all for your wonderful contributions.

Thank you, Patricia, for returning once again to this world to touch my heart and soul, reminding me of our greater purpose and ultimate goal.

And to a most wonderful, gentle soul, thank you, Lisa, for all your love and support.

And finally, I want to thank three very special people who have shared with me a lifetime of love, laughter and tears. Candace, Stacey, and David, you will always be my special Angels, and I will love you forever.

Eyes of an Angel—
"Windows to Your Soul"

This world we live in is truly a remarkable place: so many mysteries to solve, incredible wonders to marvel at, and so much to learn. But, all things considered, what's even more astonishing than the power of the human mind is the fact that none of this is new. We already know the answers to life's mysteries, we've only forgotten. It's all there, just below the surface, tugging at us, begging us to take the time to look. And the best place to start is in your own eyes, and the eyes of your loved ones.

Here's a common experience. You're meeting someone for the first time. Reaching out to shake his hand, you glance briefly into his eyes. And then a strange thing happens—you get the oddest feeling you've met this person before. Another place perhaps, another time? Even though you're sure it's not the case, you're left with an inner turmoil, a fluttering in your heart that you can't explain. Perplexed, you shrug it off as some strange quirk of the mind. But, wait a minute! What if it isn't just some weird anomaly? What if there *is* more to it than meets the eye?

It's often said that our eyes are the windows to our souls. What if this were true? What if we could somehow learn to recognize and identify these subtle, innocuous feelings and intuitions? Would it not completely alter our perception of the world? Could it possibly lead to a better, more understanding, loving universe?

Eyes of an Angel addresses some of the most revealing and astonishing aspects of the relationships binding each and every soul in our universe. It's the story of the evolution of consciousness of an avowed skeptic to that of an ardent spiritual believer. It's the kind of story I wouldn't have believed had it not happened to me.

Within these pages you'll find the details of some remarkable conversations and messages from the spirit realms—concepts, thoughts, and lessons from souls who have been through it all before, but choose, out of love, to help the rest of us remember who we really are and where we're heading. These conversations and events really did take place. Since there wasn't, obviously, a way to record the actual dialogues, their reproduction was dependent on my reconstruction of the material. To the best of my ability, I've tried to accurately present these experiences and messages just as they happened. It is my sincerest hope that from within these timeless messages of the soul, you too might recognize your own truths and pathways.

True in every respect, *Eyes of an Angel* offers a detailed, first-hand account of a remarkable spiritual adventure. It's a story about soul travel, angels, spirit guides, and soul mates. But most of all, it's a story about everlasting love.

1

The Awakening

What would you do if you suddenly awoke to find yourself floating near the ceiling of your bedroom? It happened to me, and it changed my life.

I first heard the term "out-of-body experience" in the summer of 1979. A local television station had broadcast an interview with a man named Robert Monroe. He had written a popular book, *Journeys Out of the Body*. Intrigued by the incredible story he told, I borrowed a copy from the library and read it from cover to cover.

In the book, Monroe claimed that in his early forties he began to spontaneously leave his body in spirit form while remaining fully conscious. He gave fantastic detailed descriptions of traveling in this spirit body to places on Earth as well as into the spirit world itself.

When the experiences first began, Monroe was afraid that he had become ill, or was actually losing his mind. Submitting himself to intense medical and psychiatric examinations, he was relieved when all tests found him to be healthy and normal. Eventually he just quit worrying about it. Meticulously documenting his experiences, he decided to take advantage of the continuing phenomenon, pursuing every opportunity to explore and learn.

"Fascinating story," I thought, "but the guy's obviously a brick short of a load."

Having been raised in a poor farm family with ten brothers and sisters, my grasp on reality was far too entrenched in the physical world to give this kind of fantasy much sway. Returning the book to the library, I soon forgot all about it.

To my amazement, eleven years later, my perception of reality would be changed forever.

This life-changing event took place at the end of a long and hectic week. It was late Friday night and, looking forward to a quiet weekend, I sat at my desk thinking about the recent events that were complicating my life. It had been more than five years since I was first elected to city council, and everything in my life was running smoothly. Then, one day, some important government people showed up, asking me to make a big commitment. They wanted me to run as a candidate in an upcoming election to the Legislature. With more than a few reservations, I had agreed to let my name stand. But it wasn't long before I was second-guessing my decision.

With only days remaining before the nomination meeting, I waged an internal battle. Was this what I wanted to do? Would it be good for me? With all the time I'd have to spend away, would our family life suffer? Would it be worth it? Finally, around 1:30 in the morning I gave up and sleepily crawled into bed, vowing to sleep until noon. The second my head hit the pillow, it was lights out.

The next thing I knew, I was wide-awake. But something was terribly wrong. In dazed confusion, I scrambled to get my bearings. What I was seeing was impossible! Instead of being in my bed, I was floating like a balloon near the ceiling, bumping lightly against its stippled surface.

Disoriented, a landslide of possibilities flooded my mind. There had to be a rational explanation. Below me in bed were two sleeping bodies that seemed so familiar I couldn't divert my attention from them. As I looked down, a stunning realization hit me: the woman in the bed was my wife, and the guy sleeping beside her was me.

This couldn't be happening. Here I was, floating around my bedroom ceiling, without a clue as to how I'd gotten there. Closing my eyes, I shook my head, praying that when I reopened them, everything would be back to normal again. But nothing changed. I was still floating in midair.

My thoughts reeling, I knew I wasn't dreaming. But there was another possibility. I began to wonder if I had somehow died. It didn't seem likely, though; I felt completely normal, my mind had never been clearer.

The memory of Robert Monroe's book flashed into my awareness. Maybe, I thought, Monroe wasn't crazy after all. This was absolutely real! Although it seemed beyond belief, somehow the experience felt strangely familiar. It had the feeling of routine, like I had done this many times before. I knew I was just now returning from some sort of journey, but I had no idea where I might have been.

As this insight filtered into my mind, a strange calming sensation flooded through me. Most of the fear and apprehension I had been entertaining slowly evaporated into the surrounding darkness. Far from feeling out-of-sorts, I could not remember when I had ever felt better. How could I have felt better? I was doing the impossible—I was flying.

Although it seemed such a familiar feeling, it was, nevertheless, unsettling. After a few moments I wondered if I shouldn't be returning to my body. However, I wasn't sure how to make that happen or, for that matter, if it was possible. I didn't have a lot of time to worry about it, though, because with just that simple thought, I began to slowly descend towards the bed.

To my dismay, when I finally came to a stop, I wasn't in my body. Instead, I hovered beside the bed, about two feet above the floor. At first, I worried about having somehow missed the target, but within moments my concerns subsided as I quickly became engrossed in studying this quiet, peaceful form beside me.

There didn't seem to be anything unusual or out of place. My body appeared to be in a normal sleeping state. Thinking how odd this was, I chuckled in nervous amazement. Here I was, staring at my own face from an outside perspective, examining it as if it belonged to someone else. It occurred to me that other than looking into a mirror, we never actually see our own faces, so this felt more than a little strange.

In the darkness, my face seemed a lot older than the one I usually saw in the mirror. It looked weary and surprisingly gray and colorless. The more I thought about it, the more I began to feel compassion for my seemingly abandoned body, and I had to admit that I should probably be taking better care of it.

Emotions building inside me, I thought I had better try again to get back into my body. To my surprise, at the very thought of it, I simply floated across the two foot span, and just like that, I was back inside. For the briefest moment, I felt faint. A spinning dizziness overcame me, everything faded to black, and then, with a startling jolt, I opened my eyes.

Back in my body, I could feel my thoughts slowing down. Like a genie being sucked back into a bottle, I felt squeezed and confined. And I didn't like it at all.

As I lay in bed lamenting my increasing heaviness, I became aware of a strange vibration gently rocking me. Every molecule in my body seemed about to burst with this bizarre, bubbling electrical energy. As I focused on the vibrations, they began to surge in waves back and forth from my head to feet. It was the most energized, exciting physical feeling I had ever had. My body felt like it was expanding, contracting, and rolling with the sensations. Waves of energy flooded my awareness. I could not conceive of anything more strange or delightful.

For several minutes I lay analyzing the intense energy until the feeling in my arms and legs returned. I tried to move, but the lower part of my body felt heavy, almost paralyzed. Finally managing to turn my head, I noticed the time on my nightstand clock. It was 3:02 A.M. I had been asleep for only 90 minutes.

Closing my eyes, I lay in bed struggling with my emotions, my mind desperately searching for a rational explanation. When I began to wonder why it happened, a feeling of melancholy came over me. "My God," I begged. "What on earth is happening to me?"

The word "God" stuck in my mind. It had been a long time since I'd paid much attention to God, but for some reason I felt the most compelling urge to be thankful for His blessings. As I contemplated the gift of this experience, love and gratitude slowly overwhelmed me. Tears began trailing down my cheeks.

In this euphoria, my mind began to wander. Dreamlike images of events in my life took shape and then quickly dissolved. And there were faces, so many faces. Some I knew, but most I couldn't place even though they seemed familiar. I was becoming lost in my thoughts when a sudden snap of my body brought me back to the present.

Opening my eyes, my attention was drawn to the ceiling. My eyes had to be playing tricks on me. Not only could I see the stipple on the ceiling but I could also see right through to the clouds and stars in the night sky. Hoping to correct this obvious anomaly, I closed my eyelids tightly and then quickly opened them again. But nothing changed.

My senses seemed to be reaching overload. My heart was pounding with excitement, while powerful vibrations continued flowing through my body. I couldn't imagine a more incredible sensation, but, at the same time, I worried where it was leading.

A sudden sharp surge in the vibrations gripped my attention. The electrical tingling became so intense I began to wonder if it would be possible to leave my body again. The more I thought about it, the more convinced I became that I could.

I had just begun to consider my next step, when another wave of energy swept through me. My awareness seemed to expand outward until I thought I could feel the air pressure increasing in the room. And then it hit me! A chill ran through my body. I had the creepiest feeling that I wasn't alone. Someone was watching me. I sensed the presence of other energies or beings around me. Appearing as pinpoints of light, they seemed to be everywhere. I started to panic. The thought of having unknown spirits in my room terrified me. I wanted so desperately to float out of my body again but there was no way I could force myself to do so with these "things" around.

Summoning up every ounce of courage, I projected a thought into the room asking the intruders to please leave. I waited, but nothing happened. The feeling persisted. Again I asked, this time more forcefully. Still nothing. With mounting anxiety, I mentally yelled into the room, demanding that everyone leave. There was no change. Finally, in desperation, I found myself returning to the Catholic teachings of my youth, and I prayed to God and Jesus to help and protect me. Incredibly, the moment the words became articulated in my mind, I felt a sudden change around me. In an instant every single unwanted presence in the room blinked out and disappeared, leaving me alone in the darkness.

Elated, I thought of floating up into the air, and that's all it took. A surge of energy rushed through my body while a high-pitched sound began to resonate in the center of my head, spreading through me. With the sound of air hissing in my ears, I felt a slight wobbling sensation, but then firmly and steadily rose into the air. The rush of vibrations and sounds, so consuming just a moment before, quickly faded as I separated from my physical body and floated silently to the ceiling.

As I hovered in midair, trying desperately to make sense of it all, a tidal wave of understanding swept through me. Throughout most of my life, I had doubted the existence of God. The God that we were taught about as children seemed an all-too-human, punishing, and vengeful being. I could not fathom nor accept a God like that, and decided I wanted no part of it. To me, the concept was nothing more than a fabrication by organized religion to keep control of the masses.

Since childhood, the image of God that stuck in my mind was that of a stern-faced, bearded old man—someone to be feared. But, as these thoughts flooded through me, I suddenly understood that my long-held perception of God was wrong.

Although I had no idea where these mental images originated, insights continued to fill my mind. The truth became clear. I knew about God. I had merely forgotten. God is the collective consciousness, the universal power of love and creation that gives life and meaning to everything in the universe. I found this simple revelation emotionally humbling.

How, I wondered, could I have veered so far off course? Surrounded by the beauty of creation, how could I have lost this truth? Floating in my body of energy, I also knew that this is who we really are. This pure, cosmic energy is our natural state, and the loving, powerful vibration within all of us is the vibration of God.

Returning my awareness to my floating body, I discovered that I didn't have to actually turn my head in order to see in any direction. My visual field was a full 360 degrees and was attained instantly with just a thought. As I marveled at this, the urge to test the boundaries of my new reality grew, and I began to wonder if it would be possible to float around to other parts of the house. I slowly rotated my body in midair until I faced the doorway. Setting my intention to coast out of the bedroom, and impelled by just that thought, I began moving effortlessly toward the door.

Approaching the doorway, I realized that I was too high to make it under the doorframe. But it was too late. My head and upper body were on a collision course with the wall above the doorway. Closing my eyes, I braced for the impact. And then an amazing thing happened: there was no impact. I floated through the wall like it wasn't there. The reality of this seemingly impossible act left me stunned. I had just gone through a solid wall without the slightest resistance. In disbelief, I spun around, surveying the wall as I descended to the floor in the hallway outside the bedroom, about ten feet from the door.

Coming to a gentle landing, I could feel my feet sinking into the rug. I felt the fibers of the carpet, the underlay, and finally the smoothness of the plywood below.

Motionless, I stared in wonder at the wall I had just floated through. It seemed inconceivable. If I hadn't seen and felt it, I wouldn't have believed it. But I couldn't deny the experience. It had really happened.

Standing in the hallway, I could see through the doorway into the bedroom. There, in bed, some thirty feet away, lay my physical body. I tried to rationalize how this could be possible. How could I be standing in the hallway, completely whole, thinking and feeling, while my body including my brain—the organ supposedly required for thinking—was in a different location? Pondering this dilemma, I was surprised by the sound of a soft, whispered voice.

"You are not your brain. You are not your body. You are continuous conscious energy."

Startled, I spun around. No one was there. I had no idea where the voice had come from. It felt different than my own inner voice, yet natural and familiar. The more I thought about it, the more convinced I became that it had to be only my own inner thoughts. "Just my imagination," I told myself. "What else could it be?"

Putting the question out of my mind, I decided to continue the tour. I was standing in the upper hall balcony looking down a flight of stairs into the open living room below. Reaching out with my right hand, I gripped the rounded top of the railing post leading to the stairway. The hard, smooth wooden ball felt completely normal. But when I put some weight on it to adjust my stance, my hand suddenly pushed right through the post. The feeling was incredible! Astonished, I had to try it again and again. Each time, my hand swished through the "solid" column like it was made of water.

Intent on continuing my excursion, I finally pulled myself away from this mesmerizing diversion. Looking down the stairway, I paused, wondering whether I would float down the stairs or end up falling flat on my face. Bracing myself, I pushed off. A surge of energy swept through me, and ever so gently I lifted off the floor. I gawked around unsteadily as I slowly floated higher into the air. Traveling a couple of feet above the floor, I cautiously made my way down the stairway, heading for the landing below. I prepared to touch down, and then just as my toes brushed the carpet, I felt a jolt, and in an instant, I was back in my body.

The vibrations had disappeared and the paralyzing numbness in my legs was gone. Wide-awake, I sat up in bed. The clock on my nightstand showed 3:05 A.M. Less than three minutes had passed since I decided to leave my body. It didn't seem possible. So much had occurred, I thought it could have been a half hour.

Unable to contain my excitement, I shook my wife awake, blurting out every detail. I didn't care if she thought I was crazy. This was the most fantastic thing that had ever happened to me, and I had to tell someone. To my surprise, Candace believed every word. In fact she was excited about the possibilities. "That is so amazing," she gushed. "I'm really jealous. Why couldn't it happen to me?" Candace had always been more receptive to this type of thing than I, and I was thankful for her open mind. Had our positions been reversed I doubted I would have believed the story.

Having had so little sleep, I was surprised that I was no longer tired. Pumped with energy, I jumped out of bed and got dressed. I put on a pot of coffee, and listlessly read through a couple of magazines, returning occasionally to my living room and bedroom to retrace the experience.

Although my rational mind wanted to dismiss the event as some sort of aberration or hallucination, I knew that would not be possible. This had been more real than anything I had ever experienced. My senses had been working at hyper-speed and sensitivity. I had been able to see and feel more clearly than I had ever imagined possible.

The memory of the snapping, jerking feeling I experienced upon re-entering my body kept churning in my mind. There was something familiar about it, but I couldn't place it. Then it suddenly dawned on me. I had felt that jolt thousands of times. Often when I was falling asleep, especially if I had been really tired, a jolt would bring me back to consciousness. How many times had I watched my wife and children make that same jerking reaction as they were falling asleep? I wondered if it was our spirits returning to our bodies that caused the jolt. Could it be that we all leave our bodies every time we fall asleep? I had to find answers to these questions.

When morning arrived, my decision was made. I telephoned the party president to inform him that I would be withdrawing my name from the candidacy. This was not the path I should be following. There was new meaning and direction in my life, and it had nothing to do with politics.

The library was the first stop on my morning agenda. Candace and I were sitting in the parking lot waiting when the doors finally opened. We borrowed every book we could find on paranormal and spiritual subjects. Fortunately, they had a copy of Robert Monroe's book *Journeys Out of the Body,* which we snapped up. I wanted to learn everything possible about the experience. I needed to know why it happened, but more importantly, I needed to know if I could make it happen again.

Monroe's book was even more intriguing the second time around. This time, it didn't seem so far-fetched. My own experience had opened my mind to the possibilities and power of the human spirit. This was something I could learn to do.

Although I hadn't yet realized the impact of my out-of-body experience, my world was changed. I was no longer sure about who I was or who I should be, but I knew one thing: I was on a mission, and I couldn't wait to see where it would lead me.

2

Where Was God?

I was born and raised on a farm in the west-central plains of Canada. My parents, along with everyone we knew in a forty-mile radius, were German Catholics. They worked hard all week and went to church on Sundays. That was the only day that we kids got a break from the never-ending cycle of farm chores.

Our mother, Anne, was a creature of habit. She liked the security of a routine, but mastering the rhythm method of birth control was apparently not her forte. She had eight baby girls in a row and then, when she figured out what was causing it, promptly gave birth to three baby boys. I was the tenth of 11 children.

Growing up in such a large family wasn't easy. These were the '50s. The world was recovering from the Great Depression and war. It was a time when large families were common. For many, there wasn't a lot of money to go around, but with 13 people in our house we seemed just a bit poorer than everyone else.

In the years of hand-me-down shoes, clothes, and schoolbooks, we often took life on the chin, sometimes bearing the brunt of cruel, hurtful remarks by our schoolmates. Nevertheless, probably the one thing that seemed to keep us going was our humor. When you don't have much, it helps if you can find a way to laugh at everything.

I'll never forget a schoolyard incident that happened when I was ten or eleven. A small convent of Catholic nuns operated our rural school. Classes were over for the day and, as my little brother, Dale, and I were walking across the playground, one of the nuns made a derogatory comment about how we looked like ragamuffins. Although embarrassed, I'd be damned if I was going to let it show.

"That's because we're poor, Sister," I sarcastically quipped. "Hell, it's a good thing we're boys or we'd have nothing to play with."

I couldn't believe what had just come out of my mouth. The silence was deafening. My ears and face burned as blood rushed to my head. The words echoed in my mind.

For a moment the good sister just stood there. I didn't think she had grasped what I had said, but my little brother couldn't contain himself. His hand shot up over his mouth to squelch an eruption of laughter. But it was too late.

The old nun didn't budge an inch. She just stood there in the schoolyard glaring at me for what seemed an eternity. Nervously, I glanced at my brother. Frozen in place, his hand was glued to his mouth. Tears were now running down his cheeks. It was all too surreal and funny. I couldn't believe the stunned look on the nun's face or the pathetic, muffled whimpering coming out of my brother. It was just too much. Dropping to my knees, I rolled, howling with laughter.

As expected, the rest of the afternoon did not go well for me. Unfortunately, the uptight nun didn't see the humor in my little stand-up routine. That wee bit of insolence earned me nine whacks with a leather belt across my backside—one for each remaining day of lent, wouldn't you know. Why couldn't I have waited with my smart mouth until it was a lot closer to Easter weekend?

We grew up, I suspect, like many other kids during the fifties and sixties, without any closeness to our parents. Our father was not the kind of person who could show a lot of love, or even much kindness for that matter. He probably would have considered that to be some kind of weakness.

For the most part, we grew up as a bunch of tough little realists. If we couldn't see it, hear it, or feel it, we couldn't believe it. So, although religion played a big part in our lives, and we were forced to go to church every Sunday, I wasn't really convinced there was a God. The lyrics of that old Blood, Sweat, and Tears song, "I swear there ain't no heaven, but I pray there ain't no hell," probably described my beliefs all too well.

My younger brother and I were forced by our parents to serve as altar boys until we were almost 16. That's when we finally rebelled, refusing to buy into the mind control of "hell fire and damnation." Although we would never dare talk about these things with our parents, we began to fervently resist the pressure of going to church to be preached at.

In those early years, the Catholic Church, and I suppose just about every other Christian denomination, preached "fear of the Lord" as a main plank in their religious dogma. If you did this or that, a merciless and vengeful God could fry your butt in Hell for the rest of eternity. My brother and I always had trouble with this concept. We were not about to believe that God—if there actually was a God—could possibly be so mean.

We had great difficulty believing what the nuns and the priests of the day were trying to teach us. They professed that there were basically two kinds of people in the world. There were the Catholics who would be going to Heaven, and then there were all those other people who weren't! These other people would undoubtedly be spending eternity in Hell or Purgatory, or maybe even a place called Limbo.

As young, impressionable boys, this was more than a bit unsettling to us. We had two young Presbyterian cousins who happened to be from the only non-Catholic family in the community. They were our good friends, and it made us very sad to think they were going to have to spend eternity in Limbo just because their parents weren't Catholic. We couldn't understand or accept the apparent injustices of our religion. At the very least, we desperately hoped that these things weren't true.

During our later teenage years my brother and I would occasionally go to church to please our mother, but after leaving home we rarely attended. We had seen far too much hypocritical behavior by the holier-than-thou "pillars of our community" to believe that going to church made you a good person. It seemed to me that most, if not all, of these rules were man-made. They couldn't be God's rules because every now and then the church would actually change them.

For example, back in the early 1960s, it was a "big-time sin" to eat meat on Fridays. If you did and were unlucky enough to die before you made it to confession, yours would be a most horrible fate. God would surely send you to Hell for eternity. What was equally amazing, though, was that many years later, they changed the rules and it was no longer a sin to eat meat on Fridays. One of my favorite comedians, George Carlin, had similar thoughts about this: "I always wondered," George would say, "what ever happened to all of those dudes doing time in Hell on a meat rap?"

Beyond one significant event, I think most of my childhood wasn't much different than that of a lot of other kids growing up in this era. This unusual incident took place on a warm Saturday in July of 1963, when I was 12 years old. It was an exciting day for my little brother and me. Our two cousins from the city had arrived for a weekend visit, and we had a lot of plans. My cousin Brian and I were best friends. We were the same age, we liked the same things, and we shared the same fantasies. Unfortunately we weren't able to spend a lot of time together, so whenever we had a chance to visit we tried to make the best of it. It was bound to be a fun weekend.

About a half mile from our farmhouse was a water reservoir the department of highways had dug beside a road. The purpose of these little ponds was twofold: they provided the contractors with the dirt they needed to build the road, and the remaining hole provided valuable storage for runoff water from the summer rains and melting spring snow.

Dale and I had been warned to stay away from the dugouts. We couldn't swim a stroke and had no one to teach us. Our cousins, however, had taken lots of swimming lessons in big swimming pools, and as a result were very good swimmers.

We hadn't planned on going near the overflowing dugout; we were just crossing a pasture looking for prairie dogs when one of the cousins noticed the pool of water. Tied to a stake at one end of the dugout was a small wooden raft our neighbor's kids had obviously abandoned. Well, it was just too tempting to pass up. Before long we were all aboard the raft, bobbing precariously, paddling around in the middle of the twelve-foot-deep pond.

We were having a great time until the older of the cousins discovered that my brother and I couldn't swim. Realizing we were afraid of water, he thought it would be good fun to violently rock the raft while the rest of us hung on for dear life.

On the wet, slippery planks, I lost my balance, and the next thing I knew I was toppling backwards into the water. Terrified, I didn't have the presence of mind to even try to swim. With numbing quickness, shock overcame me; my head slipped below the surface and, before I knew it, I was on my way to the bottom. In my panicked state, it wasn't long before the last bubbles of air had escaped me and my lungs filled with water.

I had always imagined that drowning would be a horrible way to die—the mental terror while one's lungs desperately screamed for air—but it wasn't like that at all. In fact, as soon as my lungs filled with water, the struggle ended. There was no more suffocating or fighting for air. Instead, an absolute peace came over me.

With my eyes wide open, I continued a slow descent. The water grew darker and darker, and soon I was up to my ankles in mud. After pausing there for a few seconds, I'm not sure why, but ever so slowly I began to float upwards. Within a few moments I was nearing the surface. I could see and feel the warm sunlight radiating into the water. My head briefly broke through, and then in a dreamlike state, without fear or panic, I began to sink again.

My senses numbing, I felt no particular discomfort, just the greatest urge to fall asleep. Soon I could feel my feet sinking again into the mud, and then everything seemed to grind to a halt. Time stood still as I hung suspended in the water, my surroundings fading. Too tired and sleepy to be concerned, I simply let go and drifted into the blackness.

The next thing I knew, I snapped back into consciousness, opening my eyes to an astonishing sight. I was being bathed in a shimmering kaleidoscope of soft, warm colors. Swirling and gyrating, they seemed to pass through my body into the core of my being. I knew I was still surrounded by water, but somehow I had gotten into a beautiful, comfortable bubble. It felt like I was inside a rainbow. Mysteriously, the colors seemed to be causing a wonderful vibrating sensation throughout my body, each shade carrying its own distinct frequency. Fanning my hands in front of me, I watched, in childish delight, the multicolored energy swirling through my fingers and hands, electrifying my senses.

I had never felt more alive and energized. In awe of the warmth and beauty of my surroundings, I sensed something important was happening—that I had somehow changed. It occurred to me that perhaps I had died. And for some unknown reason, I recalled the story of Tom Sawyer—the part when he was believed to have drowned in the Mississippi, but arrived home just in time to witness his own funeral.

Just as these thoughts settled in my mind I suddenly found myself shooting out of the water and into the air. A moment later I was hovering over the choir loft in the back of our church.

It felt so strange. There I was, floating around in our church, anxiously awaiting my own funeral. Then I noticed there wasn't a soul in the building. If this was my funeral, I thought, where were all the people? I would have expected to see my mom and dad, my brothers and sisters, and all of the other people who normally went to church. But no one was there, and I hadn't a clue what to make of it.

Fascinated, I floated over the empty pews marveling at the impossibility of the situation. I was flying—actually flying! And there didn't seem to be a darn thing holding me up. How could this be? I hadn't read anything about Tom Sawyer flying. Puzzled, I floated for several more moments, deep in thought.

Suddenly, I felt a violent convulsion. Spasms erupted through my stomach. The next thing I knew, I was back on the shore of the dugout spewing water from my lungs, gasping for air.

My face bouncing in the mud, cousin Brian had his arms locked around my waist, dangling me upside down, draining the water from my body. Sick to my stomach, I vomited for a couple of agonizing minutes.

When I finally began to collect my wits, I looked up to see the horrified faces of my brother and cousins. We were all, to some degree, in a state of shock. To make matters worse, we knew we were going to be in a heap of trouble when we got home.

We sat quietly beside the dugout, contemplating what had just happened. After a few moments, as if on cue, everyone started talking at once. Chances were we would get a good whipping if anyone found out about our little incident, so we made a pact to never tell a soul. Then we got up, brushed ourselves off, and walking as slowly as possible to dry our clothes, headed for home.

Pumped with fear and adrenaline, Brian wasn't feeling too well. He told me he had thought for sure that I was dead because I'd been under for such a long time. He had spent several terrifying minutes diving and groping around in the murky water. When he finally found me in the mud at the bottom, it took every ounce of energy he could muster to get me to the surface.

As Brian told me this, I put my arms around my little brother and hugged him. Dale had been deeply affected. Unable to speak, tears flowed down his freckled cheeks.

As we walked back to the farm, Brian and I lagged behind the other two. I told him about the strange things that happened while I was in the water, about my memories of Tom Sawyer's funeral, about floating midair in the church, and my surprise that there were no people in the building. Brian made a simple observation. Of course there wouldn't be any people in the church. It was four o'clock in the afternoon and Saturday to boot.

I told him about all the bright colors that surrounded me in the water. But what I was recounting seemed strange even to me. I remember saying "Jeez, I didn't know you could feel colors." Brian, however, didn't say much. Maybe he thought I had water on the brain or something because I'm sure this couldn't have sounded very rational.

I told him again about what it was like to fly. He listened quietly, and then as if he hadn't heard my comments, he questioned, "Tom Sawyer? Why would you be thinking of Tom Sawyer?" I admitted that I hadn't the slightest idea, but assured him that everything had seemed so real.

"Jesus, Paul," he scolded, "You scared the hell out of us. I couldn't find you. I was praying like crazy. It's a good thing you ain't dead, 'cause they'd sure be killing the rest of us when we got home."

Although exceedingly nervous, when we finally reached the farm, we tried to be as nonchalant as possible. But as twelve-year-olds, we were probably too nonchalant. It must have been obvious we were hiding something because it didn't take more than ten minutes before we were running for cover.

I can't remember who caved in, but the result was dramatic. After a lot of yelling, cussing, and recriminations, two kids were given a sound strapping on that day. Oddly enough, I was one of them.

It was, to say the least, a very strange experience. My little brother and cousins had been horrified, and our parents extremely upset. I, on the other hand, hadn't experienced it as a horrible thing at all. And I couldn't understand why everyone was so uptight. I was still alive and feeling just fine.

On thinking back to the event, it occurs to me that at no time in my young life did I ever attach to the experience any kind of spiritual or religious significance. Even though I had ended up in a church, it didn't seem to carry any consequence or lasting effect—at least that's what I thought at the time. Although I could never forget the incident, I didn't spend a lot of time thinking about it in the following years. I could not, however, have even begun to imagine the importance of this event until much later in my life.

Back then, I had been grateful to Brian for saving my life, and I told him so repeatedly. But not once did I think of thanking God. In retrospect, I'm glad that God doesn't hold grudges. Well, at least I hope He doesn't.

One of the great things about childhood on a farm is that life moves quickly. There are so many exciting things to do and lots of ways to get into trouble, so you don't spend a lot of time worrying or contemplating life. You just go out to the shed, build yourself a new slingshot, and try to improve your prowess as a marksman by shooting the glass insulators off the utility poles.

As far back as I can remember I always had a knack for getting my brother and myself into trouble. Often, the word "trouble" didn't even come close to it. Our mother didn't raise fools, but my brother and I seemed to excel at doing foolish things. By any account, it's remarkable we lived past our sixteenth birthdays.

Boredom, and sibling rivalry can lead kids to do dumb things, and on a warm, sunny day in the summer of 1966 we must have been as bored as anybody could get. We had been picking and hauling rocks from the fields, when our father announced that he had to drive 30 miles to a nearby town to pick up parts for the cultivator. And just like that, he drove off, leaving us stranded more than three miles from home. Fortunately, Dale and I had snuck along our .22-caliber rifle, which, for a while, gave us something to pass the time. But out in the middle of nowhere, we soon ran out of targets to shoot at, or things to amuse us.

Bored, we eventually ended up in the shade of an old abandoned farm building. Cradling the rifle like a marine on a mission, I made a slow pivot looking for something, anything, to shoot at. My brother suggested I looked like a dork and couldn't hit a damn thing anyway. As usual, that was more than enough to get things started. He was on his knees in the grass about 30 feet away, fiddling with a small piece of cedar roof shingle. I told him to hold the shingle up in the air and I'd show him what I could hit. He obviously didn't believe for a moment that I would act on such a crazy notion. He held up the shingle, a half-inch wide and a foot long. I shot it out of his hand. Letting out a couple of surprised expletives, he quickly struck back. "Alright, you bastard—my turn!"

This was becoming a bit serious. In Dale's mind, he was the Second Coming of Davy Crockett, but in reality he was a notoriously bad shot. Backing down in front of him was unthinkable, and there would be no purpose in arguing he was a terrible shot, because he would just call that a "chicken shit excuse."

Expecting to lose at least a finger, I finally held up the shingle. The gun sounded, and the little piece of wood snapped in my hand, and the game of "chicken" began. We passed the rifle back and forth. With each shot the shingle was whittled down until all that remained was a stub. We knew we'd have to find another target or one of us was going to be sorry.

Looking around, the only other thing we could find was an empty salmon tin. It was a standard tin, about three inches in diameter and an inch and a half high. However, in the tall grass, we couldn't find a decent place to set the tin to get a good shot at it. That's when I suggested I could easily shoot it off his head from where I was (about 30 feet away), but we might as well forget it, because he would be too chicken. "Bullshit," he said, placing the tin on his head.

My stomach muscles knotted. But with every impulse in my brain screaming, "Don't be crazy," I still found myself thinking, "Hell, there is no way I could miss from this distance." I slowly lowered the rifle to sight-in the tin. Immediately, Dale began to complain that it looked like the rifle barrel was pointed right between his eyes. I assured him that it was not, but sarcastically suggested that if it bothered him, he could just close his eyes. I should well have known the effect that that statement would have.

Eyes wide and unblinking, he steadied his stance. "Oh yeah," he yelled, "go ahead. Do it!"

My finger flexed. The shell exploded, and in an instant the can spun off his head.

Letting out a huge gasp, my brother then recited the five most horrifying words in the English language: "Okay, now it's my turn."

I couldn't believe the stupidity of the game we had gotten into. But it was too late. I was going to have to stand there and let my lousy-shot brother try to knock this little tin can off my head. I cussed myself for not having at least worn a hat, preferably one made of titanium.

There was no turning back. I was just about to place the can on my head when I had an idea. Reaching up, I fluffed up my long hair as high as I could. My brother, however, couldn't let this go unchallenged. "Chicken shit!" he jeered. My heart sank.

It was useless. There was no way I could get out of it. I put the tin back on my head and he lowered the rifle into position.

It looked like he was aiming too low; he had to be aiming too low. I could have sworn the barrel was centered right between my eyes. "Jesus," I hissed, "don't be pissin' around. You're aiming at least four inches too low."

"So, how does it feel?" he whispered, one eye peering down the sights.

The delight in his voice was more than I could bear. But there was no way I could back down.

"Quit your damn whining," he snarled. "I'm aiming right at the can."

Sweat now flooding from every pore, I wanted to throw up. I began to think how, in a strange and twisted way, I had gained a new respect for my brother. I was practically ready to faint. How in hell had he been able to stand still and let me shoot?

The abrupt sound of the exploding shell shattered the silence. I flinched as the empty tin twirled off my head.

My brother was now grinning like a horse eating thistles. I, however, thought I was about to have a heart attack. My knees almost gave out. "Okay," I wheezed. "It's a tie. That's enough. I have to take a leak."

We both relieved ourselves, and then, as we were zipping up, for some reason—nervousness, adrenaline, we didn't know why—we began to giggle, then laugh. Soon we were howling, joking about how ridiculous we looked at the moment of truth. Within a couple of minutes, though, our laughter and horseplay faded into an uneasy silence. We were both visibly shaking. With eyes wide as saucers, the insanity of the act we had just committed began to sink in. Without saying a word, we hugged each other and set off on our long walk home.

Following that day, we never again engaged in that degree of craziness and we never again intentionally put each other in harm's way. Well, almost never.

๛

Raised in virtual poverty, it seemed necessary for me to develop a practical attitude about most things in life. I quickly learned that nothing comes without a price, and the only way you're going to make it in this world is through hard work and sacrifice.

At an early age, I learned from my mother that if anything was worth doing, it was worth doing to the best of my ability. I learned the lessons of hard work almost to the point of obsession. Driven by two factors, my motivation for success was simple: I needed to succeed so when I grew up, I would have an easier life than my parents, and if I ever had kids, they would never have to know the agony and humiliation of being dirt poor.

By the time my brother and I reached the ages of 15 and 16, we were the only two children left at home. We had been born late in our parent's lives, so it felt like we were living with our grandparents. They were already in their late fifties and the generation gap grew increasingly wide.

Our mother, whom we loved dearly, hadn't had an easy life. Aside from the fact that she had been pregnant with one child after another for eight and a half years while coping with a brood of 11 kids, she had a husband who didn't spend a lot of time being caring or helpful. She would just bite her lip and do her best for us kids while going without so many things for herself. She never enjoyed anything close to a luxury. We had no running water, television, or a phone, but we never heard her complain. She was truly a saint.

One of my greatest disappointments in life was that I didn't have a father who would ever show an emotion other than anger. My brother and I would work our butts off trying to please him, but never once would he ever say, "Thanks" or "You did a good job." It seemed the only response we could elicit from him was criticism. At an early age we learned that we could never please our father. He always seemed to be angry, so we just stayed out of his way.

As a child, I did what I could to protect myself from hurt, and it didn't take long before a strong wall was built around my heart. I had learned early in life that the old nursery rhyme was wrong. It should have been changed to "Sticks and stones may break my bones, but *words can simply destroy me.*"

Sometimes when things became particularly repressive, as if to distance myself from the hurt, I would say to my brother and myself, "Quit feeling sorry for yourself and get over it." I would not understand the degree of hurt this would inflict upon me until much later in my life.

Now, don't get me wrong: If I had to do it over again, there's probably not a lot I would change. I am what I am precisely because of the hardships and lessons of my upbringing. I believe there's a lot of truth to the statement "Whatever doesn't kill you, makes you stronger." In that respect, our father may have been a good and valuable teacher.

✿

At the age of 17, I was to have another close encounter with death. It was a chilly November evening when two of my teenage friends and I were excitedly cruising down a country road. With Gerald behind the wheel, and my cousin Mervin riding shotgun, I was sandwiched in the middle of the front seat of a 1963 Ford. We were on a testosterone mission to the

Taylor farm, where awaiting our arrival were two of Mr. Taylor's finest daughters. They were fabulous and we couldn't wait to get there. Our youthful anticipation, however, could only be outdone by our lack of experience in the operation of a motor vehicle.

As we rocketed down the gravel road at 85 miles per hour, the sound of the right front tire blowing out at first registered only as an annoying hiccup in our mission. Within seconds, however, the car began to swerve wildly before spinning out of control and sliding into the ditch sideways. The wheels abruptly dug into the frozen dirt and the car catapulted into the air. Time and consciousness stood still.

With a violent explosion, the car slammed back onto the ground. Metal twisted and the windshield disintegrated into thousands of pieces. In a surreal numbness I felt the shards of glass raining in on me, then everything faded to black.

The next thing I knew, I was awakening from what seemed like a nightmare. My head was pounding. Fighting the heaviness of sleep, I tried to sit up, but fell dizzily back to the ground. Baffled, I lay for a few moments trying to get a grip on what had happened. Here I was, lying on the frozen earth in the middle of nowhere without a clue as to how I'd gotten there. After falling a couple more times, I finally made it to my feet. It was freezing cold, and I shivered uncontrollably.

Looking around, I spotted a car about 20 feet away. The door was wide open so I crawled into the driver's seat to warm up. I reached for the ignition to start the engine, but there wasn't a sound. I tried again, but still nothing. I tried to close the door, but it wouldn't budge. Something was terribly wrong!

Dazed and confused, I began to crawl back out of the car, when a stabbing pain ripped through my left side. It practically brought me to my knees. I couldn't imagine what was happening. Glancing back at the car, my breath caught in my throat. The car was horribly mangled, almost completely crushed. My eyes had to be playing tricks on me. I stood there staring, disbelieving, and then it hit me: we had crashed the car. Where were Gerald and Mervin?

Panicking, I began frantically searching for my friends. There was no one inside the car, so I crawled out of the wreckage, heading into the dark field. As I rounded the front corner of the car, I tripped and crashed heavily to the ground. Screaming in pain, I pulled myself onto my hands and knees. There beside me lay a crumpled body. In the moonlight I recognized Gerald's ashen, dirt-covered face.

A chill ran up my spine. I was frozen in place. Although my horrified mind demanded I get up and run, I couldn't move a muscle. I just knelt there, staring at his lifeless face, unable to move, unable to look away. A low growling noise began to build in my throat as I struggled against the terror that held me in its grip. Then I heard my own screams shattering the night air.

My paralysis broken, I got to my feet. My mind clicked into gear. I had to find Mervin. Through burning pain I spun around, scanning the area. About 25 feet away lay another body. Staggering to where Mervin lay, I jammed my fingers against the artery in his neck but could feel no pulse. The horrifying thought that he was dead crept through me like a slow suffocation. I became aware of great gasping sobs coming from my throat.

Frantically, I stumbled back to Gerald. He didn't seem to have a pulse either, and it looked like he wasn't breathing. I put an ear to his chest and held my breath. Nothing: no sound, no movement. In my numbing mind I heard my own pleading voice, "God, please don't let this happen."

Calling Gerald's name, I grabbed his arms to pull him up. There was no response. His lifeless body slumped back to the ground. Finally, in despair, sobbing uncontrollably, I surrendered to the cold ground. Ever so slowly, the spinning darkness overcame me.

Through the fog of drowsiness I became aware of a distant siren, and my consciousness again fought for control. In the distance, headlights and flashing red lights were approaching. Soon a police car roared into the field beside me. Two Mounties sprinted from the car, their flashlights blazing into my eyes.

I motioned in the direction of Mervin's body. The policemen checked his and Gerald's body, assuring me an ambulance was on its way and everything would be okay. Helping me to my feet, they walked me to the warm police car. It was then that I realized I had lost my shoes. My nearly frozen feet felt like blunt stubs.

I sat by myself in the back of the police car trying to warm up. Shaking, my body was numb with hypothermia and I couldn't keep my eyes open. One of the policemen opened the back door of the car and slipped in beside me. He kept telling me to try and stay awake, but I faded in and out of consciousness.

When the ambulance finally arrived, the medics loaded my friends and sped off toward the hospital. I rode in the back of the police car and drifted into sleep.

The abrupt sound of a siren rising to life startled me awake as we neared the emergency entrance of the hospital. A doctor and a nurse waiting with a stretcher wheeled me into the emergency room. Then, after taking numerous X-rays, they began to work on me. They seemed to be concentrating on the right side of my head, which up until then had been feeling numb. I could feel the bite of a needle as the anesthetic was injected. Soon, I could no longer keep my eyes open and the beckoning darkness crept over me. It would be two days before I regained consciousness.

When I finally opened my eyes, I found myself in a bright room, utterly confused. My head felt like it was about to explode. Reaching up to scratch my brow, I discovered that with the exception of my nose, mouth, and left eye, my head was wrapped in bandages.

I tried to sit up, but such a pain shot through the left side of my body that the room began to spin and I collapsed back onto the bed. Every inch of me seemed to hurt. I was becoming more panicked by the moment; I had no idea where I was or what had happened to me.

Soon a nurse entered. Noticing I was conscious, she sprinted off to fetch a doctor. The physician told me about the car accident and assured me that my two friends were okay. Gerald had suffered a smashed pelvis and a concussion, while Mervin's skull had been cracked. He told me that I was the only one conscious when they brought us in. Apparently, after the accident, I had crawled to the road and flagged down a passing car. I remembered nothing.

The doctor filled me in on my injuries. I had a ruptured left kidney, a cracked skull, two cracked ribs, a bruised lung, and my right ear had been nearly severed.

Over the next few days, memories of the accident slowly began to return, but my recollection of the two days leading up to the accident was gone. For some unknown reason it would take several more months before I had any recall of that lost time.

Recovery was a long and painful process. Physical activity was a struggle, and much of my life had to be put on hold.

This close call with fate only seemed to reinforce some of the philosophical doubts I had been harboring since my early teens when I began to question the existence of God. I had now been involved in a serious accident. I had been unconscious for a long time, but not once did I have an experience of any kind that might lead me to believe there was a God. One minute I was alive and well, and the next minute I was gone. It was like I had ceased to exist for that period of time. There was no conscious awareness of anything. In my mind, the concept of death became an act of surrender to nonexistence. . . .

Eventually I healed and returned to normal teenage life.

My brother and I could hardly wait to finish school and leave the farm, but strangely, when that day finally arrived, we did not leave without some degree of sadness.

A short time later I began dating a girl I had known in high school. She was everything I dreamed of and I fell madly in love. There was nothing I wanted more than to spend the rest of my life with her. But life, I had found, sometimes deals out harsh realities. One day she told me she needed to "find herself" and walked out the door.

Devastated, I couldn't imagine how life could continue, but somehow it did. I spent a lot of time feeling sorry for myself, and then at some point I vowed, at least subconsciously, that I would never let anyone hurt me that way again. And the walls around my heart grew ever thicker.

For a couple of years after leaving home, I drifted around, much the same as many kids in the 1970s. I worked at a number of jobs until I woke up one morning from a vivid dream and knew that I would become a radio announcer. This was an era of hippies, war protests, and most of all, rock and roll music. I couldn't imagine a better way to make a living.

The top rock station around was CKOM. I dropped in to see the manager and told him I wanted to be a radio announcer. After quickly determining that I had neither experience nor training, he said they had no openings and sent me on my way.

Talk about feeling dejected. I couldn't believe he had turned me down. It had been so clear in my dream.

A few weeks later, I stopped by to see the manager again. This time my pleading seemed more like begging. I heard myself offering to work in the station for free. I would be available day or night, I said. All they had to do was teach me about radio.

I must have been sufficiently pathetic in my pleading, because he thought about it for a moment, and was in the middle of saying, "I'm sorry," when he unexpectedly stopped, stuck out his hand and said, "Okay, I like your guts. You've got yourself a deal."

I loved radio from the start. Spending almost every available moment at the station, I filled my end of the bargain. Filing record albums, producing commercials, newscasts, and generally anything they wanted me to do, I learned all I could about broadcasting. Everything went so well that within a few months I was offered a position as a disc jockey. For me, it was a job made in Heaven. I couldn't believe they were *paying* me to do something so enjoyable.

A couple of years later, the love of a woman would again enter my life. Four years my junior, she was just a year out of high school, but carried herself with the grace, charm, and elegance of a mature woman. Candace was pretty, intelligent, witty, she made me laugh, and most of all she loved me. Our romance intensified, and a year later we were married.

For the next eight years I gave everything I could to my career. In order to advance I moved on to larger radio and television markets. Candace, a banker, happily followed me from city to city. Eventually we grew tired of the hectic pace and decided to make some changes in our lives. I said goodbye to broadcasting, bought a small insurance brokerage, and we settled down to raise a family.

Normally, what we understand about ourselves becomes less of a puzzle as we age. But little did I know that up to that point in my life, things were never entirely within my control. So much of my life had been guided and assisted, preparing me for the life-changing experiences still to come, experiences that would rock my world and challenge even my most basic concepts of reality.

This brings me again to the conscious beginning of my life's intended journey that began when I found myself floating near the ceiling of my bedroom. Virtually overnight my understanding of the world had been obliterated. It was, however, only the beginning of a long search for the ultimate truth and meaning of life.

3

Search for Truth

In the aftermath of my first out-of-body experience, I became obsessed with finding even the slightest bit of information that would enlighten me on the cause of the phenomenon. It had been the most fantastic thing that had ever happened to me and I desperately wanted to have the experience again. To the exclusion of almost everything else, I pursued this goal with a religious fervor.

The folks at the public library must have wondered about the volume of metaphysical books that I began borrowing. I read voraciously, and spent the rest of my free time trying to go out-of-body. Several books offered methods to achieve the necessary altered state. I would spend hours lying in bed, trying to reproduce the vibrations that seemed necessary for me to escape my body.

The process, however, became frustrating. The more I learned, the more I yearned to have another out-of-body experience. I prayed and I begged, but to no avail; it seemed like it was not meant to be. More than two months had passed since that first experience and I didn't seem to be any closer to my goal. It occurred to me that maybe I was trying too hard, so for several days I tried to not even think about it. But there was no escaping my obsession with spiritual ecstasy, and it wasn't long before I was back at it.

Then one night, out of the blue, it happened. I had been trying to meditate my way into an altered state. Dozing off for what seemed like just seconds, I abruptly awoke to powerful vibrations coursing through my body. My lower torso and legs were numb and heavy.

Excited by this development, I knew I had to be careful. I didn't want to risk losing the vibrational state and ruining the experience. With effort I tried to calm my mind and maintain control. The shuddering intensity of the vibrations surprised me. I didn't recall them being as choppy and strong in my previous experience. The sensations became so jarring and uncomfortable I concentrated on mentally speeding them up as a possible solution. It worked! Within moments the vibrations smoothed into a delightfully energizing wave. In my head, a high-pitched sound began to slowly intensify into a sharp oscillating tone. There was something hauntingly familiar about it; it consumed my thoughts. For a while it was as if nothing else existed.

My mind drifting, I had to remind myself of my goal. I sorted through all the possible things I could do after separation from my body. Opening my eyes, I glanced about the bedroom and found that my vision swept through the ceiling and into the night sky as it had during my first experience.

An ominous feeling swept through me. It was the unmistakable sensation that I was not alone. A chill crept up my spine. Sparks of energy invaded my senses. They were all around my room! Things. Beings. Whatever they were. I felt them everywhere. Frantically I fought to overcome the fear building inside me, but it was useless. My panic turned to terror. I wasn't ready for this. As much as I wanted to leave my body again, there was no way I could force myself to deal with this unknown horror.

Straining against the suffocating paralysis, I forced my legs to move and then my head. In an instant the spell was broken. The vibrations, along with the things or beings, disappeared.

Angry with myself, I sat up in bed. This was the opportunity I had been praying for. This was what I wanted to experience more than anything else in the world, and I had let it slip by. How could I have allowed my fear to get the best of me? I vowed never to let it happen again.

Insatiably, I read anything to do with spirituality. From the biblical teachings of Christianity to Hinduism and Buddhism, I consumed it all. Robert Monroe's books were always a comfort. He had been through it all, overcame his fear, and went on to explore the spirit worlds. I noted his and other writers' assurances that there was no reason for fear. They claimed that in our astral or soul bodies, we are pure, indestructible energy. Nothing in the ethereal realms could harm us.

Some authors recommended offering a prayer for protection before attempting astral travel. Robert Monroe had developed a prayer-like affirmation for students attempting to learn out-of-body travel. The affirmation apparently worked well in allaying the debilitating fear many students faced. Much like a security blanket, I found the affirmation a great help. I memorized it, and used it religiously before every subsequent attempt.

> I am more than my physical body. Because I am more than physical matter, I can perceive that which is greater than the physical world. Therefore, I deeply desire to expand, to experience, to know, to understand, to control, and to use such greater energies and energy systems as may be beneficial and constructive to me and to those who follow me. Also, I deeply desire the help and cooperation, the assistance, the understanding of those individuals whose wisdom, development, and experience is equal to or greater than my own. I ask their guidance and protection from any influence or any source that might provide me with less than my stated desires. (Reprinted by permission of The Monroe Institute.)

Armed with these words and assurances that nothing could harm me, I knew that the real test of my resolve would come only if I could recreate the necessary conditions to achieve an out-of-body state.

Over the following month, I spent at least an hour each night meditating and experimenting with some of Monroe's methods, but nothing seemed to work. The process was frustrating. Night after night, I managed to reach a certain degree of energy and vibration, but failed to carry it to the required intensity. The best I had been able to achieve was a deep relaxation which, unfortunately, usually resulted in my falling asleep. I began to worry that I might never be able to reproduce the experience. Then, one night, without warning, it happened again.

I had gone to bed early, quickly falling into a deep sleep. After about an hour and a half, I jerked awake as intense vibrations coursed through my body. Every molecule of my being seemed to be buzzing with electricity. A high-pitched squeal resonated in my ears.

I was ecstatic. This was what I had been working for! This time fear would not stop me. I was in such a hurry to make it happen that I even forgot to offer my prayer for protection. I simply thought "Up," and in an instant, I was floating near the ceiling of my bedroom.

It was almost too fast. A momentary feeling of disappointment came over me. I hadn't experienced the increase in vibration or the elation of pulling away from my body. I had just transported instantly to the ceiling.

Below me in the bed lay my body. Mesmerized, I studied the sleeping form. It seemed so odd to be doing this. I felt compassion and gratitude towards this body that had served me well for so many years. The blankets had slipped down to just above my waist, and it looked like I might be chilly. My wife was asleep on her right side, with her left arm draped across my chest.

I thought about the many years Candace and I had been together and our constant disagreement over what the temperature in the house should be. She preferred the bedroom cool at night, while I liked it a bit warmer. It had been warm enough when I got into bed, but as usual, it appeared that sometime during the night she had turned down the thermostat and opened a window. I turned to my right. Sure enough, a cool breeze rustled the curtains in front of the open window.

I remembered why I liked to be warm at night. There were far too many vivid childhood memories of winter nights when the fire in the woodstove, the only source of heat in our house, had gone out. Often, after nights like that, my brother and I would wake up, clinging to each other like puppies trying to keep warm. These were things I didn't want to experience again, but they were far removed from the life my wife enjoyed while growing up in the city.

I had to pull myself away from my musings. It might not be long before I would have to return to my body. With increasing excitement, I was ready for a new adventure. Having decided to first try a tour through the house, I pivoted around to face the doorway, but the door was closed.

"Damn," I cussed. "Why does she always have to close the door?" But I remembered I had floated through the wall during my first excursion. Wondering if it would work again, I braced myself and headed slowly towards the solid door. Half expecting to crash headlong into the panel, I raised my hands in front of me to absorb the impact. Instead, I sailed through it with ease. I could feel the material of the door as I passed through. It felt a bit like moving through warm water, but with no resistance.

On the other side of the door I stopped and floated to the floor. It was too tempting to resist, so just for the thrill of it, I reached back and pushed my arm elbow-deep into the door. Talk about a weird sensation. I could see only half my arm. The rest of it was undoubtedly waving about on the other side of the door. Chuckling, I envisioned what this might look like back in the bedroom. I knew that if I were on the other side seeing something like this, I'd be under the covers with the phone, dialing "Ghostbusters."

With my arm still embedded in the wood, I slowly put my forehead against the smoothness of the door and pushed. Instantly my head passed through, and I found myself looking back into the bedroom. Everything was as I had left it, my wife and my body seemingly sound asleep. Stepping fully through the door into the bedroom, I began talking to myself. "Un-frickin-believable!" Standing still for a moment, I looked around, and then confident everything was okay, I turned and stepped back through the door into the hallway.

A world of possibilities opened before me. Was there any kind of structure I couldn't go through? "Maybe steel would be a problem," I thought. "I'll have to check it out sometime."

It seemed nothing could hold me back. Leaping into the air, I floated down the stairway into the living room. Slowly, I flew up to the two-story open ceiling just to see what it would be like to be that high off the floor. It was exhilarating.

I was flying! I was actually flying, and I could hardly contain myself. Like a kid whose wildest fantasy had come true I swooped down from the ceiling, passed through the wall into the dining room, and continued on into the kitchen. The feeling of flying through solid objects was irresistible. Before long I was zooming back and forth through the walls like Casper, the friendly ghost. As I zipped through the wall of the family room into an adjacent bedroom, I came to a midair stop. It was my eight-year-old son's bedroom. Floating silently near the ceiling, I gazed down as David slept.

My heart flooded with compassion for this gentle little soul. He was one of the happiest people I had ever known. Always a smile on his face, nothing seemed to get him down for long. Even at this young age, he had a wonderful sense of humor. With a warm and generous heart, he had empathy for anyone less fortunate. David's was the bright and cheery attitude I wished I had. From my perspective, he was beautiful.

As I floated near the ceiling, my daughter Stacey came to mind. Her bedroom was directly above David's. Traveling straight up through the floor, I was soon hovering over her bed.

We were so proud of our little girl. Pretty and petite, Stacey had the dedication, intelligence, and perseverance to accomplish anything that she wanted in life. She possessed such great inner strength and, at the same time, a wonderful sensitivity to others. At eleven, she was entering that awful hormone stage of life. We were often amazed and amused at the transformation taking place before us. One moment, she would be our sweet little girl singing her dollies to sleep. The next she would become a mature young lady trying to convince her mother that she was definitely old enough to stay at Alicia's party until 10 P.M.

I was about to move closer so I could see more of that dimpled little face, when a huge spasm suddenly jolted through me and, in an instant, I snapped back into my body.

What could possibly have happened? Opening my eyes, I sat up. Candace was now facing in the other direction. She must have turned over in her sleep, bumping my body as she withdrew the arm that had been lying across my chest. Disappointed at being forced back so soon, I still rejoiced at having been able to go out-of-body again.

For several minutes, I lay in bed processing the experience. It had been a great outing. Finally I got up and, retracing my journey through the house, I ended up in our children's bedrooms. I thanked God for sharing these wonderful little souls. I knew that when the time was right, I would have to tell them about the astonishing events taking place in my life.

Encouraged by this small success, I renewed my efforts to find a reliable way to achieve an out-of-body state. Every night, before going to sleep, I experimented with various methods. Some I had read about, others I thought up. But nothing seemed to work. As the weeks dragged by, my obsession grew. It was, however, becoming more like work than pleasure.

As summer approached, my wife began preparations for a trip to Quebec where she had enrolled in a French language-immersion program. Crawling into bed a few nights before her departure, Candace asked me if I had seen her umbrella. She had searched the house without any luck. I couldn't recall having seen it for months. Speculating that we had probably left it somewhere she sighed, "Well, I guess I'd better go out and buy a new one." With those last thoughts, I drifted off to sleep.

As if awakening from some obscure dream, I suddenly realized that I was staring at the umbrella. It was lying on a closet shelf in front of me. My awareness bolted to attention.

There was no question: this was her umbrella. I reached out to grab it. Swish—my hand swept right through the handle. "Oops!" It hadn't registered on my sleepy mind that I was no longer in my body. Momentarily puzzled, I wondered how this could have happened without my being aware of it. I decided it didn't matter. The important thing was I had found the umbrella. I couldn't wait to tell Candace.

In a flash, I snapped back into my body. "Honey," I gushed. "I found the umbrella!" Then it hit me. I hadn't the slightest clue as to where I'd been. All I knew for certain was that someone else now owned our umbrella, and it would probably stay that way. I continued with dismay to tell Candace the story, admitting that in my enthusiasm I had foolishly bolted out of the closet without knowing where I was. After considerable giggling, we finally fell asleep. I was going to have to learn how to contain my excitement.

Again, I had to grapple with something new. Without warning, I had been instantaneously transported to an unknown location without any awareness that I was not in my body. How had this happened?

As summer matured, I grew more practiced at producing out-of-body experiences, but I was still far from being able to make it happen at will. Occasionally, I would feel the choppy, fluttering vibrations starting in the center of my chest, before moving slowly into the rest of my body. I would try to gain control, attempting to step up the frequency to a higher pitch. But it always seemed so difficult to maintain. More often than not, the vibrations would eventually fade, and frustrated, I would fall asleep.

Fortunately, every now and then, I would find myself briefly dozing off, then abruptly snapping back to the awareness of intense vibrations already coursing through my body. I would hear a familiar, high-pitched tone and simply wish myself into the air. Then, after checking on my body, I would be off on another adventure. I didn't know why, but I always looked back at my body. It wasn't necessary, but I felt compelled to do it.

On one of those occasions, I happened to be cruising through the kitchen looking for something to do. When I spotted the fridge, I had an idea. Poking my head through the door, I checked for any leftover dessert I could eat when I finished my excursion. For some reason, the darkness inside the fridge caught me by surprise. Reminded of a silly old joke, I had to chuckle at my expectation that the light would automatically switch on. After a few amusing moments, I simply stated my intension to see better and, in an instant, I could identify every object in the fridge. Unfortunately, there was no dessert. But I soon returned in my physical body to gobble up the leftover ham and scalloped potatoes.

In the early stages, I felt safer staying within the familiar walls of my home, but soon that became boring. One night near the end of summer, I awoke from a deep sleep to the pressure of rapidly escalating vibrations. Looking up, I found I could see right through the ceiling into the night sky. A beautiful full moon beckoned, and I decided that it was about time I sucked up my courage and ventured outdoors.

Floating effortlessly to the ceiling, I wondered what it would feel like to go through that yucky, itchy fiberglass insulation in the attic. With some nervousness, I moved slowly through the ceiling into the attic space. The insulation was hardly noticeable. Relieved, I continued up through the top of the rafters. A moment later, I was standing on the roof.

The freedom was exhilarating. Delighted with the ease of the maneuver, I thought how wonderful it would be to float up into the sky. Impelled by this simple thought, I lifted off of the roof and ascended. Rising to about a hundred feet, I stopped and hovered. I could see the entire neighborhood. It was after midnight, so very few houses were lit. I mused about how freaked out my neighbors would be if they only knew what was happening in the sky above them.

Slowly, I moved higher, stopping at around five hundred feet. It was beautiful. Lights were visible from miles around. I thought it might be fun to take an aerial tour of the city, but just as I began to move down the block, a strange tugging sensation began to draw me back to my body. I didn't want to end the experience, but the tugging was persistent. When I could no longer resist, I gave in, surrendering to the pull. In an instant, I slammed back into my body with such force that it shook the bed. It was no big deal, as it turned out, just my bladder begging to be relieved.

☙

The next opportunity came sooner than expected. Just three days later, too tired to think about spiritual journeys, I flopped into bed and immediately fell asleep. Less than an hour later, I awoke to a shrill frequency resonating in my ears. Sleepily, I closed my eyes and mentally recited my little prayer for assistance and protection. The sound in my ears seemed to intensify as I tried to gain control. Perhaps, I thought, I could use the sound as a trigger to evoke the necessary increase in vibrations. Experimenting, I found I was able to control its intensity, but could detect little change in my inner body vibration. After a while, when I could no longer maintain my concentration, I gave up, and simply fell asleep. Unexpectedly, just a few moments later, I again jerked back into full consciousness. The sound was now a high-pitched squeal. A strong vibration flowed through my body. I was ready for another journey.

Deciding to take it slower this time, I floated leisurely to the ceiling.

Skimming horizontally, I was heading for the bedroom door when I decided to try something different. Changing directions, I plunged through the north wall of my bedroom. Expecting to come out the other side near the high open ceiling of the living room, I found myself, instead, in a small, darkened space, about four feet long and two feet wide. There was a large metal pipe in the middle of it.

It took me a few seconds to figure out where I was. I had forgotten the large fireplace chimney on the other side of the wall. As I drifted inside the brick enclosure, I realized that my arm and part of my right shoulder were imbedded in the chimney pipe. I pulled back in disgust. Imagining how black and dirty my hand and arm were going to be, I pushed through the stone mantel into the living room. My arm, of course, was perfectly clean. I began to laugh at how bizarre and silly the whole thing was. When every touchstone of our reality is based in the physical world, it's difficult to leave old concepts behind.

Soot or no soot, I was going to enjoy this outing. Rather than going up through the roof, I decided this time to exit through the front wall of the house into the street. I slid easily through the inner wall and the outer brick façade. But as I was coming out the other side, something struck me as odd. I was sure that I had automatically closed my eyes as I passed through the wall. I wondered if I could ever get used to the differences between the astral and material worlds.

Everything was *strange*. To begin with, I wasn't sure how I was able to see. Obviously, it wasn't through my physical eyes. I decided to pay more attention to these pesky little physical quirks.

Propelled by a small burst of energy, I floated out into the quiet street and up into the night sky. Stunningly beautiful, the sky appeared to have a special glow. As several clouds floated nearby, I noticed what appeared to be an energy halo around them. It reminded me of the aurora borealis. Shades of luminous blue, pink, and violet began to swirl, merge, and dance together in a brilliant display of choreography.

Captivated, I watched in awe, my attention drawn to the iridescence of one cloud. It seemed to be increasing in brightness and intensity, becoming more and more animated. Suddenly, a terrific flash lit up the sky. A dazzling arc of blue-white light erupted from the bottom of the cloud and slammed into the ground. Startled, I realized it was nothing more than lightning. But in my out-of-body state, it was a sight to behold. I hadn't noticed the approaching thunderstorm, but the developing view was sensational. I could actually see electrical energy building up in the cloud before it exploded into the ground.

I studied the sky as the same cloud began to sparkle and dance, building in intensity once more. Soon it was a boiling vortex of power. I watched intently as the shimmering energy, swirling like a miniature hurricane, slowly edged its way to the top of the cloud. The bubbling formation arched across the top towards the center, and then, like a whirlpool draining through a funnel, collapsed in on itself, firing off a bolt of electricity into the ground below. Strangely, a jagged arc of orange light seemed to erupt simultaneously from the ground, leaping into the air to greet the incoming charge.

It was *beautiful.* I would never again look at a prairie thunderstorm in the same way, and I thanked God for this wonderful gift. If this was what it was like to be an angel, if this was what angels were able to see, then I wanted to be an angel.

As I continued to soak up the spiritual beauty of nature, my physical self-preservation senses began to kick in. I wondered whether I should be out in this kind of weather. As I think back on it now, I find it amusing. But at that point in my journey, I had no idea what boundaries existed. I knew that you don't mess around in a lightning storm. I may have wanted to be an angel, but not right at that moment.

Reluctantly, I headed back home through the large kitchen window. Passing through the double-paned glass was easy, almost imperceptible. Back inside I floated through the house and into my bedroom. I didn't want to end the excursion just yet. I wanted to play and thought it would be nice to have a playmate to share the experience.

Floating down closer to my sleeping wife, I hovered a couple of feet above her. I wondered if it would be possible to get her to leave her body. The problem was that I hadn't the slightest clue as to how this might be accomplished. First, I needed to get her attention without actually waking her physical body. Even that thought seemed a bizarre contradiction.

I recalled that when I was about to leave my body, the vibrations often seemed most intense in my feet and legs. Perhaps this was the key? Turning slowly in the air, I floated down towards her feet. Thinking I might be able to speed up her vibrations by sending energy into her body, I placed my hands on the blankets covering her feet and began to concentrate. After a few moments, however, it became apparent that nothing was happening. There has to be a way, I thought, and concentrated harder. All of a sudden, my right hand swished right through her foot. In surprise, I jerked my hand back. It was tingling with electrical energy.

The idea of passing through another living being hadn't occurred to me, but it was kind of fun. I began to wonder if it might be considered improper behavior. But, heck, it was way too cool. I couldn't resist. Placing my index finger gently against Candace's lower calf, I began to slowly increase the force. The tip of my finger easily passed through her skin and slowly sank to the knuckle in her leg muscle. Minute jolts of electricity tingled through my finger and up into my hand. After a few moments, I gently withdrew my finger and then poked it back in. "Boy," I thought, "this is way more fun than going through walls."

Other than an exhilarating diversion, this didn't seem to accomplish much, so I floated towards Candace's head. Hoping for better results, I focused instead on sending a telepathic signal into her brain. For nearly a minute, I continued to project the message, "Candi, come out and play," but nothing happened.

I had another idea. Placing the middle finger of my right hand on her forehead, I concentrated on the same message. Several moments passed. I could feel the energy flowing easily from my hand into her brow. Suddenly, she began to move. "Okay," I thought. "Now we're getting somewhere." Unfortunately, to my dismay, she just kept right on moving—all the way over onto her side. As she rolled over, I watched helplessly as her sleeping arm hung in the air for a couple of seconds, and then dropped onto the chest of my sleeping body. That's all it took: with a sudden jolt, I was instantly back inside. The vibrations were gone, and I was wide-awake.

While she was still partially asleep, I asked Candace if she had felt me trying to communicate with her. Sleepily, she said she didn't know, but thought that something must have awakened her.

When I casually mentioned passing my astral hand through her body, that certainly got her full attention. For some reason, she didn't think it would be so cool. She let me know, in no uncertain terms, that it was a rude thing to do, and I would be well advised to keep my damn hands to myself when she's sleeping. I tried to explain that it was purely for scientific purposes, but she wasn't buying it. The next morning, when fully awake, she did admit that it would have been great if I had been able to coax her out of her body, but she still didn't think she wanted anything passing through her.

Throughout the summer and into the fall, I continued to study anything even remotely connected to the paranormal. One author explained that one of the best times to attempt astral travel was during the pre-sleep hypnagogic state. It's the term that alludes to that narrow balance of consciousness between awake and asleep that we all experience while we're in the process of drifting off each night.

Called theta, it is the relaxed state of mind in which dream images begin to flash through our consciousness. The condition is often accompanied by small involuntary muscular jolts. In my experimentation, I had found that theta was, indeed, an ideal mental state for exploration. The problem was in trying to maintain the condition.

Try as I may, I couldn't seem to hold that level of consciousness for long. With continuous practice, I found that I could manage to extend my time hovering in the borderland, but it usually ended up with me falling asleep and waking up frustrated the next morning.

That same author also suggested that one way to help prolong the hypnagogic condition was to lie on your back with your hand and forearm held in the air. If you started to fall asleep, your arm would automatically begin to fall, which in turn would trigger you into raising your level of consciousness. You could then pull your arm back into position and in this manner stay on the edge of consciousness, extending the hypnagogic state indefinitely. I tried the method many times. After I got used to the discomfort, I found that it worked quite well, but it wasn't as successful as I had hoped. It did, however, provide me with a couple of exceptional experiences.

Late one night, while experimenting, I lay in bed for more than 20 minutes, my body practically asleep while my mind remained awake. At some point, I could feel my arm slowly collapsing onto the bed. Reacting, I opened my eyes, but to my surprise my arm was still upright. It hadn't moved.

Doubting my senses, I shook my head and shifted my awareness to my physical arm. Immediately its feeling and position were restored. Closing my eyes, I soon drifted back into my altered state. Not more than a minute later, I again felt my arm slowly dropping to the bed. Opening my eyes yet again, I was alarmed to find my arm still in an upright position.

The whole thing was intriguing. Vowing to maintain a stronger awareness of what was happening, I returned to my meditation. Moments later, I felt it begin to topple again. This time I snapped open my eyes to an unbelievable sight. As before, my physical right arm remained locked in an upright position, but now a lighter, whitish shadow of it slowly sank to the bed beside me. I realized that I was observing my physical arm and my astral arm at the same time.

The reality of the situation jarred me to full awareness. It had come upon me so gradually; I had no idea that I'd moved into an out-of-body condition. I couldn't believe how subtly it had taken place. Had I simply been so deep that I hadn't noticed the change? Or was it just becoming easier to accomplish?

I had only begun to realize the scope of the changes that were taking place in my life. My explorations were becoming more and more fascinating, and I couldn't wait to see where this new freedom would take me. Even in my wildest fantasies, I could not have imagined what lay in store for me.

4

Expanding Horizons

As time passed my obsession to learn and experience continued unabated. Reading anything paranormal that I could get my hands on, I came upon Robert Monroe's second book, *Far Journeys*. True to the author's style, it contained some fascinating revelations. Practically everything in the book resonated a feeling of recognition and truth for me.

Most importantly, the book included an address for The Monroe Institute. It was a nonprofit organization that Monroe had founded to research the out-of-body phenomenon. I phoned the Institute. They promised to send me an information package, and for ten days I waited anxiously for the material to arrive.

The Monroe Institute sounded like the answer to my prayers. They had developed successful programs to assist people achieve altered states of consciousness. Thousands of people had attended their seminars. Due to great variances in the abilities and sensitivities of each individual, the Institute would not guarantee that participants would have an out-of-body experience, but they were confident that one would not leave the program without being convinced that awareness *can* extend beyond the physical world.

The establishment of the Institute near Charlottesville, Virginia, came about as a direct result of public reaction to Monroe's books, his curiosity about the phenomenon, and his abilities as a researcher. Following the success of *Journeys Out of the Body,* Monroe received a large volume of correspondence from all over the world. Many claimed to have had experiences similar to his, but were afraid to talk about them for fear of ridicule or concern that something might be wrong with them. Monroe's books helped people understand that out-of-body travel was something every human was capable of experiencing. It was a gift, something to cherish, not fear.

Due to escalating interest, Monroe, along with a number of volunteers, set up a private lab to investigate the phenomenon. Out of the many letters and calls he received were a number of people who, like him, had the ability to travel out-of-body at will. With some of these people as volunteer test subjects, he and his technical team built a small lab containing a specially designed isolation chamber where participants' levels of consciousness could be monitored. Test subjects were connected to various biofeedback devices to study and map their states of relaxation and brainwave activity.

After hundreds of hours of monitoring and testing, they found that subjects who attained out-of-body states while in the lab exhibited very similar levels of consciousness. Monroe and his assistants postulated that if they could somehow re-create these brainwave frequencies, they might be able to help others achieve an out-of-body experience.

An accomplished audio engineer, Monroe concentrated on sound as the medium to influence the brainwaves of test subjects. He and his team spent thousands of hours experimenting with various audio tones and electronic pulses, trying to produce an effective combination of frequencies that could be fed to a subject through stereo headphones.

Their hard work and perseverance finally paid off. Through the manipulation of a small electronic pulse known as a "binaural beat," they were able to perfect an innovation in audio technology. The pulsing electronic signal was found to create a frequency following response in the human brain, which enabled automatic synchronization of the left and right hemispheres. Monroe was granted a patent for the process he called Hemispheric Synchronization, or simply Hemi-Sync.

The new technology made it possible to easily move test subjects into a state of deep relaxation in which their bodies slept while their minds remained awake and alert. In this state, subjects were able to experience expanded levels of consciousness, opening the doorway to enhanced sensory perception and the ability to access an apparent sixth sense, including the out-of-body state.

The Hemi-Sync process proved extremely successful. With the assistance of trained helpers, Monroe began to offer weeklong seminars to the public.

The more I learned about it, the more intrigued I became. There was no doubt in my mind. This was something I had to try. Calling the Institute, I signed up for "Gateway," their weeklong beginners' course, and the time until it started couldn't pass quickly enough.

When the day arrived, I could hardly contain myself. At the end of a long flight, as we approached the airport in Charlottesville, I looked out over the peaceful beauty of the Blue Ridge Mountains, and something inside me clicked. It was a moment of déjà vu. I had the feeling I'd been there before.

After a 45-minute car ride, we finally drove into the parking lot at The Monroe Institute. Like hallowed ground, the understated elegance of the rustic buildings and quiet surroundings commanded reverence. A virtual Mecca for body, mind, and spirit, it was making history here. The energy was palpable. As I walked through the front entrance, I knew that my world would never be the same.

After dropping off luggage in my room, I headed to the dining room where the other participants and instructors were gathering. The excitement was contagious. With mounting anticipation, we were all eager to get started. Once everybody had arrived, we assembled in a comfortable meeting room where the instructors began to lay out the agenda for the upcoming week. An intriguingly diverse group, we were from all over the world, including the U.S., Canada, Australia, Germany, Switzerland, and England.

Each of the twenty participants was assigned to a specific room, which would serve as our sleeping quarters as well as our own experimental lab. The instructors referred to these rooms as CHEC units (an acronym for Controlled Holistic Environmental Chamber). With a constant supply of fresh air feeding into a climate-controlled environment, the rooms were constructed to be as comfortable and quiet as possible. When the heavy black curtain was pulled across the opening to the enclosed bed, the unit passed into total darkness. It made no difference if our eyes were open or closed, everything would be black. Each encapsulated unit, however, was also equipped with special dimmer-controlled lights for those who preferred a bit of illumination. Complete with warm blankets, tape recorders, built-in wall speakers, and stereo headphones, the rooms contained everything we would need.

Finishing the orientation early, we headed off to bed. Our training would begin in the morning. With the speakers emitting the soft relaxing sounds of ocean surf, I quickly drifted into a deep, peaceful sleep anticipating my first encounter with Hemi-Sync technology.

Morning came too quickly. Still tired from the long day in crowded airports and cramped jetliners, I bolted out of bed to prepare for the exciting day to come. Following breakfast and an orientation gathering, we all retired to our CHEC units for the inaugural session that would introduce us to the deep relaxation of what Robert Monroe referred to as Focus 10. This was a level of consciousness he described as "Mind Awake, Body Asleep." After each session, we would meet in the conference room to debrief, compare notes, and share our experiences.

Closing the black curtain, I crawled into the bed and pulled on the headphones. The sound of ocean surf soon lulled me into a quiet meditative state. Within a few minutes, the surf sound faded away and a new mixture of soft pure tones began to flow through the headphones. It was a fascinating progression. In a slow controlled vibrato, the sound seemed to move back and forth, from ear to ear. Heaviness collected in my eyes. Within moments it spread down through my body and into my legs and feet. Slowly but surely, the sounds carried me to the edge of sleep.

It was a wonderful feeling. Calm and serene, I basked in the euphoria of relaxation for what seemed like 15 or 20 minutes. Much like the hypnagogic state one encounters when falling asleep, a constant stream of dreamlike images flowed through my perception. Not focusing on anything in particular, I allowed my mind to roam freely. The sensation was exquisite, and I soon lost all sense of time or connection with my body.

All of a sudden, I found myself jerking awake to the sound of Robert Monroe's voice calling us back to normal consciousness. Almost an hour had passed. To my great disappointment, I had fallen asleep. What had I missed? The trainers had warned us that this might happen. But even if we did fall asleep, they said, our subconscious would still receive the benefits of Hemi-Sync. Although they assured us it was nothing to worry about, I wasn't convinced. The long plane trip to Virginia was taking its toll.

Most of my sessions during the first couple of days were similar. I often fell asleep and had little to report. But the energy of the place was starting to have its effect on me. Each day we were introduced to progressively more powerful Hemi-Sync signals. We moved from the "Mind Awake, Body Asleep" level of consciousness on to Focus 12, the state of "Expanded Awareness," and finally to Focus 15, a level of consciousness beyond our concept of linear time.

By the third day, I was nearly bouncing off the walls. The energy flowing through my body was so strong that a tingling vibration rippled from my thighs all the way up to the back of my neck. The high-pitched tone, normally only present while I was in an altered state, now seemed to be with me all the time. By late afternoon, as we headed to our rooms for another session, the sound in my ears had become so loud, I worried it might be distracting.

After settling in to the relaxing Hemi-Sync tones, I could feel the changes slowly spreading through my body. At first, as my thoughts drifted, I began to lose all awareness of anything physical. But when I finally refocused my attention, I couldn't believe the amount of electrical activity playing through my muscles. I could feel my lower legs tense up and then slowly relax. The stiffness and tightness moved to my thighs, which also contracted and then relaxed. Soon, the lower half of my body began to feel heavy and immoveable.

Floating ever closer to the borderland of sleep, as had happened so many times before, my consciousness began to click in and out. One moment I would be awake and alert, and the next I'd be snapping back to awareness, knowing only that I had somehow fallen asleep. It was from one of these unconscious voids that I suddenly clicked back into awareness, just as I was lifting off the bed, floating toward the ceiling. My excitement was almost uncontainable.

As I approached the ceiling, I turned as usual to look down at my body. But this time there was something different—I didn't seem to be in control of what was happening. I kept on rising through the ceiling of my CHEC unit. Before I knew it, I was sailing right through the lower body of a participant in the unit above me. Startled, but only somewhat concerned, I floated up through the roof of the Institute.

With every molecule buzzing, I began rising into the sky. One hundred feet, five hundred feet, a thousand feet, I quickly picked up speed, moving ever higher. Soon, watching the landscape shrink below me, I felt like a rocket blasting into space. This, I thought, must be what the Shuttle crews see as they leave the Earth.

The Virginia landscape became a blur of green as I moved higher. To my right, the vast sweep of ocean blue came into view, and still I continued climbing. Within moments, the entire planet became visible as I hurtled into space. The sun took on a distinct brilliance I had never seen before. Moving ever faster, I continued on until the Earth itself appeared as a tiny blue ball. Finally, many thousands of miles into space, I slowed and came to a stop.

The panorama was stunning. In every direction, I could see and feel the beauty of creation. A blanket of stars lay in every direction. It occurred to me how small and insignificant I was in the midst of this beautiful sea of creation, yet I knew I was a part of it all. Everything was intimately connected, and perhaps even the tiniest particle was no less important than the largest.

For an indeterminate period of time, I floated quietly in space, absorbed in the beauty around me. Monroe was right. This level of consciousness, Focus 15, was unaffected by time.

In my contented solitude, I became aware of a strange, distracting sound. It seemed to surround me, while at the same time resonate within me. Although I couldn't pinpoint the source, it appeared to be a deep, low frequency like the roaring of the wind or pounding ocean surf. Continuing to grow louder, I soon found it impossible to ignore. Concerned, I thought perhaps I should get back to my body.

In one swift movement, only a flicker in time, I snapped back into my body in the CHEC unit. To my astonishment, I could still hear the sound, and it was even louder. Then the realization hit me. *The sound was coming from me!* It was my body, snoring!

My mind completely awake, I lay in the darkness, amused and astonished at the power of this anomaly. I was listening to my own body snore as if it were someone else. There was no doubt about it. Our minds and bodies could certainly operate independently of each other.

Moments later, Robert Monroe's voice was calling us back to end the session. Briefly, I entertained a strange notion. I wondered how I was going to awaken my body. With a mere thought, though, I coaxed my fingers to move, then my arms. Soon I was back in control.

Taking off the headphones, I stretched out. The debriefing session would have to go on without me. I needed some additional time to process the significance of this latest experience.

My flight into space had been profound. Almost too powerful, it had the effect of creating within me a high degree of performance anxiety. I became so determined to have another out-of-body experience that I'm sure I ruined the next few sessions by trying too hard. Rather than just relaxing and letting it happen, I kept trying to *make* it happen. I was defeating myself.

By the last day of the seminar, I was so energized by the Hemi-Sync process, I was practically buzzing. We had been warned about this possibility and had been advised to do a grounding exercise. Running, swimming, hugging a tree—any of these activities would help to ground the energy and bring us down to Earth. Most of the participants paid serious attention to these suggestions. I, however, didn't want to. I loved being high on psychic energy. It wasn't until later, when I was finally back trying to manage in the business world, that I began to understand why grounding was a good thing.

During the week, we had progressively made our way into deeper levels of consciousness. The final and deepest level of the "Gateway" seminar was Focus 21. Bob Monroe called it "The Bridge to the Other Side." It was from this level of consciousness that one could access the spirit world, visit with angels and spirit guides, or even deceased relatives and loved ones. Although intrigued by the possibility, I didn't think I was ready for it. I wasn't sure I wanted anything to do with anyone who had died.

As one of our last sessions got underway, I began to contemplate how I might integrate some of the new things I had learned into another meaningful experience. Offering my usual prayer for protection, I also asked to be given an experience that would most benefit me at this stage in my development. I sent the prayer out into the universe and trusted that all would go as intended. Then I relaxed and waited.

As the Hemi-Sync frequencies carried me into deeper and deeper levels of consciousness, time seemed to drag. I was beginning to wonder if I would get any response, when a sudden, powerful surge in vibration swept through me. In the next instant, I almost leapt out of my skin. There at the foot of my bed, bathed in light, stood a blond-haired boy. It startled me so much I had to fight the urge to jump out of bed and turn on the lights. I saw him clearly. He appeared to be about 12 years old. His freckled face and sparkling blue eyes beamed with delight. I didn't know what to do. Who was he? Should I try to talk to him? Say, "Hi"?

As I struggled to control my fear, an expression of understanding and compassion spread across his face. I was sure he knew my thoughts. As if in apology for frightening me, he smiled ever so gently, lowered his eyes, and in an instant he was gone.

A heavy sadness flooded through me. I couldn't get over the feeling that this young spirit had wanted to communicate with me, and I had let him down. Why hadn't I been able to deal with my fears? Perhaps he could have helped me. I wondered if I would ever see him again or find out who he was. Through the remainder of the session I repeatedly invited him back, but it was not to be.

When the session ended, I sat quietly during the debriefing. I had been deeply affected. The image of the boy would not leave my mind. There was something hauntingly familiar about him and I couldn't shake the feeling I'd known him before. It felt like he could have been a part of me, a distant memory. I wanted to call him back, to tell him I was sorry.

When the final session got underway, my consciousness dropped quickly as a persistent numbing sensation enveloped my legs. Ready for another adventure, I knew that I would shortly start to feel electrical spasms in my body. For a moment I seemed to fall asleep, but snapped back with the usual jolt. I had been startled yet again by the sound of my own snoring. This was amazing, as ordinarily I seldom snore. On rare occasions when it did happen, I would usually be immersed in a deep sleep.

I began to think about the autonomic processes of the body and how complex and intricate our physiology is. How ridiculous the official accepted view of our reality had become. Our scientific community was still insisting that we, and all that we have become, were the result of a freak accident in which precise quantities and types of amino acids came together in primeval pond scum and evolution took care of the rest.

How ignorant that was. At one time, I may have bought into such concepts because I wanted to deny the existence of a Creator. But even though I had preferred this left-brain linear view of the universe, deep inside, it didn't sit comfortably. I knew intuitively that there had to be something more. Now I was living and learning about this "something more." Now I was experiencing firsthand the beauty and complexity of creation. I was beginning to understand the order in which everything existed.

The more I thought about our existence, the more intrigued I became with the concept of consciousness. Where exactly was the seat of consciousness within a human? If it is within the brain, as science dictates, then what was it that allowed me to travel thousands of miles away from my brain and remain a thinking, self-aware individual? It was becoming obvious to me that consciousness is not at all dependent upon the brain. The brain is only a secondary factor in control of our physical existence. It is merely an electronic relay system—something that translates the mind's thoughts into actions and reactions within our physical bodies.

I began to wonder if it would be possible to focus the thinking process at another location within the body other than the brain. Would it be possible, for example, to move my consciousness into my foot? I wanted to try, but couldn't imagine how this might be accomplished.

I decided to just go for it. Almost immediately, I felt a change in internal vibration, and my perception became clouded and confused. I hadn't a clue where I was, but I could feel the flow of liquid surging past me in a steady rhythm. Too disoriented to make any sense of what was happening, I decided to withdraw to an external point of view. After a brief feeling of movement, I found myself floating several inches away from my right foot.

I had somehow become a mere microscopic version of myself. With no perception of having any type of body, it felt like I had been reduced to the tiniest spark of conscious energy. Reorienting myself, I settled on re-entering my leg just above the ankle. In an instant I found myself back where I had started. It felt like I was inside a main artery, but with my vision extremely blurred, I couldn't be sure. If this was going to be of any value at all, I needed to be able to see. I recalled the incident within the darkness of my refrigerator and thought if it worked once, it should work again. I asked for clarity. Almost as quickly as the thought entered my mind, everything around me came clearly into focus.

The sensation was overwhelming, almost too much to handle. Surrounded in a flood of red and pink, a beam of light seemed to come from within me, lighting the way. It reminded me of TV medical shows where tiny cameras had been inserted through small holes into a patient's body. I could feel the flow of the liquid surging past me, and I could hear the sound of blood swishing through the artery. It seemed as though I was moving steadily along, against the flow of blood, pulled in the direction of my upper body.

In just a few moments, the sound of swooshing liquid swelled and I knew I had arrived at the center of my body. Surprised at the loudness of my pumping heart, I felt jostled about, the motion and flow of blood, agitated and powerful. But why, I wondered, was my heart beating so fast? It seemed a lot faster than usual. Considering the possibility that my own mental excitement might be contributing to the increased pounding, I decided I should find another place to hang out. This was new territory for me, and I wasn't sure how this might be affecting my body.

As I thought of other places to go, I felt a tug at my consciousness, distracting me, drawing me out of my altered state. I tried to resist, but to no avail. A moment later, I was back to normal awareness, wondering what had happened.

At some point during the session, I had rolled over onto my side. The headphones digging into the side of my head had become extremely uncomfortable—and that's all it took.

Thrilled with my short excursion, I lay in bed contemplating the potential inner bodywork such as this might have for medicine. If trained medical people could be taught to make similar journeys into patients' bodies, the diagnostic possibilities could be enormous. Maybe this was how Edgar Cayce, the famous medical psychic, had been able to give accurate readings on the medical conditions of his clients. If only this inner-body exploration could be duplicated at will, I thought, the ramifications for the future could be exciting.

⟨♡⟩

Our last session over, everyone was sad that we would soon be leaving such a wonderful place. There were hugs and tears all around. It had been a great week. We had learned so much about consciousness, the reach of the mind, and the power of the spirit. But most of all, we had all come to a greater understanding of our own existence.

Back home, the energy I had generated during my time at the Institute stayed with me for weeks. My recall of nightly dreams increased dramatically, the images and emotions often remaining throughout the day.

I thought about how much simpler my life had been before these experiences began. I knew the answers to many questions that previously I hadn't even contemplated. It was becoming increasingly obvious to me that we know so little about the nature of our own reality. We just go about our lives, working, eating, and sleeping, trying to survive and maintain our existence in this material world. Forgotten are the times in our childhood when almost anything was possible, a time when we truly wondered about who we were and how we got here. I felt like I was inching closer to some answers, but there was so much more to learn.

Occasionally, while dreaming, I encountered the boy who had visited me in spirit form at the Institute. Although it was never entirely clear, I had the impression we were brothers, spending hours together in boyhood fantasies. Intrigued by the familiarity and friendship his presence evoked, I was nonetheless shocked by my next discovery.

My sister, Josie, and I had been close for years and I often shared with her my experiences and the things I was learning. It was during one of these long conversations I mentioned my encounter with the boy and my subsequent dreams. When I suggested that he felt like a brother, I was taken aback by her reply. "Well, don't be surprised if he really is your brother," she stated, excitement in her voice.

"What do you mean?" I asked. "How could he be my brother?"

Josie then went on to tell me a story I had never heard, or at least didn't recall. She recounted that when I was about two years old, a year after my brother Dale was born, our mother became pregnant with her twelfth child. Several months into her pregnancy, she had gone outside to fetch a pail of water from a well in the yard. A thunderstorm had just passed through the area and the pump-handle was still wet with rain. While she was working the handle, a bolt of lightning struck the pump. A huge jolt of electricity exploded down the wet handle sending our mother flying. Although she wasn't seriously injured, the baby didn't make it. It was a boy.

I couldn't believe my ears. How could I not have known this? Why hadn't I been told? Josie explained that we were very young at the time, and it was something our mother never felt comfortable talking about. There was no reason to tell us.

Although angry at being left out of the loop on this bit of family history, I was grateful for the validation. Strangely enough, since that day, other than one fleeting glimpse of his smiling face, I have neither seen nor dreamt about him. Perhaps, the contact served its purpose and there is no longer a need to maintain the connection. But I know in my heart that someday we'll be together again.

During the summer of 1992, my sister Evalina was rushed to the hospital with a ruptured pancreas. It's a very serious ailment and, within a short time, it advanced to the point where there was little medically that could be done for her. Within a couple of days, she lapsed into a coma and was put on life support with little chance of recovery.

Our family was in shock. Other than our brother-in-law, Albert, and our mother's earlier miscarriage, we hadn't lost any members of our immediate family. Suddenly we found ourselves facing our own mortality. Even though the doctors had expected her to live only a few days more, we took up a vigil at the hospital, praying that they were wrong and that Evalina would somehow make a miraculous recovery. To everyone's surprise, the days stretched into weeks, the weeks into months. Some days she would show small signs of improvement, only to dash our hopes in the following days, sliding ever closer to death.

While at The Monroe Institute I had learned methods of remote healing. We had been taught how to send healing energies to others, even at great distances. Scientific studies had shown compelling evidence that the healing process could be dramatically assisted through focused prayer. Sending healing energies while out-of-body could be even more effective.

Although I felt the need to contribute to the healing efforts of my family's prayers, I struggled with the appropriateness of doing so without my sister's permission. But how do you get permission from someone in a coma?

A statement I had heard at The Monroe Institute contributed to my mental struggle. "Every disease known to man can be cured, but not every person can be healed." They said that some things were just meant to be. According to some, everyone has a plan as to how their life will play out, the challenges they'll face, and the lessons they hope to learn. I felt the truth of this statement. As much as I loved my sister, I wasn't sure I should mess with her soul's karmic choices.

Eventually, I decided I couldn't just sit back and do nothing. I didn't know if there were consequences for someone who interferes with another's spiritual plans, but on several occasions, when I was able to move into an altered state, I attempted to contact my sister's spirit to ask permission to send her healing energy. I could never seem to get through. Perhaps it was because I was too involved emotionally. Or maybe I hadn't yet learned enough about the spirit world to make the connection. Each time, after trying unsuccessfully to connect with her spirit, I asked for forgiveness if I was intruding and then with great focus, mentally bathed her body in healing energy. Each time, I hoped and prayed I was doing the right thing, but if her healing was not meant to be, I knew that we might only be delaying the inevitable.

Staying in contact with the family, we checked on Evalina's condition almost daily. I did find on a few occasions that her condition seemed to improve shortly after I had sent the healing energy. However, in my still skeptical mind, I could never be sure that it wasn't just coincidence.

For months, our roller coaster ride continued. Day to day, our hopes were raised and then dashed. Beyond the doctor's amazement that she continued to defy the odds, it seemed that we had little to be hopeful for. It was rare for anyone to survive as long as she had, and this in itself gave us hope that perhaps another miracle was possible.

One night in early November, after going to bed late, I attempted another spirit journey to help Evalina. After trying for an hour without headway, I gave up and dropped off to sleep.

The next thing I knew, a rush of vibration jarred me back into awareness. There followed a swift movement and I found myself floating over the nurses' station in the hospital's intensive care unit. It took me a moment to figure out where I was, but I was able to look directly into my sister's room. Although I couldn't actually see them, I was aware of beings on either side of me. They had brought me to this place, and I was not afraid.

Focusing my attention on Evalina's room, I saw her lying on the bed. To the right side of the bed sat her daughter, Jackie; on the other side, a nurse was busily checking monitoring equipment. Realizing that it had to be nearly 3:00 A.M. I wondered why Jackie would be there at that time of the night.

It soon became apparent that something was wrong. While the nurse scurried about, Jackie appeared agitated. As I watched intently, a wispy, shimmering energy-form began to emerge from my sister's body. Floating into a vertical position a few feet above the bed, she paused for a moment to look in Jackie's direction, and then turned toward me.

Although appearing a bit confused, Evalina looked radiant. A warm smile of recognition spread across her face. I tried to smile back, but the excitement was too much. In a flash, I was back in my body.

Immediately awakening my wife, I told her I thought Evalina had either just died or had suffered a major trauma. Candace suggested that I phone the hospital, but, in the wee hours of the morning, it might have seemed weird, so I resisted. I reasoned that if something had happened, we would undoubtedly receive a call in the morning. I didn't want to be spooking anybody.

Morning arrived and then midafternoon, but no one called. I'm not sure if Candace was beginning to doubt me, but I knew what I had seen. I also knew one thing more: Evalina was ready to make her transition. I somehow knew that she was now looking forward to the release. It was meant to be. I would not be attempting any more healing sessions.

Two days later, Candace and I made the three-hour trip to the hospital. While I sat with Evalina, my wife visited with other family members. After a while, I headed back to the waiting room where Candace and my niece were in conversation. Jackie addressed me immediately, "Uncle Paul, how did you know about mom?"

A bit surprised, I asked, "How did I know what?"

"Aunt Candi was just telling me that on Wednesday night you knew that Mom's heart quit, and you knew that I was at the hospital with her. That's so amazing, it's scary."

I sat down and told her what I had seen. Wiping away tears, she confirmed that indeed, early on Wednesday morning, at about ten minutes to three, her mother's heart had temporarily stopped. The nursing staff had previously been instructed to not attempt resuscitation. Believing Evalina might be dying, they had called Jackie in from the waiting room.

Jackie told us that it was just coincidence that she was in the hospital at the time. She normally would have been home with her family, but her husband was spending a few days away with their sons. Rather than stay at home by herself she had decided to spend the night at the hospital. She was sleeping in the waiting room when the nurse came to get her. Evalina's heart had stopped for more than two minutes before starting again. Even though I had been certain of what I had seen, the validation sent chills up my spine.

I still wondered who had brought me to the hospital at that precise moment. Somebody had been guiding me. I knew it would be just a matter of time before I found out who.

5

To Die Again

The autumn of 1992 proved to be very mild across the Midwest. While our sister continued to defy all odds by clinging to life, distracted as the family was, our lives went on.

I had been an athlete and hockey player all my life. But, by the age of 41, I was already too slow and old to be playing a young man's game, so I contented myself with a position on a local old-timers' team. It was a lot of fun, and we got a bit of exercise at the same time. We were, however, your typical "weekend warriors," going from relative inactivity during the week to all out battles on weekends. It was during one of these robust outings that providence dealt me another unexpected hand.

Although my leg muscles felt stiff, everything else seemed normal as I made my way to the arena for our Sunday morning scrimmage. Looking forward to a good workout, I laced up my skates and headed out onto the ice with my team. It wasn't long before we were racing up and down the ice, firing frozen pucks at our aging goaltenders.

After only a few minutes of play, I was becoming surprisingly tired, when midstride, it felt like I had been hit in the chest with a sledgehammer. My legs nearly buckled beneath me. I had no idea what was happening. Utterly exhausted, I stumbled off the playing surface.

I couldn't believe how winded I had become. Even after several minutes on the bench, I still struggled to catch my breath, and, to top it all off, a sharp, deep pain began to develop in my left elbow. I couldn't remember hurting myself and had no idea why it should be so sore. The pain, however, seemed to grow more severe with each passing moment. Nauseous and sweating profusely, I was beginning to think that I might have come down with food poisoning or flu.

As the minutes dragged, the pain in my elbow became unbearable, my breathing difficult and labored. It was obvious that I was too sick to continue playing, so I decided to go home. Heading to the dressing room, I changed into my street clothes, and in less than five minutes I was ready to leave.

My equipment bag in tow, I pushed the door open and, struggling to keep my balance, staggered into the hallway. I was beginning to think that my problems might be more than just food poisoning. Instead of heading home I should be going to the hospital. Fortunately, an alert rink attendant took one look at me, and rushed off to call an ambulance.

With each passing minute my condition seemed to worsen. Before long, I was leaning against a wall, trying to maintain my balance. Just the simple act of breathing was painful. No longer able to stand, I dropped to my knees and slumped to the floor just as a couple of my teammates popped around the corner to see how I was doing. Alarmed, they propped my head up on a towel as the rink attendant returned to announce an ambulance was on its way.

Soon the rest of the team gathered around me in the hallway. Their hushed tones and concerned looks suggested that this probably wasn't one of my better days. Closing my eyes, I tried to ignore the numbing pain and slowly I drifted towards sleep.

The sound of running feet and clattering wheels jarred me back to awareness. I opened my eyes as two paramedics, aided by a couple of my teammates, lifted me onto a stretcher. In a moment, we were whizzing through the halls of the arena and out the front doors to the ambulance.

increasingly energized with delight and anticipation. Powerful vibrations coursed through me, and then, like a jet accelerating down a runway, I started to move through the darkness. Before long it felt like I was traveling at a tremendous rate. I was drawn toward a pinpoint of light in the distance ahead and could barely contain my excitement. The urgency and yearning to reach the light became consuming. It seemed I had waited so long for this moment. I was finally going home, and there was nothing I wanted more.

Oblivious to everything else, I became absorbed in my goal when, suddenly, a huge spasm virtually exploded through my awareness, jarring every particle of my being. The next instant, I was back inside my body.

I couldn't believe the assault on my senses as I opened my eyes in the emergency room at the hospital. The pain had returned, flooding through my body in waves. In shock, I knew only one thing for sure: I didn't want to be back.

A nurse struggled to insert an IV needle into a vein in my left wrist while a doctor barked his instructions. Everything around me seemed too bright, too harsh. My jacket and shirt were pulled back, exposing my chest, and I found myself screaming, "No, please, this is a mistake. Let me go. Please let me go!" The words, however, seemed caught up in my mind; there was no sound.

In a surreal haze I could see and hear everything around me, but I had lost control of my body. I felt like a rag doll as a doctor pulled off my shirt and flopped me back down onto the table. While one of the physicians injected me with drugs, another put his face in front of mine. Slowly, but firmly, he spoke to get my attention. "Paul," he said, "you're having a heart attack. You've got to relax."

His words sounded bizarre and incomprehensible. Me, having a heart attack? Ridiculous! And if it was true, how in hell did he expect me to relax?

The pain was more than I could handle. It felt like there was a huge weight on my chest squeezing the life out of me, but it was nothing compared to the pain in my left elbow. If I could have spoken, I would have begged them to cut it off. I would rather go through the remainder of my life missing an arm than have to endure another minute of that pain.

IV bottles flying, they rushed me out of the emergency room and into the intensive care unit. For more than an hour, the doctors worked frantically to clear the blockage from my heart. The pain, somewhat lessened by morphine, continued to be excruciating. In my horrified state, time dragged agonizingly slowly.

The most mind-bending part of the whole experience came about while *watching* the drama unfold around me. It was intriguing. If I hadn't been feeling so lousy, I'm sure I would have enjoyed watching all the action even more.

Especially spellbinding was the minidrama of the ECG machine as it displayed a continuous graph of my heart rhythm. It would show a steady rhythm of heartbeats, and then it would go crazy. There might be as many as five rapid beats in a row as my heart fibrillated, and then it would stop and miss several beats. Continuing this way for almost an hour, the erratic display was more than a little scary and surreal. Often when my heart stopped beating or began missing beats, I wondered if this would be the time when it wouldn't start up again.

As time wore on, the doctors became increasingly concerned I would not survive. They decided they had better allow my wife in to see me. Candace appeared shaken, but not as badly as I thought she might be. To her credit, not once did she say, "I told you so," although she later confided that she had certainly thought about it.

The situation was becoming critical in more ways than one. If I were to survive, the longer the blood-flow was blocked, the more damage there would be to my heart muscle. Too much permanent damage wouldn't leave me with great prospects for a future.

Finally, after an eternity and an arsenal of drugs, the blockage dissolved. I became nauseated for about 30 seconds, and then, like someone had thrown a switch, the pain disappeared and I felt instantly better. My heart rhythm returned to normal and so did my thought processes. When it was all over, exhausted, I fell into a deep, deep sleep.

Later, when I awoke, the episode seemed like a bad dream. I couldn't believe it had happened to me. Several days would pass before the totality of the experience settled in. My recollection of the pain was all too real, but the memory of the near-death experience was wonderful.

Such a paradox: one of the most wonderful experiences in my entire life had been dying. For the first time in years, I recalled my previous encounter with death at the bottom of the murky dugout when I was 12. All the details flooded back into my mind, releasing with it countless long-forgotten childhood memories and emotions. It was too much to bear. Tears welled up in my eyes, and I cried.

Death, I realized, would be a glorious event. Rather than something to fear, it was something to look forward to. The physical pain of a heart attack I wouldn't want to repeat, but the dying part was beautiful. Strangely, although thankful for the spiritual experience, I was somewhat disappointed. I had read numerous accounts of other people's near-death experiences. Some of them had had fabulous encounters with light-beings who guided them through life reviews. This hadn't happened to me. I hadn't received the full deal, and I felt gypped.

In the weeks following the heart attack, I went through a range of emotions. In the beginning, I didn't want to believe that it had happened to me, but when it was confirmed that 25 percent of my heart muscle had been permanently damaged, self-pity often overwhelmed me. I had been physically active through most of my life. When it became apparent that I could hardly walk up a flight of stairs without becoming winded, it shook me to the core.

My family seemed to handle everything in stride, but they were at times perplexed by my emotional swings. One moment I would be fine and the next practically reduced to tears. The doctors explained that this gamut of emotions was normal for most heart attack victims, but to me it didn't matter. For the first time, I didn't seem to be in control of my own body. The possibility that I could, at any moment, drop dead in front of my children was greatly distressing. Over the next year, there was hardly a day when I didn't consider how vulnerable I'd become.

Following the heart attack, I came to realize the degree to which my children had been affected by my previous out-of-body experiences. Prior to the incident, I had shared many of the stories with them, and they had been accepting of the spiritual changes taking place in my life. Candace told me that after receiving a call from the emergency room that Sunday morning, she had bundled the kids into the car, apprising them of the seriousness of my situation. During their long stay in the waiting-room, our daughter Stacey became teary-eyed and said, "But Mom,

Daddy likes it on the Other Side so much, what if he doesn't come back?" To this day, I cannot think about that without a lump in my throat.

A month after I was released from hospital, my sister Evalina finally made the transition to the Other Side. Along with the rest of our family, I was relieved she would no longer suffer. Her six-month coma had been hard on the family. Everyone was emotionally and physically exhausted. The funeral seemed anticlimactic as most of us had all but completed our grieving. I, however, had a different perspective on her death from the others. I knew that she was in good hands and that I would be seeing her again.

☙

In the first few months following my second near-death experience, I found out-of-body travel virtually impossible. Try as I might, I couldn't free my mind enough to relax. Whenever I tried, the vivid images of my dying would play over and over in my mind. I was haunted by strong emotions. The experience itself had been extraordinary, and even though I had been initially upset at being brought back to this painful physical world, I wasn't ready to leave. I still had a lot to learn, and there were so many things I needed to do. Time, however, heals all things, and although it took more than a year, my life, along with my spiritual quest, slowly returned to normal.

Reading in bed one night, I became so droopy-eyed I set the book aside and turned off the lights. After tossing and turning for several minutes, it was becoming apparent I wasn't ready to sleep, so I decided to try to move into an altered state. Within a short time, a high-pitched tone began in the center of my head and I thought it might be possible to do some exploring.

Just as the familiar vibrations started, I felt an annoying itch in the calf muscle of my right leg. I didn't want to ruin the altered state by scratching, but it was driving me crazy. So, while lying on my back, I thought that perhaps if I moved my arm very slowly I could reach the itch and still maintain my level of consciousness. Slowly I inched my fingers forward, but it soon became obvious that I might have to either twist my body to the side or lift my legs in order to reach the spot. Concentrating,

I continued to stretch, reaching farther and farther until I realized that my fingertips were already well below my knee. This was impossible.

There was no way my physical arm could stretch that far. My body, however, felt completely normal, and I began to wonder how far I might be able to reach.

Again I stretched with ease and I soon felt the tips of my fingers moving down my calf to the bottom of my leg. What a bizarre feeling! An image of a monkey popped into my mind and I almost laughed out loud. Regaining control, I pushed on. In no time, my hand was reaching past my ankle and making its way through the blanket at the bottom of the bed. The absurdity of it was too much to believe, and I had to giggle at the strangeness of it all.

Committed, I was having too much fun to stop. As I continued to reach out into the darkness, I thought, "Jeez, I sure hope Candi doesn't wake up. She'd be in for a hell of a surprise."

My arm, or at least my perception of it, continued to stretch until the tips of my fingers bumped into a solid object. Feeling around, I discerned a smooth, raised wooden surface. It had to be the dresser, but that was at least 12 feet away from the foot of the bed. For this to be possible, my arm would have to be at least 18 feet long. The whole thing struck me as terribly funny, and I struggled to maintain control.

Slowly but firmly I pushed against the smooth surface of the dresser. After a slight resistance, my fingers slid easily through the cabinet door and into the sweaters stacked on a small inner shelf. I kept going. Soon I was through the thin panel at the back of the dresser and into the wall behind it. As I continued on through the drywall and into the wall cavity, my hand brushed lightly along the side of a two-by-four-inch stud where I felt something sharp. Sticking out of the edge of the stud was a drywall nail. Poorly aimed, it had almost missed the stud entirely. I'm not sure why this stood out in my mind, but it occurred to me that perhaps some day I could cut into the wall to check it out, if for no other reason than to verify for myself that what I felt inside the wall was really there.

I had just begun to consider what to do next, when something pulled at my awareness. A cough was building in my throat. I tried to resist for a while, but the urge finally overcame me. In an instant my consciousness was back to normal, and so was my arm.

Over the next several months I occasionally thought about the bent nail I had found in the wall. Although my curiosity had been piqued, the prospect of all of the work involved in cutting open the wall and repairing it kept me from checking it out. Almost a year later, however, I ended up doing some renovations in an adjoining bathroom and my curiosity got the best of me. The work involved some drywall patching on another part of the room, so I thought if I have to patch and paint anyway, why shouldn't I just cut a hole in the other wall too?

In no time I had finished cutting a sizeable hole through the wall where I calculated the bent nail might be. With my heart pounding, I slowly removed the piece of drywall, looked inside, and there it was, exactly as I believed it to be. Running my fingers along the stud, I grasped the nail. You can't imagine how delighted I was with the confirmation. Astral and physical realities had blended perfectly.

☙

Even though my out-of-body successes had been few and far between, I continued my crusade. One night, while Candace was away for the weekend, I tuned our bedroom television to an easy-listening music channel and got into bed with a book.

At some point, I must have drifted off while reading. Later, through the fog of sleep, I slowly became aware of my surroundings. For some reason, the music playing on the TV began to cause a similar vibration in my body. The sensations became more and more jarring, until I felt like a huge tuning fork. Finally I could stand it no longer. I had to get up and turn off the television.

Sitting up, I swung my feet over the edge of the bed and stood up. An odd feeling came over me. Something didn't feel right. A chill ran up my spine. Out of the corner of my eye I caught a glimpse of someone in the bed behind me. In a rush of adrenaline I spun around to face the intruder and stopped dead in my tracks. There was no one in the bed but me. It was my own body that I had just left behind.

Relieved, I turned away from the bed, intending to take advantage of my out-of-body state. I had only taken a couple of steps when I felt a pull near the back of my neck. Something was holding me back. Again I looked behind but saw nothing, felt nothing. It occurred to me that it might be the so-called silver cord. (I had read accounts of people who reported noticing, while out-of-body, a thin silvery cord connecting their energy bodies to their physical bodies. Even the Bible contains references to a "silver cord.")

Whatever it was, there was no way I was going to let it stop me. Straining like a horse in harness, I pulled with all my might. Suddenly, as if someone had let go of the other end of a rope, the resistance released and I cartwheeled across the room. Half expecting a burst of laughter from some hidden audience, I spun around. There was nobody there but my sleeping body. A little chagrined but more determined than ever, I headed across the room towards the TV.

The small television sat on the left side of a long dresser. At the center of the dresser was a large mirror. As I passed in front of it, it occurred to me that this would be an opportunity to examine myself in a mirror while out-of-body. But to my surprise, there was nothing there, only the reflection of the room behind me. It was so weird to be looking directly into a mirror from less than two feet away and not see myself.

In the mirror, I could clearly see my sleeping body on the bed behind me. Looking for some rational explanation, it occurred to me that maybe my eyes weren't open. Concentrating, I made an effort to open my vision and instantly found myself looking through my physical eyes. All I could see was my hand draped across the open book splayed across the bed covers. Well, that didn't seem to help, so I let my eyes fall shut and immediately I was back in front of the mirror, which again reflected only the room behind me.

Again I opened my eyes, and again I was instantly transported back to my body, seeing only the fallen book in the light of the reading lamp. Closing my eyes once more, I found myself back in front of the mirror, staring at the room behind me, marveling at the peculiar physics of the out-of-body state.

The annoying music, however, was still playing so I decided to try another experiment. I wondered if it would be possible to affect physical matter and shut off the TV while in my energy body. Reaching the knob on the front panel, I twisted it counterclockwise. There was a distinct clicking sound and, to my amazement, both picture and sound went dead. But almost immediately it came back on. I tried again. There was a click, the TV seemed to shut down, but then came back on.

This was beginning to unnerve me. The irritating music continued, and I was no further ahead. I had to find out what was going on. In frustration, I turned back towards the bed and dove into my body. Sitting up, I then leapt out of bed and headed over to the TV. As I got to within a couple of feet of it, I stopped in disbelief. To shut off this particular set, you had to push the button in, not turn it. I reached out with my physical hand, pushed the button to "Off," and returned to bed.

Sleep, however, was not possible. After tossing and turning, I got up and retraced my steps through the room. Why had I so clearly felt the button turn and click off? Previously, I had read accounts of others who reported similar anomalies while out of body. On astral journeys, they had noticed oddities such as furniture or other objects out of place. Since that night, I've never again encountered such an anomaly. Over the years, I have often contemplated the details of that particular experience, and the TV quirk still remains a mystery to me.

For some time, I also wondered why I hadn't been able to see my astral body in the mirror. I have, however, come up with a possible answer to that question. A mirror in our physical world can only reflect that which is visible in the physical world. Our astral or energy bodies operate at much higher rates of vibration, beyond the spectrum of physical light. So even though I could look down and see my energy body, I would not be able to see its physical manifestation in a mirror, because it is simply not physical.

6

Guidance

Throughout our lives, most of us encounter moments of déjà vu, those elusive memory jolts that give us the impression that we may have had the same experience before. It might be a conversation, an incident, a feeling of familiarity with a place we've never been, or a knowing that we've had the identical experience at a previous time, but just can't remember it clearly. Other times, we receive flashes of intuition or receive answers to difficult problems seemingly out of nowhere. Occasionally I had such experiences and wondered what it was all about.

To my delight, I had been able to arrange another trip to The Monroe Institute. They referred to this second weeklong seminar as "Guidelines." As its name suggested, the program was designed to help participants search within to identify and experience the subtle communication from so-called spirit guides.

Based on the experiences of Robert Monroe and numerous other out-of-body explorers, it was postulated that every person has one or more spirit guides assisting them throughout life. This wasn't a new concept to me. I had been taught as a child that we all had guardian angels looking after us. My problem was that I had never seen evidence of anything like an angel and had difficulty buying into the idea. However, considering some of the seemingly impossible experiences I'd been through, it was certainly worth checking out.

The "Guidelines" protocol was the same as before. We were each assigned to our own specially designed rooms, where all sensory distractions could be blocked out, enabling us to move easily into controlled altered states.

Unfortunately, the first couple of days were a rerun of my first visit to the Institute. Tired after the long trip, I could hardly make it through a single session without falling asleep. I decided not to waste time worrying about it, and by the afternoon of the second day, an energizing vibration began building within me.

As the morning session began, it wasn't long before I felt myself settling into a deep hypnagogic trance with the now familiar flashes of hyper-consciousness. Slowly my thoughts and attention drifted away from my body, leaving me in a warm, comfortable void.

I loved this part. The clarity of mind was such that I could drift for hours in the euphoria of expanded consciousness. I always felt a strong connection with what seemed like a never-ending universal awareness of all things. Images, thoughts, concepts, and living scenes played out in my mind. Sometimes it felt as though I was watching my own dreams, but without the confusion and scattered emotion that normally accompanies them. Absorbed in my thoughts, I lost track of time; I could spend an hour or a moment, it didn't matter. It was so utterly enjoyable.

The abrupt sound of Monroe's voice shunted my attention back to the present. He was asking us to return to normal waking consciousness. I couldn't believe that 45 minutes had passed.

I didn't want the session to end. A powerful energy had just begun rippling through me. It was an opportunity I couldn't pass up; they would have to do the debriefing without me. Concentrating on the vibration, I thought about separating from my body. The next thing I knew, I was floating towards the ceiling.

It would be just a matter of minutes before the waking signal would pull me back to my body, so I had to make a decision. Where to go? I thought about my wife back home and wondered if it would be possible to make the long trip to see her. In the next instant, I found myself hovering in bright sunlight over the front entrance of a building with a strange roof design. I wasn't sure where I was, but the street seemed familiar. A few moments later, as I glanced around for clues, a vehicle pulled up to the sidewalk and stopped. It was a car I knew well.

I realized I was floating over the front entrance of the primary school where my wife worked as a secretary. Delighted, I watched intently as Candace hurried up the long sidewalk, and passing right below me, opened the door and rushed into the building.

I took a mental note of what she was wearing: a matching outfit with a blouse and walking shorts, white with light blue flowers throughout. These details would help verify the fact that I had made the three-thousand-mile trip home in a fraction of a second. I would be able to describe the weather as well as my wife's clothing.

Something, however, seemed amiss. It occurred to me that it had to be nearly ten o'clock. Why was Candace only now arriving for work? She had to be two hours late.

I was just about to drop down through the roof to follow her into the office, when I felt an insistent tug. It was the beta signal on the headphones calling me back to Virginia. The session had obviously ended. Surrendering to the pull, I slammed back into my body.

Puzzled, I remained still for a couple of minutes, contemplating my journey. Why would Candace be going to work at almost ten o'clock? Then it occurred to me. I had forgotten about the two-hour time difference between Virginia and home, where it was only 8 A.M.

During the debriefing and chat sessions on the previous day, our instructors talked about the various experiences that some participants commonly reported during Guidelines seminars. Some reported encounters with spirit guides, loved ones who had passed on, and some even talked about previous lifetimes.

I had serious reservations about things such as past lives. As a Catholic, reincarnation wasn't part of our belief system. To us, it was just some silly illusion of those Eastern religions. In retrospect, I can't believe what a skeptic I was. For almost two years I had been floating through walls and flying into outer space. I had seen the spirit of my dying sister. Yet I still resisted the possibility that we could live more than one life.

The concept of guardian angels had been somewhat easier to swallow as these beings were actually alluded to, albeit in vague terms, in the Bible. I reasoned that the term "spirit guides," might well refer to the same beings. It could have been just a different name for angels. I filed this stuff under the "I'll believe it when I see it" category, and got up to join the group.

※

The afternoon session began later than usual. But it didn't take me long to settle into a relaxed state. While my mind wandered in a dark, comfortable void, I soon forgot about my sleeping body.

The purpose of the session was to introduce us to a new type of frequency. Designed to create a shift in our vibrations, it would give us the opportunity to experience a new dimension. As Monroe's calm voice reverberated over the headphones, I was having difficulty concentrating on his directions. The energy within me was strong, but I kept drifting off into my own thoughts, barely aware of Monroe's instructions. To make matters worse, my mind also seemed to be falling asleep. I kept clicking in and out of consciousness.

It was from one of these lapses that I became aware of a spinning vibration in the pit of my stomach. Different than anything I had experienced before, it was nearly nauseating. I was trying to get a grip on it, when I suddenly found myself floating in strange surroundings, about 15 feet above the ground. Wherever I was, it was nighttime.

In the dim glow of a small yard light, my attention was drawn to a gleaming object lying in the thick, dew-covered grass below. It appeared to be a polished, nickel-plated handgun like some of the semiautomatic pistols I had seen on television. I was puzzled. I hadn't the foggiest idea where I was or why.

As I floated in place, trying to figure out what was happening, I felt another surge of energy and, a moment later, I was looking down on a pair of hands over a washbasin. Beside the basin, an old, hand-operated water pump was bolted to the counter top. Below me, someone reached out, pumped water into the basin, and began to wash his hands. To my surprise, the wash water quickly turned to red. It looked like blood.

My thoughts were all questions. Whose hands were these? My hands? It didn't feel like they were. Whose blood? Had I killed someone? Had somebody killed me?

The scene faded and I next found myself in a long frame building looking down at a dirty wooden floor. Feeling suddenly fatigued, my mind reeled at the realization that I was now inside a physical body wracked with pain. At the front of the building, a uniformed army officer sat at a wide official-looking desk. Pacing in front of the desk was another soldier in combat gear. He was screaming at me in a Slavic tongue. I couldn't understand a word he was saying, but somehow I knew that this man was going to kill me. Almost faint from prolonged, intense pain, I couldn't bear much more. I just wanted him to get it over with.

A moment later, I was again floating in the night air, looking down on tall green grass. I had a startling realization. This was indeed another place and time. It was a scene from a previous life. As if in answer to an unstated question, I heard the words "nineteen-forty-four" in my mind. I understood. This was the year of my previous death.

The next thing I knew, I was back in my body in the present world. Pulling off my headphones, I drew a deep breath and stretched out on the bed. There was a lot to think about. No longer did I doubt the possibility of past lives. Reincarnation was a reality.

Upset that the session ended so quickly, I had many unanswered questions. Who was I in that lifetime? How did it end? As I finally got up and prepared for the debriefing room, I could only hope that someday these questions would be answered.

The rest of the day was a blur. I spent most of the time wrapped up in my own thoughts. I couldn't shake the images. Each scene played over and over in my mind. The questions and possibilities were endless. As I finally drifted off to sleep for the night, it was clear that there was so much more I needed to learn.

The next morning I awoke early and trudged off to the washroom. Upon checking my wristwatch, I noted that it was only 5:30. Since the wakeup call on the room speakers came at 7:00 A.M., I headed back to bed, hoping to get at least another hour of sleep.

With the soothing sound of ocean surf playing in the background, I settled in under the covers, reflecting on the experiences of the past week. There hadn't been anything earthshattering, but I had learned a few new things. Most significantly, I had actually experienced a piece of a past life. That meant another big shift in my perception of reality.

As I pondered the recent changes to my worldview, I began to notice a subtle vibration exerting pressure against the inside of my forehead. A new sensation, it seemed to be slowly but steadily increasing in intensity. With the exception of the vibration, it felt a lot like the beginning of a sinus headache.

Deciding to let the process unfold, I relaxed and waited for what would follow. The pressure continued to build, growing increasingly uncomfortable. When I began to wonder if I could stand much more, it abruptly released. It was as if a jet of air had puffed through the center of my forehead, creating an aperture that I could see through. At first only a small speck of light appeared, but the vibration inside my head began to surge and, ever so slowly, the opening grew wider. Soon, it seemed like I was peering through a long dark tunnel. I wondered if this vision was what some referred to as the third eye, or was it instead the type of tunnel people described in near-death experiences. Then I began to worry. Why was this happening? Could I be dying? No sooner had this thought crossed my mind, than a feeling of peace and well-being began to flow through me.

The exquisite vibration, which earlier seemed to be confined to my head, now surged through my entire body, intensifying as it spread. It wasn't long before my every molecule felt as if it were being gently massaged from within. As I drew nearer to what appeared to be the end of the tunnel, my anticipation became almost unbearable. I was shaking like a leaf in a breeze.

Softly, like sunlight filtering through the morning mist, a wonderful golden light began pouring into the opening, enveloping me, bathing me. Overwhelmed by powerful emotions, I found myself irresistibly drawn into the light. There was nothing I had ever wanted more.

For several moments I floated in place, soothed by the vibrating glow. Whatever this light was, it filled me with the warmth of complete love and acceptance. I would have been willing to stay forever, but as the minutes passed I felt a compulsion to move on. I thought I heard someone calling my name, and I could not resist. Someone was waiting for me to move through the brightness to the other side.

I had to know what the next step would bring. With increasing excitement, I moved through the opening. The golden light faded, and before me appeared the most beautiful vista I had ever seen. Billowing white clouds floated through a pristine sky. In the distance, my eyes were drawn to a horizon of beautiful snow-covered mountain peaks. Spilling out of the mountains, a forest of magnificent blue green trees cascaded down the slopes to the valley below. Alive with every imaginable color and variety of flower, dazzling grass-covered hills swept up from the valley and across a small clearing to a stand of vibrant fruit trees beside me. The smell of the blossoms, flowers, and grass was intoxicating. "If this isn't Heaven," I mused, "then it sure ought to be."

While soaking in the natural beauty of my surroundings, I began to have the feeling that someone was watching me. Cautiously turning to my left, I was surprised by the presence of two men a few feet away. Dressed in tan, monklike robes, warm smiles spread across their faces as they bowed their hooded heads in greeting. My mind raced with excitement. Who were they? They looked so familiar. I was certain I had seen them before.

As if in answer to my thoughts, the man on the left reached up and pulled back his hood. Deeply tanned, with short black wavy hair and a full beard, his beautiful dark eyes burned their way into my soul. Appearing to be around 35, he had a trim, but stocky physique. With eyes twinkling, he greeted me. "Hi Paul. My name is Meldor." The other man, a bit younger and slimmer, was cleanshaven with medium brown hair and blue eyes. Smiling warmly, he just said, "Hi."

I was stunned. They had actually spoken to me. It was the same as speaking with any person in the physical world. I clearly and distinctly heard their voices. But how could they know my name? For some reason I thought communicating with a spirit would be different from this. I'm sure that my thoughts must have been as plain as the confusion written all over my face.

Meldor's expression took on a look you might expect from an amused, loving parent answering a child's question. "We have known you through eternity, in many, many lifetimes. It's taken a while in this incarnation, but we are delighted that we have finally been able to make you aware of our presence."

With that, he smiled, and a beautiful golden aura began to form around the two beings. Growing in brightness, it enveloped both of them, slowly radiating towards me. Cautiously, I pulled back, bracing myself as the wave of energy hit. Within seconds, my body began to vibrate with the purest feeling of love and acceptance I'd ever experienced. At first, it practically took my breath away. But when I felt the love and trust it engendered, I closed my eyes, allowing the wonderful energy to envelop me.

How long I basked in their aura I didn't know, but at some point I began to feel the embrace of Meldor's mind within my own. I could feel his vibration and hear his thoughts: "We are pleased that we have been able to spend this short time with you, but it is now time for us to withdraw. In a moment your consciousness will be drawn back to your body and you will not be able to see us, but please know that we are always available to you. You need only to search within. Call us and we will be with you."

The love and appreciation that I felt for these two beings seemed unlimited. My heart ached. I wanted them to know this, but I was speechless. I managed to express only two simple words. "Thank you."

A moment later, an electrical spasm shot through my body. I was being called back. I didn't want the experience to end, but the pull to return to the physical was powerful and unrelenting. The morning wakeup music had begun to play over the room speakers, along with Monroe's voice bidding us to "rise and shine." For a moment it seemed that my consciousness was simultaneously in two places. Although I was back in my bed, I could still see through the aperture. Finally, when I could no longer maintain this level of consciousness, the vision of the two beings faded and the aperture closed. Completely back in my body, I remained alert, but emotionally shaken.

Turning down the speaker volume, I lay back to process the experience. I couldn't believe the time that had actually passed. It felt like I had been gone for only a few minutes and yet nearly two hours had evaporated.

Previously, I had read about spiritual helpers and guides. I had never given the idea much consideration, but now I somehow knew that these two beings were my spirit guides. I sounded his name over and over in my mind, "Meldor. What a strange name." My thoughts then turned to the other spirit, and it dawned on me that he hadn't told me his name.

There had been such a powerful connection between us. I had the feeling that nothing about me was or could ever be hidden from them. Meldor had said that all I had to do was call, and that was exactly what I planned to do, at the first opportunity.

The remainder of the day was a washout. I couldn't chase the experience out of my mind. For some reason an uncomfortable pressure formed in the center of my chest. I wondered if it was my heart reminding me that it still required more time to heal. Perhaps the opening of my third eye and meeting my spirit guides had been a bit too much emotional stress.

During each of the remaining sessions, I had difficulty remaining focused. When I was able to relax into an altered state, I felt my heart pounding so loudly it seemed to drown out the Hemi-Sync tones. It destroyed any chance of success through the last day of the program.

I would be heading home the next morning, and even though I had lost a day of sessions, I certainly wasn't disappointed. It had been an incredible week. I had been blessed with experiences that would keep my mind busy for days to come.

Back at home, the power of the visions and experiences continued to occupy my mind. Floating invisibly through walls or flying home to watch my wife arrive for work paled in comparison to experiencing a past life and meeting my own spirit guides.

As usual, I eagerly shared all my experiences within minutes of walking through the front door. Always an enthusiastic listener, Candace couldn't wait to hear about my new adventures. When I told her I had been floating above the school just as she arrived for work, she confirmed that on that day she had, indeed, been wearing the outfit I had seen. A small, relatively unimportant confirmation, but to me, it was greatly reassuring.

The new energy that had built up in my body during my stay at The Monroe Institute continued unabated. Still buzzing from the revelations I had experienced, I wanted so much to reconnect with the two spirit entities. The memory of their faces, their vibration, and the love I felt in their presence was continuously with me.

A couple of weeks after arriving home, the end of a long business day found me sitting in my office chair daydreaming about the encounter with my guides. Wondering if I would ever see them again, I lolled deep in thought when the abrupt sound of a distinct male voice jolted me to attention.

"We are here!"

It startled me so much I bolted upright. At first I thought there had to be someone else in the room. Where else could the voice have come from? I glanced around, but I knew that there was no one else in the building. The more I thought about it, the more I felt that the voice had to be inside my head. It sounded like the same voice I had heard a few weeks earlier at The Monroe Institute. It had to be Meldor.

Sitting back in my chair, I calmed my mind and moved into a meditative state. Within a few minutes I was hovering at the edge of sleep, when a sudden chill went up my spine. The hair on the back of my neck stood on end. Fighting every impulse to jump up and run, I refused to move. Moments later a warming vibration began to move down the back of my skull to the bottom of my spine, and then back up to the top of my head. With it, a wave of heat spread through my upper body. Everything began to spin. I felt like I was about to faint, and then I heard the voice again.

"We're sorry we startled you." Meldor's words were quiet and soothing. "We have been working with your internal energies to help you become more receptive to our communication. We wanted you to know that it's not necessary for you to be separated from your body in order to be aware of our presence."

Breathing in deeply, my body shuddered as I exhaled. I had a vague sense of slumping into the chair, my mind riveted to the new impressions inside my head. It felt different than anything I had ever experienced. I could clearly hear words and thoughts which were not my own.

I wondered if the spirits were able to hear my thoughts. Meldor's clear and measured response came quickly.

"Yes, we can hear your thoughts and your spoken words, but only if you have directed them to our attention. If you call us, we hear you."

I tried to remain calm. There were so many things I wanted to know. Although unsure of my ability to communicate, I began, "I think I've seen you in my dreams. You seem so familiar, but I need to know who you are. Are you my guides or guardian angels?"

I heard a soft chuckle. "No, we are not angels in the sense that you have come to understand. We are helpers. We have been with you through many lifetimes in this physical world. We have agreed to assist you in the challenges and goals that you've set for yourself. The circumstances of your early years were tougher than expected, but you have overcome many barriers and are now beginning to remember and reconnect with your true essence."

"But if you've always been with me," I questioned, "why haven't I been aware of you before?"

"When you first begin an incarnation as an infant," Meldor replied, "you are still closely bound to the realms of the spirit. As your physical form grows and you become more and more involved in the physical aspects of survival, your connection to the world of spirit begins to fade. Incarnated spirits, for the most part, slowly forget their origin and true identity. The consciousness of the soul, operating through the human brain, can be very slow and dense. Therefore contact between the helper and the soul is easier when the body is asleep or in an expanded state of awareness. We are able to communicate with you in your dreams and meditative states, sometimes to simply put a thought into your mind."

This was all so fantastic. I didn't doubt his words, but being the type of person I am, I needed proof. Meldor was way ahead of me. With a small titter, he admonished me, "Okay, Missouri."

Instantly I was transported back in time driving my car through British Columbia. It was a long haul through the mountains and I was having difficulty staying awake. At some point I had fallen asleep while approaching a long curve in the road. All of a sudden, I became aware of a voice screaming in my ears, "Paul, wake up!"

Jerking back to consciousness, I found to my horror that I was in the wrong lane, heading straight for a truck coming from the opposite direction. Jamming on the brakes, I cranked the steering wheel. With tires screeching, the car lurched across the centerline, missing the truck by inches.

The mental imagery came to an end, and I recalled the entire incident. I remembered having had to pull over to the side of the road while I waited for my heart to crawl back into my chest.

"That was you?" I asked. The question needed no answer.

Before I could refocus my thoughts, another memory started playing out in my mind. It was the terrible car accident I had been in years before. I was back in the car as it careened down the ditch, crashed, and spun wildly into the air. Everything went black, just as it had during the crash. The next scene, however, was not part of that memory. It was something new. As I lay unconscious in the frozen field, I became aware of someone calling my name, urging me awake, telling me to get up. I had to get help or I would die.

Only vaguely aware of my body, I drifted in and out of consciousness. Then, out of the darkness, a luminous mist began to appear beside me. It continued to expand and grow in intensity until it surrounded me. At its center appeared a radiant being. As he loomed over me, I was enveloped by an overwhelming feeling of love and compassion. The glowing form bent down and, putting his arms around me, drew me close. I could feel the warmth flowing from his body into mine. I thought that I must be dreaming or hallucinating, but it didn't matter. Completely at peace, I slipped again into the blackness of sleep. The next thing I knew, I heard my name called again, this time more forcefully.

"*Now*, Paul, you must get up *now*."

Jerking awake, I sat up in the field. The being was gone. I was alone. In the distance I could see headlights approaching. Although it had to be more than two hundred feet to the road, I had to get someone's attention. Desperately, I began crawling. But it soon became apparent that I wouldn't get there in time. Struggling to my feet, I ran for all I was worth. Just as the car was approaching, I lurched to the edge of the road, frantically waving my arms. The car careened by, but then with a spray of gravel, it came to a skidding stop. The driver put the car into reverse and backed to where I stood. The passenger side window rolled down, and someone exclaimed, "Jesus! Take it easy, man. We'll go and get help."

With that, the engine roared, gravel flew from the tires, and the car sped off into the night.

The scene faded, and a moment later I was back in my office chair.

I was stunned. This episode had never been part of my conscious memory. All of these years I had no idea that a spirit had come to help me in that frozen field. As feelings of love and appreciation flooded through me, Meldor continued his narrative.

"We would never interfere with your intentions or free will, but there have been times when we have interceded to prevent a transition before your intended time. There have been many instances in your life when we have been in direct contact with you, in times of trauma or at critical points in your development. The two examples you have been shown are the extreme. Normally, we merely try to provide a subtle guidance to nudge you along, to help you achieve your goals."

I was deep in thought. What an opportunity! A new question occurred to me.

"Meldor, you said that you have been with me through many lives. A few days ago at The Monroe Institute, as I'm sure you're aware, I had an experience that seemed to be from another lifetime. It left me with a lot of confusion and a number of questions. Was that a past life? Did I kill someone, or was it me that was killed?"

"Yes, it's unfortunate that the experience was cut short," Meldor replied. "As you now understand, you have had many incarnations. The one you experienced was the most recent life in your linear concept of time. We know that having the experience interrupted left you in confusion. If you wish, we can assist you with a continued look at that short life."

Although a bit apprehensive, I certainly wanted to unravel the mystery. "Yes, please," I responded, tentatively. "I'd like to know."

Immediately, I began to feel a slight pressure at the center of my forehead. There followed a surge in vibration and a blur of colors. The next thing I knew, I was gasping for air, wracked with pain.

The assault on my senses was unbearable. A moan escaped from my throat. My head hung down, my chin resting on my chest. Opening my eyes, I realized it was nighttime. I was outdoors in the cool air. Looking down at my body, a wave of shock spread through me. I was naked and filthy, my chest blackened and covered with blood. On my inner left thigh, a large gaping wound was crusted over with blood trailing down my leg to a pool of scarlet beneath my feet. The entire left side of my body felt like it had been crushed. An incessant pain throbbed in the left side of my chest and I was having difficulty breathing. The salty taste of blood filled my mouth. I knew there must have been a hole in my lung; I could hear bubbles as I drew each painful breath.

My hands had been tied behind my back and bound tightly to a pole. Overhead a dim yard light shone from the top of the pole, and about 15 feet in front of me stood a gable-ended building covered with tin. Exhausted and in agony, I couldn't take much more. I knew they were going to kill me, and I just wanted them to get it over with.

Moments later, two soldiers stepped out of the building, slamming the door behind them. One of them, a man I had seen in my first vision of this life review, strode up to me, raised his pistol to my left temple, and pulled the trigger. In an instant I found myself floating above my body, which now hung awkwardly from the pole. With a dizzying spin, everything faded to black, and I was back in the quiet of my office.

Emotionally drained, I needed time to recover from the intensity of the experience. Meldor's voice focused my mind once again. "We are pleased that we had this time to communicate with you. But we must now withdraw our vibration so that your energy may be restored. We are with you always."

With that, the vibrations disappeared and the ringing telephone brought me back to the physical world. It was Candace, wondering when I'd be home for dinner. It was almost 6:30. The encounter had gone on for more than an hour.

7

We Are Not Alone

Life in the aftermath of meeting my spirit guides grew ever more compelling. My days were divided between operating my business and performing my duties at City Hall, but at night I would shut out the rest of the world to investigate the nature of human existence and who I really was. My experiences with Meldor led me to realize that my understanding of life had been rather limited. There was so much more that I needed to learn about the universe and my place within it.

So many profound experiences had occurred during my last trip to The Monroe Institute that I had almost overlooked a significant event— the opening of my third eye. Although it had been a fairly recent discovery for me, it was a powerful and intriguing portal to the spirit world. In those early days, however, this new psychic vision would, more often than not, leave me confused.

I found that the best time for successful out-of-body exploration was just after awakening from a night's sleep. One morning, I woke up but stayed in bed watching dreamlike images in my mind.

As I lolled in comfort, the high-pitched sound I had become accustomed to while entering an altered state gripped my attention. My eyes closed, I began to see a tiny ray of light in the center of my forehead. Anticipating another trip to the Other Side to see Meldor, I was surprised when the opening merely widened into an oval-shaped viewing portal. Through this aperture—about an inch in diameter—a clear and vivid scene materialized.

It appeared that I was in a lecture hall with people seated around me listening intently to a presentation. I could hear a male voice droning in the background. Everyone looked like ordinary, everyday people, but the vividness and color of their faces was astounding. My own flawed physical eyesight had never revealed such depth and clarity. Where was this place? Who were these people? Opening my physical eyes, I shook off the altered state. The vision disappeared and the aperture closed.

I couldn't imagine where I had been. Had I been watching an event in the spirit realm or had I somehow remotely viewed another physical location on Earth? It was unfortunate I hadn't maintained the vision for a while longer. If I had listened to the lecture it may have given me some idea as to where I had been. Whatever was happening to me, I was grateful and excited by the possibilities. There seemed to be no end to the changes taking place in my life. As if meeting my spirit guides wasn't enough, a new means of travel and perception had opened up for me.

Over the next few weeks, it became clear that my sensitivity to many different forms of psychic phenomena had increased dramatically. I noticed subtle changes occurring when I hovered in the borderland before falling asleep. I began to see faces—all kinds of faces. Usually, a face would momentarily appear in my third eye, then, after a few seconds it would fade out, and another would replace it. Where they were coming from, or who they were, I didn't know. Sometimes as many as a dozen vivid beings passed before me. I couldn't tell if they were checking me out or I them. Some looked vaguely familiar, but I could never place where I might have seen them.

One of the strange things I noticed about these visual montages was the difference in the quality of those occurring in the morning and those I saw at night. The morning apparitions were usually clear and in color, while the nighttime visions were mostly black and white and not nearly as vivid. The only explanation that made sense was that in the morning, after a good sleep, I was more relaxed than at night. Perhaps the degree of relaxation had a direct effect on my ability to see the Other Side. The frequent visions became so interesting that most nights I could hardly wait to get to bed to see who or what would show up.

Over a period of three months, "the parade of faces," as I began to call them, materialized on numerous occasions. Mostly, it was like looking at a series of still photos. Their features didn't seem animated, and there was no indication that the spirits were either willing or able to communicate with me. Although I had become comfortable with it, I wasn't sure why the phenomenon continued to work that way. That, however, was about to change.

During a weekend convention in another city, I sat in a lecture hall with comfortable seats and a boring speaker (not a good combination at any time). Late to bed the previous night, I grew drowsy as the speaker droned on. The lights were dimmed, so I thought nobody would notice if I were to doze off. Closing my eyes, I quickly relaxed into a hypnagogic state.

Within minutes, a procession of faces, male and female, began parading before me. After several had passed, the face of an attractive young woman appeared. Struck by her beauty, I thought to myself, "Hmm, pretty." To my surprise, the moment the thought formed in my mind, a smile spread across her face. Batting her long eyelashes, she beamed with delight. Completely surprised, I exclaimed, "Jesus, she heard me!" In an instant, the vision was gone, and I opened my eyes.

I didn't realize I had blurted these words out loud until a guy sitting in front of me turned around and said, "What?"

Embarrassed, I mumbled a feeble apology.

For some reason, I had always assumed that the beings I saw couldn't hear or communicate with me. It was a surprise to discover they could do both. Another bridge had been crossed. The journey was becoming even more interesting.

<hr />

As I continued to read and learn, I occasionally came across new spiritual concepts I had difficulty believing or accepting. One of these notions was the suggestion that animals had souls and that they, too, could be found in many of the spirit realms. During a previous seminar at the Institute, Robert Monroe spoke of being visited by a couple of his house cats that had passed on. I had also read books on shamanism that often referred to "power animals." These were the spirits of animals who, in much the same manner as spirit guides, dedicated themselves to the guidance and protection of humans. Refusing to allow for even the possibility of such a concept, I had always considered this some sort of uneducated primitive myth.

Most nights, I read for an hour or two before falling sleep. One night, I had become so engrossed in a book that I kept reading into the wee hours of the morning. As I read, a peculiar feeling came over me. It felt like someone was in the room watching me. Setting the book aside, I glanced around, but noticed nothing out of place. I returned to my reading, but couldn't shake the persistent sensation. It was becoming more powerful and distracting. Putting the book down, I again scanned the room. This time, my attention caught something moving just outside the door.

Floating in the doorway, two feet above the floor was a round, swirling mass of energy the size of a basketball. The iridescent globe seemed to be made up of millions of small particles, orange and black in color. I had the impression that I was seeing something at a molecular level.

I watched as the shimmering sphere expanded, spreading outward from the center until it took the shape of a huge spotted leopard. Standing in profile 20 feet away from me in the doorway, the cat was spectacular. It was entirely real and alive. I could hear and see it breathing, its belly moving with each breath. Slowly it turned its head in my direction. When our eyes met, an instant flash of familiarity swept through me. A warm vibration swirled in my chest.

The leopard's beautiful eyes seemed to stare directly into my soul. I felt I had known this spirit for an eternity. Captivated by its gaze, I became immersed in the memories of its love and protection. Finally turning its head away, the majestic beast promptly dissolved into millions of multicolored molecules, and then abruptly disappeared.

My throat felt dry. I was having trouble breathing. I was wide-awake and yet, right in front of me a ball of molecules had appeared, turned into a leopard, and then disappeared. It was real in every sense. I had heard it breathing. I could even smell it.

Shakily, I got out of bed and headed cautiously to the doorway. I wanted to be sure of my own senses. This had not been an out-of-body experience. I had watched all of this with my own physical eyes, yet I was still having trouble believing it. I stood in the doorway where the leopard had materialized. The unmistakable, musky odor of the big cat lingered, but all other remnants of its visit had disappeared. Something magical had just happened and I felt truly blessed. Why had this beautiful animal visited me? What was the connection that I felt? Was the shamanic belief true? Could this be my *power animal?* I lay awake for hours, pondering it all.

For weeks following the visitation, I often found myself reliving it. It was difficult to pass through my bedroom doorway without thinking about the leopard, re-experiencing its mesmerizing eyes, or feeling that vibration in my chest.

About a month after the incident, I had another strange experience. One night, I snapped awake with a falling sensation in the pit of my stomach. It felt as though I had just returned from an excursion, but I had no idea from where. Vibrations still coursed through my body so I prepared myself for another adventure.

Trying to decide on a destination, I floated to the ceiling. Curious as to where I had been, I concluded that although my conscious mind didn't know, my subconscious could probably return me to the same place. I decided to go with the flow, and almost instantly I felt a shift and found myself floating in an unfamiliar room in what looked like the lower level of a two-story home. There was nobody around, but I could hear a commotion on the upper floor. Deciding to check it out, I slid up through the floor into the next level. Just as my head and shoulders began to pull through the carpet, I was startled by the hiss of a cat and the sensation of something slashing through my face. If I had been wearing pants, I'm sure they would have been soiled. I had come up into the hallway right beside where a cat was sitting. As soon as it saw me, it tried to claw a chunk out of me.

Gathering my courage, I floated up to the ceiling high above the hissing ball of fur. In terror, it finally tore out of the hallway and down the stairs like it had seen a ghost. I didn't know whether to feel good about it or bad. This was the first living animal I had encountered while out-of-body. I couldn't believe the poor little creature had seen me. I had scared the crap out of it, and it returned the favor.

When I finally got my wits about me, I noticed an open door at the end of a hallway. The light was on, and I could hear the sound of giggling kids. Floating through the doorway, I rose up to a corner of the ceiling. Below, four young boys, about ten years old, were having a great time jumping on the bed, batting each other with pillows. This seemed to be an adult's bedroom. Their parents obviously away, the boys were taking advantage of it.

As I watched their amusing high jinks, one of the boys stopped dead in his tracks, looking up in my direction. His mouth fell open. He stood there, frozen. I was astounded that he could see me! When a couple of the other boys stopped to look, I decided to make my exit. I thought of returning to my body and, in an instant, I was back in my bed.

I didn't think I would be trying that again soon. Whether or not my subconscious had taken me back to where I was previously, I didn't know, but it didn't seem likely. Somehow, I had gone off course. I wondered why the boy had been able to see me. I hoped I hadn't been responsible for scaring the poor kid into therapy. I couldn't help but laugh, thinking of the wild story the boys would be telling when their parents got home. Some guy in blue jockey shorts floating around the ceiling isn't the type of report most parents want to hear.

⊗

As time wore on, I became more familiar with the feeling and vibration of my spirit guides. Although my life had become extremely busy, I tried to spend at least a few minutes each day communicating or attempting to make contact. Depending on my level of stress and ability to relax, sometimes I felt their presence and sometimes I didn't.

One night I awoke at about 3 A.M. with the familiar high-pitched tone in my ears. I knew that if I could keep from falling asleep, it would be a good opportunity to leave my body. Within just a few minutes my mind calmed and I dropped through the threshold into superconsciousness. Before long a wave of energy flooded the top of my head and began to radiate throughout my body. Concentrating on the frequency of the vibration, I pushed the energy higher. When every molecule in my body seemed to be buzzing with electricity, I was ready to leave. With just the thought of floating, there came an abrupt surge and I lifted off the bed towards the ceiling.

Elation momentarily overwhelmed my senses. When I regained control, I had difficulty deciding what to do. Should I fly around the house? Head out into the night sky? Perhaps I could find my way back to the beautiful park where I had met my spirit guides. The thought had hardly registered when I felt a shift, a feeling of movement, and I was standing in a parklike setting. Sensing a familiar presence nearby, I turned in the direction of the vibration and was greeted by two smiling faces.

"Welcome back. We're glad you could join us." Meldor's voice was clear and strong. "We know you have many questions. Reopening awareness to your own spiritual reality can be very exciting. We are pleased to assist you in any way possible. You need only to ask."

I wasn't sure what I should be asking. My mind was racing. Finally, I thought of a good beginning. "Thank you for helping me," I said. And referring to the second guide I added, "But you know, I don't know your name."

"In our plane of energy," he replied, "names are not necessary. Every being has an identifiable and unique vibration. You will know us by our vibration and feeling, but if you feel more comfortable with a name, you may call me Raylon."

"Sometimes," I continued, "when I try to connect with you, I'm only able to feel Meldor's vibrations. I can't seem to feel you."

"Raylon," Meldor injected, "is my assistant. He is what you might call an apprentice, learning to work as a teacher. He has other assignments and is therefore not always able to accompany me."

I thought of another question. "Sometimes, when I'm trying to communicate with you, the volume of information is overwhelming, and yet now I can clearly hear and understand what you're saying. Why does this happen?"

Meldor nodded his head and smiled. "Communication in the spiritual realm is more encompassing and proficient than in the physical world. Human language concepts are extremely limiting. When the consciousness of your mind is operating in this realm, it is easy for you to assimilate the complexity of the communication. However, when you are back in your body, trying to process the information through your physical brain, you may have difficulty remembering or interpreting aspects of the information. The human brain, in its present development, simply cannot handle the assimilation of so many levels of data.

"You may have noticed this phenomenon in your dream states. While you are engaged in the dream, your mind is operating at its spiritual level. Although everything may seem entirely understandable during dream consciousness, as soon as you awaken and begin to process the data through your physical brain, the details may seem completely nonsensical.

"To answer your question, we are communicating in this simple manner to enable you to fully process and remember the experience when you are back in your physical body. As you become more adapted to our form of communication, you will find that you are able to assimilate information at more complex levels."

A thought that had been nagging at me ever since my near-death several months earlier came to mind. I had heard about near-death experiences where people had gone through a review of their life. I hadn't made it to that point before being brought back from the Other Side. I had always wondered what the experience would be like.

Reading my thoughts, Meldor was way ahead of me. "As you are beginning to realize," he said, "when each incarnated soul returns to its origin, there is no judgment by any other entity. Each soul making the transition is assisted by loving guides in a review of their immediate past life. Very often, perfected higher beings such as the Christ Consciousness, Krishna, Mohammad or other deities and masters—depending on the individual's beliefs—will be present to offer support and guidance to the returning soul. They do not judge, nor does anyone mete out punishment of any kind. The concept of a judgmental, punishing God is purely dogmatic, a manmade construction. God does not punish. God only loves.

"We know," he continued, "that you have wondered about the experience of a life review, and to further your understanding, we will assist you in this aspect of the higher vibration. Nothing of energy is ever lost. All thoughts, actions, and deeds are retained to provide the basis for assessment and reflection. In a moment," he warned, "you may feel a shift in vibration, which is necessary to engage the higher energies that hold the imprint of the life vibration."

I felt a burst of energy, brief motion, and then a montage of images began to play through my mind. Like fanning through the pictures in a photograph album, my life flashed before me. Everything was there: incidents, events, thoughts long forgotten, good experiences, traumatic and uncomfortable experiences—all whirled by in chronological succession. If at any time I wanted to take a closer look at a particular event, the process would stop and, instantly, like a videotape playing in my mind, I would be immersed in reliving the occasion. I was on an emotional roller coaster—the highs, the lows, the sadness and grief, along with jubilation and happiness, forever imprinted on my mind.

I could not be sure of the amount of time the processing took. It could have been a minute or hours, I didn't know. I saw why there was no need for someone else to pass judgment on my life. Nothing was lost. I was the only judge necessary, and I would be the harshest critic. I knew when I had failed and when I had succeeded, but there was an unexpected twist.

Not only could I relive how I had felt during any particular incident, I could also feel the pain or happiness of others whom I had affected through my words and actions. I could feel again the anger I felt as I lashed out at a playmate in the schoolyard, but I could also feel the pain and injury he felt at the humiliation. The good and the bad all passed before me. I watched the effect that even a small act of kindness could have on others. Something as small as my cheery greeting had lifted someone's spirits, and they, in turn, felt better about themselves and treated others more kindly. I was astonished at how the lives of so many people could be inadvertently affected by my actions, whether positive or negative.

Inevitably the chronology of my life brought me back to the time of my heart attack and near-death experience. I needed to see no more. The images stopped. I felt the love and support in Meldor's embrace. I was emotionally drained, yet at the same time rejuvenated. I had a better understanding of who I was and what I needed to do.

Meldor's soft voice interrupted my reverie. "It's time now to return to the physical vibration. There is much processing that you will need to do, and your energy needs to be restored. We are pleased to have been able to assist you."

In a snap, I was back in my body. Wide-awake, I rolled over in bed and glanced at my nightstand clock. It was just after 5 A.M. More than two hours had passed.

For another hour I lay in bed, reviewing and contemplating the experience. The images of my past life were engrained in my consciousness. I would never forget them. The message was clear: it didn't matter one bit in life who won or who lost, or how rich or successful we became. When we finally pass from this world, the only thing that will matter, the only thing of lasting importance, is how we treated others along the way.

8

The Ultimate Mission

Just when I thought that I'd seen and heard more than my share of strange things, I learned of a bizarre yet intriguing concept from Robert Monroe and his researchers at The Monroe Institute.

In the late '70s Monroe had spent a great deal of time monitoring lab sessions with a gifted out-of-body explorer, Rosalind McKnight. Following numerous sessions, he became familiar with McKnight's spirit guides who often communicated through her vocal chords as she lay in an altered state. McKnight's guides began to reveal the reality of so-called "lost souls." They explained that due to the circumstances of some people's deaths, instead of moving on to the spirit realm, occasionally some souls become trapped in a moment of their own reality. Unaware that they have died, these poor beings are incapable of escaping the confines of their own trauma or belief systems.

Normally, when the physical body dies, the spirit passes easily into the higher vibration of the spirit world. It will be met by spirit guides and loved ones who have previously passed on. From there, the soul is lovingly assisted and escorted into the realms of spirit, often referred to as Heaven. But in some cases, due perhaps to the extreme violence or trauma of their deaths, some souls become trapped in a reality of their own construction for varying periods of Earth time. As they don't realize they have died, they're unable to perceive the nonphysical world they now inhabit. Although their guides and loved ones may be trying desperately to get their attention to assist them home, they are unable to make the transition. Locked into the slower Earth vibration, they cannot easily escape until they realize the truth of their existence and consciously seek the Light.

What McKnight's guides further imparted to Monroe seemed to be even more astonishing. They claimed that living human beings in an out-of-body state could be of invaluable assistance to these lost spirits. As they are still of the Earth vibration, astral travelers can be easily seen and heard by the trapped souls. Due to their lower physical vibration, living humans can gain their attention and make them aware that they have died. When these souls realize the truth of their predicament, they are then able to see and communicate with their own guides and loved ones who are waiting to help them complete the transition.

After hundreds of hours of research with McKnight and other out-of-body explorers, Monroe mapped out the specific level of consciousness in which these lost souls could be found. Thanks to improving technologies they were able to duplicate the required brainwave frequencies through their Hemi-Sync process, allowing them to guide an out-of-body explorer into this realm. Monroe and his staff also committed themselves to developing a new program to teach what they considered the ultimate service to humanity: "Lifeline."

Although a bit skeptical, I was intrigued by the possibilities, and knew I had to give it a try. Calling the Institute, I registered for the first available program.

Through several previous months, my work and other commitments had kept me extremely busy and I hadn't had much contact with my guides. I was sure that another week at the Institute would help to bridge the gap.

Time passed quickly. Soon I was back in the beautiful blue hills of Virginia meeting a new group of explorers. Although the relaxing surroundings of The Monroe Institute were just what I needed, it was not without some anxiety that I approached the week to come. The idea of trying to help people who had already died was more than a little unnerving.

The first days of the program reacquainted us with territory we had explored in previous programs. As usual, I ended up falling asleep during most of the early sessions with very little to report. The full day in noisy jets and airports always seemed to take its toll. I came to the conclusion that arriving a day earlier, to catch up on sleep, would be a good idea for future seminars.

On the second day, I awoke rested and eager to get into the program. Although I couldn't remember much, I knew that I had been dreaming about my spirit guides. I looked forward to reconnecting with them.

The morning session began and, in the quiet darkness of my CHEC unit, the relaxing Hemi-Sync tones carried me quickly into a deep, altered state. Within moments I began clicking in and out of consciousness, hovering tentatively at the edge of sleep. After three or four clicking-out episodes, I found myself in the grip of a strong vibration. My body shook from head to toe. Fighting for control, I willed the slow choppy cycles into higher, smoother frequencies. In a short time, the pulsing tremor rose into a high-pitched whine. Soon, a series of small energy rushes coursed through my body. Although I couldn't seem to exert any control over them, I lay back and welcomed the experience. It wasn't long before I realized that someone else had taken charge. My body rose into the air as if being drawn by a huge magnet. A light briefly flashed before my eyes, and the next thing I knew I was speeding towards a familiar energy.

The iridescent beauty of what I now called the Park greeted me with the warmth of a long lost friend. Meldor's powerful presence was pervasive. I could feel his distinct vibration flowing through me. Within moments he was standing beside me, softly touching my shoulder. "Hello again," he greeted me. "Welcome home."

"Thank you," I eagerly responded. "Meldor, this is so incredible. Why can't I come here everyday?"

"Actually, you do, quite often. Most nights while your physical body sleeps, at some point you travel here in your spirit body to join with those who love you. You come to learn and to rejuvenate your energy within the vibration of *The All*."

"*The All?*"

"Yes, *The All That Is.* Many refer to it by various names, but the energy you feel here permeates all things. It's the universal energy of Love. Nothing can avoid or escape its power. It is essentially the energy vibration of all souls. Considering the religious concepts that you've been taught, you may think of it as the energy of the Holy Spirit or the essence of God. It's all the same, and it's the source of *All That Is.*"

Deep within, I felt the truth of Meldor's revelations, but I was still puzzled. "It's a wonderful feeling, but if I come here every night, why don't I remember it? In fact why doesn't everyone remember it? Wouldn't the world be a much better place if everyone knew and remembered that this is our real home? If everyone could experience this and remember it, there would be no wars, there would be no crime, and no one could hurt another being."

"That is true," Meldor acknowledged. "But if everyone knew and remembered, there would be little reason to incarnate. There would be little challenge to the human experience. The challenge and the quest to improve, to overcome and to remember, is what gives real value to the experience. The value and power of human existence is in the experience itself. We all benefit from the lessons and experiences of each soul. We are, in reality, all one."

His answer made sense to me, but I struggled with the idea of being all one. I needed more of an explanation. Meldor sensed my confusion. "To truly experience something," he continued, "is the best tool for understanding. Knowing is better than believing. The human mind experiences itself as distinct and separate, but this is an illusion. To fully understand the reality of 'all as one,' and the connection of all things to each other, it is helpful to experience the polarity of separation and connection."

With that, Meldor placed his index and middle fingers on my forehead. A surge shot through me and I felt as though I was about to lose consciousness. Where just moments before I felt clear and rational, now I couldn't seem to hold a coherent thought in my mind. I was dizzy. Nothing made sense, and very quickly my entire existence seemed to be closing in on me. As I fought to maintain consciousness, the image of a television screen loomed before me. It was as if my entire view of the universe was from inside a television tube from where I looked out.

There was an electronic snap as if someone had shut off the power to the television. The screen to my perception of the world went blank. All that seemed to remain of me was a tiny dot of energy in the center of the screen. A virtual sea of blackness surrounded me. The feeling of isolation and darkness creeping into my spirit was almost too much to bear. I was alone in a universe of emptiness. A profound sadness overcame me. I wanted to cry out in desperation, but even my thoughts had begun to fade. My consciousness, my awareness of self was dying, and I knew that in another moment I would cease to exist. Then everything went black, and I was no more.

As if from an eternity of sleep, I slowly began to reemerge from the nothingness. Vestiges of dream images and fleeting thoughts tugged at me like the rescuing hands of a loving parent. In a few moments I was again awake, my consciousness fully restored. I was still me, but I felt somehow different—changed in some unfathomable way.

I'm not sure how to best describe this, but I was no longer aware of being in any particular form. I felt instead like I was a floating sphere of microscopic particles. I had no idea where I was, but it felt as if I was hovering in outer space.

With each passing moment I felt the power of spiritual energy growing within my form. Even though I was composed of hardly more than a mass of seemingly nonconnected particles, I felt more alive and together than I had ever been. My awareness of self was acute. Somehow, every individual particle of my being seemed to contain the totality of my consciousness.

As I floated in space, relishing the immensity of the experience, I became aware of a concentrated power approaching me. It was nothing that I could see, but the energy of this presence, whatever it was, was awesome. Every fragment of my awareness began to shake and then to resonate in harmony with the vibrations of this enormous force. Suddenly, I found myself exploding into the universe.

It felt as if the very essence of my spirit was being blown like dust into the far reaches of the cosmos. Expanding and growing in perception, it seemed that I had somehow joined with the energy of every living thing. I felt a baby's cry and the anguish of its mother. I experienced the joy of a puppy as it bounded happily after a child. I felt the power of a whale swimming in the ocean. From the mindless destruction of war to the purposefulness of a hummingbird in flight, I experienced and became a part of everything that I touched. It was at the same time an explosion of emotion and a mystical encounter with the love of God. I suddenly understood the perfection of creation. The entire experience was so overwhelming, so illuminating, that I became lost in the beauty and complexity of it all.

It began slowly at first—small shifts of consciousness tugging at me, reminding me that I was still attached to a physical body. Tears of gratitude and joy started welling up in my eyes until I could no longer resist the pull of the physical. In an instant the experience was over and I was back in my CHEC unit.

My heart pounding, I remained in the silence of my room, contemplating the emotions and images newly imbedded in my mind. The montage of revelations had been almost overpowering. So much had happened simultaneously that I couldn't even hope to remember, much less describe the totality of the experience. Sitting up, I tried to make notes of the session, but the effort seemed futile. After scratching out a few inadequate phrases, I summarized it with one word: "Wow."

❦

Initiations complete, we were ready to get down to business. With the help of Hemi-Sync, the trainers slowly led us into new territories of exploration. The basic plan of action called for us to be guided by the frequencies to the Park. This was a place Monroe often came across in his journeys to the Other Side. Others had described it as the "meeting place," the "receiving station," or, more elegantly, as Heaven. This was where the souls of the newly deceased arrived when they first made the transition. Here, they were greeted by spirit guides and deceased loved ones, who then accompanied them to their place for orientation to their spiritual surroundings. In the program's Hemi-Sync terminology, the level of consciousness where the Park could be found is referred to as Focus 27.

This part excited me. I felt sure that I had already been to the Park. Focus 27 must have been where I first met my guides. We were told that this level was where we could unite with our guides or other helping spirits who would then escort us to other levels of consciousness where the lost souls were trapped.

Although nervous, I couldn't wait to get going as we began our first guided tour of the various levels. With the powerful, brainwave-altering frequencies humming in the background, Monroe led us through the steps we would repeat many times in the coming days. After several palpable changes in vibration, to my delight, I suddenly found myself standing in the Park welcomed by Meldor and Raylon.

"This is a wonderful service you've made yourself available for," Meldor began. "And we are very happy to assist you."

Nervous, I remained silent as Meldor continued. "There are many beings that require assistance and we hope to help as many as we can. We do want to make you aware that you may be faced with some very powerful emotions and disturbing scenes, but we are certain you will be able to handle it. We will first accompany you on a tour of this level to help you understand and acclimate yourself to the coarse and sometimes uncomfortable vibrations that you may encounter."

With those words, Meldor and Raylon positioned themselves on either side of me. "When we begin to move through the various levels," Meldor continued, "we may not be visible to you, but you will be able to feel our energy and know that we are with you."

At that point, they placed their hands on my shoulders. I felt a dizzying shift in vibration and my senses seemed to turn inward. Within moments I had the sensation of moving at high speed through a dark, mistlike atmosphere. On and on we flew, until without warning, it felt as if I had burst through the other end of a dark tunnel in the sky. The landscape dropped away below me, and I found myself shooting through the air a couple of hundred feet above the ground. A scream caught in my throat. I felt like Wile E. Coyote shooting off the edge of a cliff, desperately clawing the air when he discovers there's no ground beneath his feet. Shocked, I virtually hit the brakes in midair, finally coming to something of a skidding stop.

"Holy shiiiit!" The words blew out of my mind before I could stifle them. Floating motionless in the air, I needed a moment to calm my thoughts and regain my bearings. "Jesus! Meldor," I muttered, "take it easy."

From somewhere beside me, I heard Meldor chuckling. "Oops, sorry about that."

The whole thing suddenly struck me as terribly funny, and I burst out laughing. It occurred to me that Meldor had probably done it on purpose. I had been nervous, perhaps a bit too uptight, and needed to relax a tad before taking on whatever lay ahead.

My wits somewhat recaptured, I began to check out my surroundings. It seemed like a real Earth environment. Below me was a large body of water, like an inland lake. A 12-foot-high cliff wound its way along the perimeter overlooking a thin strip of beach at the water's edge. I noticed a couple of people swimming in the lake, perhaps a hundred feet or so from the shore. I floated down for a closer look.

As I drew closer to the surface of the water it dawned on me that these people weren't swimming. They weren't even moving. The bodies of a man and a woman appeared to be floating just below the surface. They were dead, obviously drowned. It was then that I first noticed a man sitting on the beach, agitated and distraught. Just as I was about to move closer to him, I heard Meldor's voice in my mind. "Don't worry about him; we'll come back for him later. He'll be okay. But for now, we should continue on. There are other souls we want you to see as well."

With Meldor's reassurance, we resumed our travels. The scene below began to fade and I was soon floating over a small country home in a flat agricultural area. I noticed the absence of roads in the prairie below. There was only a small, worn, rutted path leading to the property. A short wooden fence surrounded a large, well-treed back yard containing a huge vegetable garden. Dropping lower I was drawn to the back of the house and a pathway into the garden. It was then that I understood why I was there. A rather plump elderly woman in apparent difficulty lay on her side at the edge of the path. I knew we'd be returning to try to help this poor soul, and at Meldor's bidding, we continued on.

Through scene after scene our tour continued: from visages of armored soldiers fighting bloody sword battles in medieval times to more modern forms of warfare, we journeyed on. The brutal reality was numbing. I wasn't sure that I was prepared for the depth of the emotional trauma I was witnessing. Still we continued, mostly just flying over the sites, but occasionally stopping to get a closer look at some of the souls we would return to help later.

Two of the more traumatic scenes stunned my senses, leaving a heaviness in my heart. While flying over a barren, hot and dry grassy plain of what I took to be Africa, my attention was drawn to a small, one-room, stone building. The roof was gone. It looked like the structure had been destroyed by fire. Meldor's voice surfaced in my mind, telling me that two African tribes, the Hutus and the Tutsis, had been at war. In one of the skirmishes, a number of the local people had been rounded up and locked into this building, which was then torched. There was a young soul there who needed assistance. We would return for him.

In the last encounter, we floated down into a jungle in South America, perhaps Columbia or Peru. Vegetation was thick and green. As I neared a small clearing I spied the body of a young man draped over the bottom rail of a ranch-type fence. It looked as if he had been crawling through the fence when he died. A large wound cut through the back of his neck, nearly severing it. I wondered about the circumstances of this gruesome scene, but knew we'd be back.

With that, Meldor brought our tour to an end. "It's time for us to depart," he said. "Your emotional energy needs to be restored. You will have much to process before we return for this work."

A second later I was back in my body. The session hadn't ended yet, but I pulled off my headphones and stretched out on the bed. Meldor was right; I would need some time to think about all I had witnessed. As shocking as these scenes were, I was surprised at my calmness and detachment. In my physical body, the horror of the experience would have been difficult to deal with, but in my spirit body I understood that there was no such thing as death. There were no accidents. Each and every event had its purpose.

Stark images still playing in my mind, I got up and headed out into the warm Virginia sunshine. Enjoying the peaceful sounds of nature, I wandered aimlessly through the lush grounds of The Monroe Institute. In the shade of a large old tree I sat down, resting my back against its trunk, and while the birds and frogs sang a lazy lullaby, I fell asleep.

Sometime later, I awoke to the chirping of an angry squirrel in the branches just above my head. He was, no doubt, scolding me for invading his territory. With the fading images of a dream retreating into my subconscious, I crawled to my feet, apologized to the squirrel, and headed off to dinner. At the dining room I was surprised to find that most of my friends had already finished their meals. I had slept for more than an hour.

The following morning, rested and alert, I couldn't wait to get going on my first soul rescue mission. Following breakfast and an early briefing session, I anxiously headed to my CHEC unit. By the time the vibrations of the Hemi-Sync tones surfaced in my headphones, I was already deep in an altered state.

As Bob Monroe's voice guided us through the various levels of consciousness, I was having trouble focusing on his words. I kept clicking in and out of awareness. The stereo frequencies were designed to lead us through the various levels in ascending order until we finally reached the Park at Focus 27. Halfway there, I began to feel a familiar vibration that could only be coming from Meldor. In anticipation, I relaxed and waited for the sound of his voice. Instead, I was unexpectedly jolted by the sound of a squirrel. It was so startling, I almost sat up in bed. Then I heard his distinct laugh.

"That was *you* waking me up under the tree yesterday?" I asked.

"What, you didn't recognize me?" Meldor chuckled. "You'd probably still be out there if I hadn't awakened you."

"Very funny, Meldor," I replied. "You do that type of thing often?"

"Only when I need a good laugh," he chortled. "You'll never be able to look at a squirrel in the same way again, will you?"

"Not likely," I mused. "It's a neat trick, though. You'll have to teach it to me some day."

"Oh, I can assure you, that was no trick. What makes you think I can't be a squirrel if I want to?"

"I don't know. But trick or not, I'd still like to learn how to do it."

"You already know how to do it, you've only forgotten. Someday you'll remember."

Meldor changed the subject. "So, are you ready to get down to business? We have a busy day ahead, you know. Places to go, people to meet."

"To tell you the truth, Meldor, I'm still a bit nervous about it. How will I know what to say? What if I screw up or can't get through to them?

Meldor's voice softened. "Don't worry. You'll be just fine. You were becoming a bit too emotionally involved yesterday. You've got to lighten up a little or you may end up blocking your own efforts. That's why I've been trying to cheer you up. Just remember, even if you can't see me, I'll be right beside you."

With that, there came a surge in vibration, and a moment later I found myself hovering in the air above the lake we had visited the previous day. Below me the same two bodies floated beneath the surface, one male, the other female. About a hundred yards from shore I noticed a small boat lying on the bottom in relatively shallow water. I somehow knew that it had been swamped in a sudden storm. The man and the woman had drowned.

My attention was then drawn to the lone male sitting at the edge of the water. Rocking back and forth in apparent grief, he appeared extremely agitated. Tears streamed down his face.

At that point I became aware of another being floating in the air beside me. I felt his vibration but I couldn't get a close look—his shimmering image faded in and out of view. Not alarmed in the least, I wondered who he was and why he was there beside me. Meldor interjected, telling me telepathically that this entity was the spirit guide of the man on the beach. His was the soul we had come for, and his spirit guide was along to assist in leading him to the Light. It was my job to get this poor man's attention and bring him to the realization that he had died.

As I descended to the shore, I wasn't sure what to expect. From there I walked slowly in the sand until I drew to within just a few feet of the man. He appeared to be in his mid-thirties, a bit stocky, but of average height. With a mop of dark matted hair, and a week's growth of stubble, he looked like he'd seen better days. Undoubtedly supplied by his spirit guide, the name "Randy" resounded in my mind.

I was about to step closer, when a wave of energy almost toppled me. Inundated with a jumble of frantic, overwhelming emotions, I realized I was actually hearing and feeling the man's thoughts. Imprisoned in his own reality of unthinkable horror, he was paralyzed with shock. The sheer intensity of his mental anguish was staggering. I found myself backing away, begging, "Oh God, I can't do this. How am I supposed to help him?" Instantly, Meldor's reassuring voice calmed my fear.

"It's okay, Paul. You'll be just fine. Nothing can harm you, and this soul can use your help. Use the power of your mind to help him relax. Send him loving energy. You'll see."

I decided to give it another try. Hanging back, I tried to project soothing, calming thoughts that everything would be all right. To my surprise, after two or three minutes, his thoughts began to slow, his terror subsiding. When he had calmed down a bit, I tried probing his mind to see if I could make sense of his dilemma.

Slowly the details began to emerge. This poor soul had somehow made it to shore after their boat capsized and sank, but his wife remained in the lake. Unable to swim, he was terrified of water. Frantically crawling on his hands and knees at the edge of the lake, he had screamed in horror and disbelief. He wanted desperately to dive back in to save her, but found himself frozen with dread. His fear was simply too great. Not realizing that he had actually drowned without making it to shore in his physical body, he now sat trapped in the horror of his own reality. He was already in his spirit body, but because of his dilemma he could not escape the confines of his own illusion.

How could I get him to realize that he was dead? I wondered if I could somehow get him to float into the air with me. Perhaps if he saw his own body he would realize the truth. Not sure of anything, I decided to play it by ear. Summoning up my courage, I took a couple of steps forward and called his name. "Randy." There was no response. I repeated my call, this time a bit louder. "Randy, can you hear me?" Suddenly, jerking his head in my direction, he looked up at me with wild eyes, screaming.

"My wife! She's in the water. Please help her. I can't swim!"

Shaken by his outburst, I tried to remain calm. "She's okay, Randy," I stuttered. "Marlene is . . . she's just fine." My own words surprised me. Where had her name come from? How did I know it?

"What do you mean, she's okay?" He stammered, wide-eyed, disbelieving.

"She's okay, Randy. She made it out of the water and went to get help."

"She's okay? How did she do that? I didn't see her."

"She's just fine, Randy. You might have been unconscious for a while and didn't see her. Marlene is just fine, but right now we're more concerned about you."

"Oh God, thank you God," he wailed. "I thought I'd lost her. Thank you. Thank you." Staggering to his feet, he hugged me. I gently patted his back, thinking to myself, Well, that wasn't too bad. Now how the hell am I going to tell him he's dead?

"Where's Marlene?" Randy asked as he stepped back from the embrace. "God, I can't believe she's okay. She's not hurt or anything, is she?"

"No," I said, wondering how I was going to get out of the hole I was digging. "She's okay, but now you're the one we need to help."

"Me? I'm okay. There's nothing wrong with me."

Now what would I tell him? I began to grope for the right words. Would mere words be enough to convince him that he was now in the spirit world? Not likely.

"Show him his body." The sound of Meldor's voice filtered into my mind carrying with it images of looking down at the two bodies from above the water. I wasn't quite sure how to pull it off, but decided to give it a try.

"When our bodies die, Randy, we may not even notice the difference for a while. It might seem like we're just our normal selves, but there is a difference; we can do things we couldn't possibly do if we were still in our bodies."

Randy's eyes widened and a sort of disbelieving "Say what?" expression came over his face.

"Haven't you noticed anything different since you got out of the water?" I asked. "Don't you feel a bit strange and tingly, a little lighter?"

"Aaah, no, not really." His incredulous look said it all. Knitting his brows, he looked me in the eyes and in an agitated voice retorted, "What the hell! Of course I feel a bit tingly. I just about drowned, for Christ's sake."

Trying to soften my demeanor and wishing I had used a different tack, I continued. "What would you think, Randy, if I told you that you *did* drown?"

"What . . . then, how the hell could I be standing here talking to you?"

I needed to somehow get the message across without further upsetting him. I had an idea. "I'm sorry, Randy, I didn't mean to upset you," I said. And in a conciliatory gesture I reached out to shake his hand. His features softened as he tentatively accepted my offer. In that moment I begged Meldor to help me out. Projecting every ounce of energy I could muster into the connection between our hands, my hope was to try to boost his vibrations beyond the physical field that limited his perception. The flow was powerful and instantaneous.

It hit him with such force that he appeared stunned. His eyes widened. For a moment he hesitated, trying to pull away, but I maintained my grip. Then all hell broke loose! To my surprise, I began to rise slowly into the air. Disbelief spread across Randy's face as he too started lifting off the sand. Stretching his toes, he tried desperately to reach back down to the beach, but we continued our slow ascent. As we approached a height of about eight feet, he desperately threw his left arm around my neck, hanging on for dear life. I had no idea what to expect next, but I knew one thing for sure: Meldor had taken charge of this operation.

Leveling off at around 12 feet, I tried to calm my racing thoughts. Still clinging to me tightly, Randy seemed to be taking my cue, and I could feel his stress begin to subside. As we began to slowly float out over the water, he looked around in amazement. When we were finally in position overlooking the two bodies, our movement stopped. Releasing my grip on Randy's right hand, I directed his attention towards his own limp remains. He looked down, and upon seeing the body he flinched, tightening his grip around my neck. With intense curiosity, he continued to stare at his corpse until a look of sheer amazement spread across his face. Finally recognizing it as his own, a tremor rolled through him. And then, ever so slowly, his vibrations seemed to change. Without diverting his gaze he began to speak in low subdued tones.

"I didn't know. This is so strange. I feel perfectly fine, but that's my body. I guess I don't really need it." He then turned his head, looked up at me and asked, "Who *are* you?"

A feeling of relief and compassion came over me. "Just a friend," I whispered. "I came to help you to the Other Side."

Perhaps without even realizing it, Randy released his grip, floating freely in the air beside me.

I knew the next step might be a bit more painful for him, but I wanted him to understand that his wife would be waiting for him on the

Other Side. I pointed again to the water, but this time towards the woman's body floating about 50 feet away.

His eyes followed my direction. "Oh no! Marlene. It's Marlene," he sobbed. "But you said she was okay."

"But she *is* okay, Randy. She's never been better. She just went on ahead of you. If you want, just take my hand and I'll try to take you to her." Without hesitation he reached out, gripping my left hand with his right.

The moment of truth was approaching. Nervously, I closed my eyes to send a quiet thought-message. "OK, Meldor, it's up to you. Please take us where we need to be."

A rush of energy swept through me. My consciousness plummeted, and everything began to turn black. Seconds later we emerged through what seemed like a dense mist into the warmth and brightness of the Park.

The power of the place was stupefying. For a moment Randy tried to shield his eyes from the tremendous light, but quickly realized that it wasn't necessary. Dropping his hand, he let out a whistled exclamation as he drank in the beauty of the surroundings. Soon, our attention was drawn to the sound of someone approaching. On a pathway just to the left of us appeared a dark-haired woman beaming with light and happiness.

"Mar?" Randy could hardly believe his eyes. "Oh Jesus, Mar. You're okay!" He bolted down the path to embrace his happy wife.

This was one of the most wonderful and rewarding encounters I had ever experienced. I felt blessed and honored to be able to help another soul in this way. Breathing a quiet thank you to God, I felt the warmth of Meldor's voice in my mind.

"A wonderful feeling, isn't it? You've done well. We're very grateful for your assistance with this soul, but it's now time to return to your body. You'll need to become a bit more grounded and rested before our next journey. As always, we are with you."

Suddenly dizzy, I seemed to lose consciousness. A moment later I was back in my body.

The rest of the day flew by. Although we followed up with two more sessions, I just couldn't get my mind into it. When I did manage to stay awake, my thoughts kept returning to the previous experiences. Meldor was right. I needed grounding, some physical activity to take the psychic edge off my vitality. Heading outdoors, I ran the half-mile trail to a small lake. There, the Institute kept a couple of canoes for participants' use. I crawled into one and paddled hard around the pond before returning. The sweating and hard work did the trick. My body and my mind were once again attached to the Earth.

❧

After a good night's sleep, I was ready for another adventure in the spirit realm. Soon into the first session, I made contact with Meldor. Now that I had a bit of experience helping lost souls, he indicated that he would leave me more on my own. He felt confident I'd be able to handle almost any situation, but assured me he would still be there if I needed assistance. All I had to do was ask.

The Hemi-Sync frequencies carried me quickly to the Park. Once there, I was immediately approached by a wonderful, loving spirit who'd been trying to break through to a soul trapped in her country garden. It was the elderly woman I had seen a couple of days earlier.

This time the transition to the necessary level of consciousness was quick and direct. After only a moment I found myself floating in the air directly above the elderly woman. She lay on her side on a well-worn garden path. Beets and tomatoes she had been carrying remained strewn across the path. Although I knew there was no connection, she reminded me of my grandmother.

There didn't seem to be a lot of trauma surrounding the woman's death, and I wondered why she'd become trapped. Her guide told me her name was Maria. He explained that throughout her life, she had maintained an inordinate sense of duty to her husband. In addition, she had never believed in God or any kind of afterlife. Her rigid belief, or lack thereof, dictated that when someone died, that was it. There was nothing more. So, refusing to accept existence beyond the body, when Maria died, she was unable move on. Thus for her, time stood still.

As her guide telepathically communicated these messages to me, I wondered how long she had been caught in her own time warp. The crude construction of the cabin, along with the apparent absence of any utilities or even roads, suggested that her death must have occurred many years earlier. I was wondering what year it might have been, when the voice of her guide popped into my mind: "1853."

Unbelievable! More than 140 years had passed in the physical world since this poor soul had become locked in her illusory reality. Her guide, however, assured me that it was not nearly as bad as it seemed. Our perception of time didn't exist on the Other Side. In her mind, very little time had passed.

I began to consider the possibility that this particular soul might be tougher to get through to than I had at first imagined. Convincing her that she was dead might not be so easy. Asking Meldor for assistance, I immediately felt him contributing to my thought process. With his guidance, I decided to try something that might be in opposition to her beliefs.

I floated down near the woman to a position about three feet off the ground. Seeking to determine her state of mind, I focused my attention on her thoughts. To my surprise, I found she was almost frozen with fear. Terrified of her husband, Maria knew he would be very angry if his lunch wasn't ready by the time he got home. She had long ago convinced herself that Herbert was a good, hardworking man, and it was her duty to see that he was happy. If he wasn't, it would always somehow be her fault.

Even more significant to the present moment was her fear of dying. She did not want to cease to exist. For several weeks before she died she had felt increasingly strong pains in her chest that began whenever she worked too hard or became upset. She hadn't said anything about it to Herbert. Now, even though the severe pains had passed, she was perplexed and upset that she couldn't get up. It became clear to me that she had died of a heart attack. Her fear of both living and dying had locked her into her illusion.

From my position, hovering a few feet above the ground, I softly called her name. "Maria."

She lifted her head in my direction, but said nothing. Through squinting eyes, she appeared to be trying to make out what she was seeing. After a few seconds she finally responded, "What do you want?" Her voice revealed a strong Polish or Ukrainian accent.

"I came to help you, Maria. Everything will be all right." I said.

"But I just can't get up," she replied.

"Sure you can, Maria. You can get up. All you have to do is take my hand, and I'll help you."

"But you're not even touching the ground. How can you do that?" She asked suspiciously. "Who are you? Are you an angel?"

"No, Maria. I'm not an angel." I said softly, "But I can help to take you to Heaven."

"Heaven, there's no such thing," she argued.

"It doesn't matter if you believe in Heaven or not, Maria. It still exists, and it *is* real. You didn't believe what the Bible said, but it's true. You remember the pains in your chest? You knew there was something wrong with your heart, didn't you? Well, now your body has died. You can leave it behind and go to Heaven. All you have to do is take my hand."

I floated down to the ground beside her. As if testing the reality of what she was seeing, Maria closed her eyes and shook her head. When she reopened them and saw that I was still there, she let out a sigh of resignation and slowly reached for my hand. Grasping her arm, I gently guided her to her feet. Although she didn't realize it, in her energy body, she was virtually weightless.

A look of relief and amazement spread across her face. She was finally ready to leave. Holding her hand, I focused my thoughts on her spirit guide, asking for assistance. Almost instantly, a vibration surged through my body like a high-voltage transformer. I felt a shift in consciousness, and in less than a heartbeat, we were standing in the beautiful green grass of the Park.

Maria's eyes widened. Overwhelmed by the beauty and power of the place, she mumbled in disbelief. There was hardly time for a quick look around as her attention was drawn to a group of people approaching on a small pathway beside us. Tears of joy rolled from her eyes as her two children, her mother, and her husband welcomed her home.

An emotional moment for me as well, I felt a lump building in my throat, and decided it was time to leave. Sensing my thoughts, Maria's guide expressed his gratitude with a wonderful parting gift. Placing the palm of his right hand flat on my chest, he closed his eyes in concentration. A moment later, like someone had opened a tap, my body was flooded with a radiating energy. I closed my eyes to more fully enjoy the exhilarating vibrations. The force began to swirl and expand throughout my chest. It felt like my heart was about to burst. Wonderfully dizzy, my consciousness began to slip. Soon everything turned to black, and the next thing I knew, I was back in my body.

Elated, I got up and headed out into the morning sun. The energy infusion had been so powerful, I felt like I could take on the world. Grateful for the tremendous opportunity for spiritual growth, I offered a quiet prayer of thanks.

☙

The last day of the program was eventful and emotional. I had been having the best results during the morning sessions, and this morning would not be a disappointment.

Within minutes of the session's start, I floated quickly through the levels of consciousness. Meldor's familiar vibration accompanied me as we began to move into the spirit planes. By the time we reached the area of the lost souls, we were joined by a bright and intensely focused being. There was something new and different about this guide. Though I caught only glimpses of it, it didn't seem to have a physical form at all. Instead, it appeared only as a bright, vibrating oval of light. Even without a physical shape, this entity seemed to project a powerful feminine energy.

With a determined but gracious manner, she led us quickly to the soul who had been entrusted to her. Without any feeling of movement or direction, we were suddenly standing before a mudstone building on a wide, open plain. It was the burnt-out building I had been shown a few days earlier on my tour with Meldor. The building had been burned black. The roof was gone, and what had once been a window and door, were now just bleak sooty openings. I stepped closer, peering in through the window.

The sight of more than a dozen burnt and charred human bodies almost staggered me. Repulsed, I wanted to get away from the place. Even though it was difficult to discern the features of most of the bodies, it appeared that nearly all of them were either quite young or very old.

They were male and female, strewn across the floor. At least five of them were small children. The suffering that must have occurred seemed too horrible to comprehend. This had been done deliberately! What kind of fear and hatred would cause someone to do such a thing?

It was then that I began to sense the presence of a soul trapped in deliberation. Near the far corner of the room, a young black African boy, perhaps 10 or 11 years old, lay face up in a crumpled heap along the wall. His thin hands were clasped to the sides of his head covering his ears. The horribly burnt body of an older woman lay across his legs, pinning him down.

This was simply too much. I didn't want to see what this young man had experienced. Closing off my perception, I begged Meldor for help.

Almost immediately the warmth of his energy began flowing through me. Like a powerful sedative, the effect was calming. For several moments I stood, languishing in the intense vibrations. Soon Meldor's reassuring words filled my mind. "The more horrific the prison," he said, "the more wonderful the release."

The words pierced powerfully through my being. He was right. This unfortunate soul certainly needed our help. I began to imagine how wonderful it would be to see the young man's transformation from desperation to joy. There was no question; this was something I had to do.

Reopening my perception, I began to focus on the boy's thoughts. Bracing myself for the mental shock that would surely follow, I prepared for the worst. But it didn't happen. Instead, I heard only a small voice quietly singing a simple tune. To my surprise, I found his mind engrossed in thoughts of being safely hidden beneath thick, comforting blankets. It was like he was absorbed in a daydream. Probing further, I understood what was happening.

As a young boy, he had endured a terrible existence. All too often, he had witnessed atrocities of mind-numbing consequence. His mother had been frightfully abused and beaten so many times that he had learned to protect himself by crawling into the safety of his bed. Pulling the blankets over his head, he would put his fingers into his ears to block out the sound. Now, at the horrible ending of his young life, he had again protected himself by mentally crawling into his bed and blocking out the terrible reality. This time, however, he was locked into his self-induced daydream.

Although saddened by what this young boy had endured, I was immensely relieved I didn't have to experience his terror. This would be a lot easier than I expected.

Stepping through the doorway, I crossed the floor until I stood over him. He looked like such a lost little creature it tore at my heart. Asking for God's help, I reached down and placed my hand on top of his head. Startled, his eyes flashed open. He jerked his hands away from his ears, staring up at me in complete surprise. I couldn't help but smile. Feeling a deep empathy and tenderness for this child, I began softly. "Hi," I said. "What's your name?"

"Lelanee," he whispered back.

"Lelanee," I repeated. "That's a nice name." His eyes widened. I slowly continued. "You're okay now, Lelanee. You can get up if you like. How would you like to see your mother?"

He nodded his head.

I reached down, took his hand, and began to help him to his feet. All of a sudden, the building, the horrific scene, and everything around us dissolved before my eyes and we were instantly transported to the Park. Lelanee's eyes were wide with amazement as he scanned the surroundings. Before I could say a word, he bounded past me yelling, "Mama, Mama!" Elated, I turned to watch as his mother swept him into her arms, and hugging him close, spun in circles, laughing happily.

Gratified, I just stood there, grinning. When tears began building in my eyes, I wanted to be back in my body, and a moment later I was.

There was so much to think about. I lay in bed contemplating the power and meaning of all that I had witnessed. At the beginning of the week, I had been more than a little apprehensive and skeptical about the program, but it had turned out to be a miraculous learning opportunity.

Even though I had experienced many remarkable encounters in the spirit world, the final session of the week proved to be the most profound. After moving quickly through the various levels, I was joined by two spirits who wanted to take me to their lost charge. One of the entities was a spirit guide, while the other had been the grandfather of the soul we were to retrieve. Although I wasn't given the name of the guide, I was told that the grandfather's name was Alejandro. The name of the young man we were searching for was Marcos.

Following a short burst of movement, we emerged on the ground in a heavily vegetated, jungle-like area. It seemed to be about midafternoon. The sun shone brightly in the warm, humid air. This was the same place Meldor had taken me on our first tour. My impression was of a rural area somewhere in South America. I could feel the vibrations of both spirits that accompanied me, but could only make out the faint form of the grandfather.

As I stood in the green grass of a small clearing, the memory of the disturbing scene of my earlier visit returned. We would be looking for a body with a vicious neck wound, draped over a fence. Our immediate surrounding was familiar. The old weathered three-board ranch fence was right in front of us, but there was no one to be seen.

I stood for a few moments peering about when, to my left, the sounds of someone running caught my attention. A soldier in green camouflage came charging out of the dense underbrush and stopped short in the clearing. Obviously looking for someone, he crouched, anxiously scanning the fence line. The view of the other side of the railing, however, was obscured by dense brush and foliage. From a distance I could hear the sounds of machine-gun fire and barking dogs moving in our direction. The thought entered my mind that this was a drug raid.

There came a flurry of motion, and I spotted a dark-haired young man crashing through the foliage on the other side of the fence. Diving to his hands and knees, he began desperately crawling through the horizontal planks towards the clearing. The soldier, now less than a hundred feet away, quickly raised his rifle and fired twice. The bullets ripped through the back of the young man's neck just as he was part way through the fence. His head dropped, and his body collapsed lifelessly over the bottom rail. Then it was as if time stood still.

Long moments passed as I stood riveted to my spot. Stunned by what I had witnessed, I was also puzzled. This was different than the other retrievals. All of the earlier cases had been presented after death had occurred, not *while* it was happening. Previously I had either been given the details by my guides or had probed the thoughts of the affected soul. This time, however, I was right there, as if it were just happening. Could it be that we had actually traveled back in time to the exact moment of the event? Not knowing what to make of it, I returned my mind to the task at hand.

Marcos's thoughts were frantic. In that instant he knew his neck was broken and that he would soon be dead. In shock and disbelief, he began to pray.

Moving to within just a few feet of him, I called his name. "Marcos," I said softly. Continuing his Spanish prayer, he obviously hadn't heard me.

"Marcos," I repeated more loudly and firmly. This time he stopped praying and fell into a dead silence. Then as if deciding that he must have been hearing things, he returned to his prayers with renewed vigor.

At this point, I wasn't sure what to do, but I had to get his attention. Offering a quick prayer of my own, I asked for help and guidance. A moment later I felt a strange new energy swirling through my body; it intensified until it began to literally radiate from my fingertips. My hands felt scorching hot.

Knowing there must be a good reason for the energy flow, I bent down and, placing my hand on the back of his head, I again called out his name.

Breakthrough! In the middle of a word, he stopped praying. Then with gushing sobs he began to cry.

"Marcos," I repeated softly, trying to sooth him. "Everything is okay. Your neck is all right. You can get up now. Look, your grandfather, Alejandro, is here to see you."

As the words were coming out of my mouth, a stunning realization hit me. I couldn't believe what I was hearing. My thoughts were in English but my words were not. I clearly heard myself speaking Spanish, yet I hadn't a clue how to speak Spanish! Momentarily dumbfounded, I didn't have time to give it much thought.

Marcos began to stir. Slowly raising his head, he glanced at me, and then turned in the direction of his deceased grandfather. With a loud cry, he let go a burst of unintelligible expletives. I didn't know if he was cursing or praying, but suspected a bit of both.

Seemingly forgetting his injuries, Marcos jumped to his feet, his energy-body passing through the upper fence boards like they weren't there. A big smile spread across his face. Fixated, he gingerly stepped around me and rushed to his grandfather's embrace. As I turned to follow him, in the next instant, Marcos, his grandfather, and everything around us, abruptly vanished. With a resounding jolt, I slammed back into my body. The session was over.

As I lay in the darkness reliving the fascinating images, numerous questions plagued my mind. Had I actually gone back in time to view an event *while* it was happening? A fluent Spanish dialogue had flowed from my mind. Where did it come from? Had I spoken Spanish before? Perhaps in another lifetime?

I knew I might never know the answers to these questions, and perhaps it didn't matter. The questions themselves could be more intriguing than the answers.

⊛

Our final debriefing session ended with the expected rounds of teary-eyed hugs and goodbyes. We would soon be heading back to our busy lives in every corner of the globe. It had been a most remarkable week for me. I hadn't shared many of my own experiences with the group, but I had certainly been enthralled by some of the emotional stories I heard. Just a week earlier, I had had serious reservations, but now there was no doubt in my mind. We *had* made an important difference in the lives of some people.

9

Spiritual Connections

Life, I had always believed, was for the most part a crapshoot. Fraught with unexpected twists and turns, it could lead us down some peculiar paths. I was beginning to discover, however, that regardless of the roads traveled, eventually we all arrive at the same place—home. Although often an endlessly confusing struggle, the path we end up following is likely the very same one we ourselves designed before we came here.

I was gradually learning that there weren't many coincidences or accidents in life. Instead, there seemed to be a definite plan including some built-in roadblocks and obstacles that each of us envisioned before incarnating.

Following my return home from the Lifeline Program, I spent a lot of time in contemplation and meditation. My recent experiences had been profound, and I needed to know how it all fit into the path I was taking.

It felt like my life was becoming something of a giant jigsaw puzzle without the benefit of a guiding photo. Every now and then I was given a new piece to put into place, but I couldn't yet grasp the entire picture. There were still more pieces missing than found. On top of that, I had no idea how big the completed puzzle was supposed to be or if I could ever hope to put all the pieces together.

Some things I knew to be true without a doubt. I knew there is definitely a God but I wasn't as sure about what or who God is. From Meldor's revelations, it seemed that we are all part of God, and even more incredibly, as a collective unit, we *are* God.

I accepted the premise that we are eternal and that the great majority of us do not come into the world just once, but incarnate many, many times. Working through our goals and trials, we hope to eventually achieve perfection and ultimately the realization of being one with God.

I also understood that we—and apparently every other living thing in the universe—are connected at a spiritual or pure energy level. Being all part of the experience, we could also experience all of the parts. These things felt right and true in my heart, but there were still so many things that I didn't know and couldn't comprehend. In terms of spiritual knowledge, I was still in kindergarten. My education had only just begun. . . .

Having lived a difficult and tormented life, my mother, wracked with cancer and Parkinson's disease, finally gave up her body on her 81st birthday. Although grief-stricken at her passing, our family was relieved that she would no longer have to endure the suffering of her final years. Most of us were with her in the hospital when she made her transition. By that time in my life, I had a completely different view of death than my devoutly Catholic siblings.

A few months earlier, as it became apparent her condition was terminal, she had been afraid of dying, uncertain if she was good enough to be allowed into Heaven. Undoubtedly, throughout her life, she had heard far too many sermons of hellfire and damnation. Although we all thought she could be sainted, she worried she might be somehow lacking.

In those final moments, while holding her hand, I spoke to her with my thoughts, encouraging her to let go, to go to the Light. I promised her that she would be going to a wonderful place where she would be happy and free of her crippling diseases. I assured her that Grandma and

Grandpa would be there to greet her, and I told her that she would be able to fly.

Although my sisters and brothers wept with grief, and a large lump formed in my throat, I tried to maintain positive thoughts. This, I told myself, was a wonderful occasion, and we should be happy for our mother's return home. I would not and could not cry.

Near the end, as her life force began to withdraw, a noticeable change came over the energy in her body. I knew she was ready to leave and closed my eyes, hoping to be able to witness her transition. But it was not to be. With all the anxious thoughts flooding my brain, I wasn't able to step up my vibrations or see beyond the insides of my eyelids. Although I couldn't see her, I was able to feel her subtle vibration as she floated to the ceiling in the upper right hand corner of the room. I sensed her elation and wonder. Moments later, while I strained to open my inner vision, her vibration faded and she was gone. My eyes still closed, I projected a final message. "Bye, Mom. I'll see you soon."

This had all happened about a year before my Lifeline seminar. At various times during the ensuing year I attempted to make contact with my mother while out-of-body, but to no avail. Out of frustration I stopped trying. I knew that if it were meant to be, someday I would meet her again on the Other Side. I had learned through trial and error that if I became obsessed with trying to achieve a certain experience, it would usually elude me until I least expected it.

About a month after my return from The Monroe Institute, it was my mother who came to visit me.

I had gone to bed late. As I floated at the edge of sleep, a fluttering vibration began to slowly surface in my awareness. Tired as I was, I couldn't resist the opportunity for an adventure. Taking mental control of the vibrations, I moved quickly through the threshold of consciousness, attempting to home in on the frequency that led to the Park. But nothing happened. For several more minutes I lay in bed, trying to focus my thoughts while fighting off sleep. It appeared that I was going to lose the struggle and slowly I drifted into oblivion.

A loud thud quickly brought me back to awareness. To my surprise, I found myself floating near my bedroom ceiling, the sound of a woman's soft voice calling my name. Startled, I turned in the direction of the voice. To my total bewilderment, a large portion of the bedroom wall began to swirl into a dim mist before opening into a tunnel-like vortex about six feet in diameter. Near the center of the opening moving in my direction was an oval of shimmering light.

Projecting my senses, I probed the light to identify the approaching entity. Almost immediately a vibration of familiar love permeated my entire being. I had not the slightest doubt. It was my mother!

The anticipation was exhilarating. I watched as the light moved slowly in my direction. Was this the form that my mother now inhabited? Was this the true form of all spirits?

Within moments the glowing oval floated through the wall and into my bedroom. Once inside the room it stopped, and with a gentle mes-merizing swirl, it began to transform into a familiar human shape. My mother did not appear at all like the withered, tired, 81-year-old I had last seen. She looked to be in the prime of her life, between 35 and 40 years old. She was simply radiant.

Even though I wasn't in my body, I could feel the pounding of my heart. I had not anticipated anything like this. My mother exuded such a wonderful peacefulness about her that I ached with happiness. As she stretched out her arms, I moved to embrace her. The instant we touched, I felt a rush of energy; the bedroom faded, and the next thing I knew, we were in the Park.

Surprised, I had no idea how this movement had taken place. Pulling back from her embrace, I looked into her eyes. They were beaming with happiness and reassurance. In my mind I heard her voice. "It's easier to talk to you here."

For a moment I felt Meldor's vibration nearby, then it faded. I had the impression that he had been assisting in this reunion and then with-drew to give us privacy.

"Mom, you look wonderful," I gushed. "It's so great to see you."

"It's beautiful over here," she said. "All the pain is gone, and see [she held up her hands], I don't shake anymore."

I couldn't take my eyes off hers. Beaming brilliantly back at me, they carried the knowledge and memories of so much of my life. How many times had I looked into those wonderful eyes to see the pain and tears of a hard and unrewarding life? How many times had I fought back my own tears for the deep disappointment I saw in those eyes? Disappointment and frustration at the things that she wanted to give but couldn't. How many times, as a boy, had I been comforted by the warm, unconditional love that shone in those eyes when the rest of the world seemed cruel and unforgiving?

All of these thoughts and feelings flowed though my mind. For the all-too-few times that I would see happiness in those eyes, I would also see years of sadness and yearning. Now it was different. No longer was there sadness or disappointment. I now saw only happiness and the kind of contentment that could perhaps only be realized by someone who had gone through great tribulation and triumphed.

Bursting with joy, I wouldn't have traded that moment for all the gold in the world.

"It's okay," she said, knowing my thoughts. "It's all part of the learning experience that we chose. It might have seemed pretty hard at the time; sometimes I wanted to quit, but it was worth it."

I was puzzled. "You mean you wanted a life like that?"

"Yes, of course. It wasn't actually so bad, you know. We've been through tougher lifetimes than that. In order for us to get what we need out of it, it's important that we don't remember that we ourselves chose the kind of life we wanted to experience. You and the rest of your brothers and sisters are part of the plan we all put together. That's how it works."

"We all put together?" I was confused. "You're saying we all wanted a life like that? You mean we came here knowing what was going to happen and how it was going to turn out?"

"Well, sort of." She smiled coyly, a gleam in her eyes. "We don't always know how things will turn out, but we put ourselves into circumstances where there can be a number of possibilities and outcomes. It all depends on the choices we make and how we deal with the situations we put ourselves into. Before I was born, I already knew how I was going to die."

"Jeez, Mom, that's kind of spooky," I said in a serious tone. Almost immediately, the silliness of my statement became glaringly apparent. We both burst into laughter. Here I was, talking to the spirit of my dead mother, proclaiming that what she was telling me was spooky. We giggled about this for some time.

For several moments we stood with arms entwined, enjoying each other's vibrations and our own memories. This meeting was so completely different than I had ever imagined it might be. I marveled at the remarkable change in my mother. Yes, she was still the same wonderful person I had always known, but it was our relationship that was different. We seemed to be relating to each other like old friends meeting again after a brief separation. It wasn't the same type of mother/son relationship we had experienced in our physical bodies. It was much deeper and older than that. It was like we had known each other for a long, long time.

Finally, I broke the silence. "You know, it's been amazing. Sometimes I can hardly believe everything that's been happening. My life has changed so much in the last few years."

"Yes, I know," she smiled. "I've been keeping track of you."

"You have . . . ? Thank you," I responded. "I think about you a lot. Sometimes I dream about you."

"I know," she said, her eyes hinting of sadness. "You've been punishing yourself because you thought you could have spent more time with me in those last few years. But you didn't need to worry. I knew how you felt. I knew how it hurt you to see me wither away, and I hurt for you. I still felt your love. You don't need to feel that way anymore."

I was now beginning to fight off tears; I didn't want to be crying. I didn't want to be sad. I changed the subject. "So, how does it feel?" I asked.

"Oh, you mean how does it feel to die? You mean you don't remember? Oh, of course you don't, but you've come close a couple of times, haven't you?

"It was wonderful! The dying part, that is. The sickness and pain beforehand wasn't so easy, but the actual dying was great. Oh, and I want to thank you for your help when I was finally able to leave. And thank the rest of the kids for their prayers too. It did help a lot. I was really scared. It was kind of strange at the time, because I could hear your voice in my mind. I thought I was dreaming, but I could hear you and some of the other kids. It made me feel better, though, and then Grandpa came and told me I could come with him."

Pausing for a moment, she had an idea. "Here's a better way to show you what it was like."

A visible stream of mental energy began flowing from her to me, and I became immediately immersed in her reality. I felt her emotions. I saw what she saw. I experienced what she experienced.

Instantly transported back to her old hospital room, I felt myself and her float to the ceiling. Below me I could see myself sitting beside her bed. I could see her frail withered body, and my sisters and brothers sitting quietly in the hospital room, tears in their eyes. I felt the sympathy and love that she felt. I felt the tug at her spirit as my grandfather's face appeared in her mind. Amazement transformed to elation as I felt myself drawn through a tunnel-like darkness, moving towards a powerful vortex of light.

At first only a small glow in the distance, the light became brighter as I sped along. Anticipation and yearning consumed me, pulling me along. Then, as waves of energy swept through me, the journey ended and I felt myself bathed in a beautiful golden light. The warmth and love of all consciousness overcame me like a narcotic. Soon, everything began to fade, and in a dizzying, spinning euphoria, I lapsed into a blissful sleep.

I wasn't sure how long we slept, but my next awareness was of awakening from a peaceful, dream-filled sleep. Through my mother's eyes I awoke to a softly lit, immaculately clean, white hospital room. Around her were a number of loved ones who had passed on before. I recognized the beaming faces of my grandmother and grandfather, my brother-in-law, Albert, and a number of aunts and uncles, all there to welcome my mother home.

With that final scene, the thought-transference ended, the vibrations subsided, and I was left with a wonderful sense of peace and happiness.

It took me a few moments to recover. This method of communication—telepathy, thought-transference, or whatever it was—was incredible. Complete in every respect, there was no room for error or interpretation. I experienced what she had experienced. It did, however, leave me puzzled. Why had my mother awakened on the Other Side in a hospital room? I thought everyone was whole and healthy in the spirit realm. There should be no need for hospitals.

Picking up on my thoughts, Mom explained. "They tell me that if a person has had a long, painful death in an Earth hospital, their spirit energy can also become weak and run-down. Disease in the physical body can also affect the energy body and vice versa. People in that condition can also become very accustomed to their surroundings. It helps make the transition to spirit so much easier if they wake up in a familiar room where they're being cared for. It can also take time for a person to restore their energy after they arrive. A hospital is a comfortable and natural way to do it. There's nothing but love and caring here."

While she was explaining these things to me, a remote tug on my awareness began urging me back to my body. I tried to resist the pull. I needed more time. There were still so many questions to ask. I wanted to find out about other lives that we might have lived together, how my brothers and sisters were connected, and how she now spent her time. I was about to ask if she planned on reincarnating when it became apparent that I could no longer fight off the pull to return. Finally, I told her that I had to leave. My body was calling me back. With an understanding smile she reached out to draw me near. I had time for only one last parting thought. "I love you, Mom."

A moment later, I was back in my body. My right arm was throbbing. I had rolled over onto it, cutting off the circulation. As I sat up and began rubbing my arm, my eyes were drawn to the wall in front of me. I would never forget the sight of my mother in her brilliant energy form, floating into my life once again.

Some of the concepts my mother had told me about intrigued me. Do we really lay out a plan for our lives before we take on a physical body? I couldn't imagine that she would have chosen the type of life she had endured for 80 years. For that matter, if I had any choice in the matter, why would I have chosen the circumstances of my childhood? Certainly there must have been any number of easier options. Why wouldn't I have chosen to be born into a rich family? And did this mean that we *choose* our parents?

What about the starving, emaciated children we often see on television in some far-off country? Why would they have chosen such terrible existences where they could die of starvation or disease before reaching the age of five?

The questions were endless, the possibilities mind-boggling. Fortunately, I knew just where to go for the answers. At my first opportunity I would pay Meldor a visit.

My schedule during those next few weeks was hectic and opportunities for a spiritual adventure were few. The rare times when I did make an attempt to connect usually resulted in my falling asleep within minutes.

Then, one Saturday morning, it was Meldor who decided to take the initiative. I remember awakening in a dreamy relaxed state. But as I lay in bed, I began to feel a gentle tingling in my forehead. This usually meant that the aperture of my third eye was about to open. Anticipating the usual parade of faces, I was surprised to find myself peering out into the peaceful setting of the Park. On a large boulder sat Meldor, looking for all the world like a canary-swallowing cat. With a twinkle in his eyes, he greeted me.

"Good morning, sleepy head. Are you ready for today's lesson?"

He looked so funny I couldn't help but laugh. "Aahh, it's the squirrel guide," I chortled. "Where have you been?"

At this, Meldor burst into such an uproarious laugh that he almost rolled off the boulder. "Very funny," he howled. "Squirrel guide, girl guide. And you do this while you're still half asleep.

"Hey, Mister," he roared, "you wanna' buy some cookies?"

Meldor continued laughing so hard; he appeared to be hyperventilating. Tears streamed down his face.

As infectious as his mirth may have been, I tried to remain unaffected, looking on with feigned bemusement. "A regular bloody comedian," I quipped. This, however, only sent him into more spasms. No longer able to hang on to his perch, he rolled off the boulder and fell howling, to his hands and knees where he continued to carry on.

When he finally began to catch his breath and settle down, Meldor let out a big sigh. "Boy, it's times like these I sure miss having a body. There's nothing quite like laughing until your sides hurt. Thank you for the memory."

After a few moments of chuckling, he got down to business. "So, you have some questions, and think I have the answers."

"I'm not so sure that there are answers to my questions," I began, "but I thought if anyone would know, you would."

"Well, I don't know if I'll have all the answers, but I'll certainly give it a try."

"I want to learn more about how things work in the spirit world," I continued. "Do we actually decide, before we come here, the type of life we'll have and even how we'll die? Do we choose our own parents? Do we set up our own challenges to overcome? How does it all work?"

"Aahh, the big question," Meldor replied. "Yes, I think it's something we can communicate to you." He sat back down on the rock, pondering where to begin.

"First, as I have alluded to before, you should know that you and most every other incarnated being already knows most of the answers to these questions. It's not so much a matter of learning about these things as it is a matter of remembering what you already know.

"Most of us have made the transition from spirit to physical life and back, many, many times. Each time we return, the memory of our origin slowly fades from awareness. By the time a child has reached the age of six, most of the memory of its true spiritual nature has been filtered out by physical consciousness, leaving the imprint only in the subconscious, and the soul. The denseness of the physical body puts a tremendous restriction on the sensory perceptions of the spirit. As a child grows in size and physical awareness, the genetics of the species, with its powerful built-in survival instinct, becomes more and more dominant, leaving a decreasing memory of its true spiritual reality.

"Our teachers have told us that we all began as part of the one great consciousness. In order to experience diversity and to honor ever-continuing creation, we, as parts of the Creator, agreed to become individuated, and split off from the source. By doing so, *The All*, which you refer to as God, could experience itself in endless evolving form and reality. Like individual drops of water in the ocean, we are still one, and flow together as part of the whole ocean of consciousness. Therefore, what we experience as individuated beings, seemingly in isolation, is actually also experienced by *The All* at various levels of understanding and consciousness.

"God, as you understand it, continues to seek perfection. It is never at rest, but continuously moving, creating, and experiencing through all aspects of its colossal energy. As individuated parts of the Creator's energy, we seek the same perfection that is sought by God; that is to become fully aware, flowing and vibrating together as one unified consciousness. We seek, as a part of God, to bring every individuated aspect, every soul, to the perfect love of God realization."

"Meldor," I interrupted, "you made reference a few moments ago to what your teachers have told you. Are you saying you have teachers?"

"Oh, most definitely. We all have teachers. There are many, many levels of spiritual vibration and realization. The physical world that you now occupy is among the lowest levels of vibration and consciousness. Because the Earth is of such a dense physical nature, with harsh realities, it is one of the most powerful levels to gain experience and meaningful development. There is tremendous opportunity for growth and advancement in the Earth plane.

"Each soul or aspect of *The All* continues always to work toward higher and higher levels of vibration and understanding. As we are in reality all one, it is a natural desire for all souls to want the very best for every other soul. The evolution and advancement of each individuated soul is extremely important to souls in all planes of consciousness. Regardless of the levels of vibration and realization that we have attained individually, we can never be completely happy or content until every aspect of *The All* has attained the God realization and perfection that we seek.

"We are our brother's keepers," Meldor added, "not because we have to be, or because we are told to be, but because we want to be. For this reason, out of pure unconditional love, many advanced souls volunteer to assist others in progressing through levels that they, themselves, have already assimilated. I have enjoyed many teachers and I will have many more."

"But, if we were already in the spirit world before we came here," I asked, "why would we bother to incarnate into a slow and dense physical body?"

"The greatest opportunity that the physical world offers is the experience of human emotions. It is for these powerful learning tools that most souls choose to incarnate, and return again and again to Earth."

"You said *most* souls choose to incarnate," I interrupted. "Do you mean there are souls that don't?"

"Oh, Heavens, yes," Meldor explained. "Billions upon billions of souls have never incarnated into a physical being as you understand it.

Many souls choose to experience and contribute to *The All* entirely from the spirit form. Every soul has complete freedom to contribute to the well-being of the collective consciousness as it sees fit."

"But why would a soul be attracted to experiencing human emotions?"

"Let me put it this way," Meldor explained. "In this higher vibration, a spirit, other than vicariously, cannot really experience or understand the many powerful emotions that an incarnate spirit can. Being part of *The All,* a spirit on this side, who has never been exposed to human or similar incarnations, is not normally able to experience feelings other than the emotion of *love.* A spirit could not, for example, experience or understand emotions such as pain, hate, fear, jealousy, sexuality, or lust.

"Knowledge gained from experience is the key. Some of my compatriots argue that to really know and appreciate a complete understanding of love, it may be necessary to experience the opposite of love through emotions like fear and hatred. The challenge and experience of all these powerful emotions can be like a very strong magnet, an almost irresistible drug, to those in spirit. These are very potent and compelling learning tools.

"But let me get back to your original questions. Through various incarnations, souls develop special friendships and bonds with certain other souls. They quickly learn that with each other's help they can achieve better results, and a more profound learning experience. So, together they agree to return again and again to the Earth environment, learning, evolving, and experiencing. Often they will switch roles in each other's lives. In one life, a soul might play the role of a parent, only to return in the next life as the other's child. Numerous scenarios can be played out time and time again, all for experience and accumulated knowledge. Experience and knowledge are, after all, the only things you can take with you when you leave the physical world.

"When souls become intricately involved in the numerous rotations of incarnations, the learning can be great. A group or family of souls may become involved in planning out the challenges and general circumstances they hope to experience or overcome in the next lifetime. The lessons and roles they agree to play can be very harsh in the physical realities of Earth. But the soul knows and understands that the experience itself will be like a fleeting dream, the batting of an eyelash in the cosmic reality of nonlinear time.

"There is also great sacrifice by individual souls to help fulfill another's chosen lessons. Like your most recent Earth mother, they may agree to put themselves into a difficult lifetime to help facilitate the learning and experience of others. For those souls who wish to accelerate their growth and spiritual advancement, the quest for experience and knowledge is tremendous.

"The human experience is a very powerful lesson. With few exceptions, those who choose to incarnate make their way through hundreds, even thousands of lives. They will experience both male and female bodies. Most, at some point, will also become murderers, thieves, and vagabonds. They'll experience lives of happiness and productivity as well as lives filled with grief, despair, and human failure. Always seeking to improve, a soul might make significant gains in one life, only to fall and digress in the next. The paths are as many and varied as the number of souls participating.

"As you have heard and read, there are many who refer to life experiences as karma. They may refer to karma as a spiritual system of justice and balance. They believe that if a soul performed badly, perhaps causing injury or even death to others, that soul would be forced to endure the consequences of its actions and make amends. This is not necessarily true. No one is forced to do anything.

"From the physical point of view, karma can be considered with both positive and negative connotations. But in the larger spiritual sense it is neither good nor bad. It is merely experience. For example, human societies may view the actions of some souls as incurring negative or bad karma where an apparent wrong has been done to another. What if that same soul had actually agreed to perform the seemingly cruel act to assist another soul in its learning experience and development? In reality it may be that an act judged by human society to be cruel and hurtful was actually a great sacrifice by the soul carrying out the act. The soul may have agreed to provide the lesson or experience for others, all the while knowing that he would incur the wrath and punishment imposed by human laws.

"But, please do not misunderstand my message here. These types of laws that hold people accountable for their actions in Earth society are very necessary for the order and well-being of the physical world. In the spiritual world, retributions and punishments are not necessary. The responsibility for actions is readily accepted by souls in the course of their development.

"For example: a soul, having lived a life as a cruel and violent womanizer, may very well choose to return in a subsequent life as a woman who may become the victim of abuse. But, I should also make it very clear: a soul caught up in cycles as an abuser or abused should not accept this as their fate, but rather strive to conquer and triumph over these powerful lessons. The soul learns and experiences from both polarities, and the slow wheel of cause and effect in human endeavor continues to turn."

My mind was spinning. Meldor's words were profound and engaging. I only hoped that I would be able to remember and integrate the message in my physical world.

I thought of another question. "I can understand, Meldor, that it may be possible for two or more souls to plan on a relationship by being born into the world as another soul's child or as brothers and sisters. But, how could two souls plan to meet and become involved with each other as husband and wife? Given the freedom of choice by their parents and the many variables involved, how could they ever hope to overcome the tremendous odds against finding each other?"

"Well," Meldor smiled, "that's where we come in. Each and every soul that chooses to incarnate into the physical world has the help of one or more beings to guide and assist them towards achieving their goals. Guides and other helpers also work together in this realm to assist the individual souls with the lessons they hope to accomplish. This is by no means foolproof, and there is certainly no guarantee that the intended outcome will be achieved. Even as incarnated souls, you always have the freedom of choice, which could negate the possibilities, but the power of the guidance can be quite strong.

"Usually, guidance will appear in small, almost undetectable, subliminal ways. A simple thought or idea could be put into your mind, causing you to turn onto a certain street or to go into a certain store where you may encounter another specific soul or circumstance designed for your development. It could also involve working with totally unrelated people, causing them to take a certain action that would assist in bringing the two souls together. The possibilities and circumstances are endless. It's very interesting, enjoyable work."

"Jeez," I interjected. "That's amazing. I never thought of it that way. That would certainly improve the possibilities for almost anything if you guys on the Other Side decided you wanted something to happen."

"Well, not exactly." Meldor grinned. "We would never do anything to interfere with a soul's higher purpose or wishes. But you should understand that our assistance might also help to achieve what may be considered by human society as bad or destructive. If a soul, for example, wanted to experience a tragedy resulting in his body or brain being handicapped, we would also assist in providing the circumstances for the accident to happen.

"We realize that from a human's physical perspective, it might seem unthinkable or cruel that anyone would assist in what may seem like an unfortunate or needless tragedy. But, from a spiritual perspective, it is only the temporary physical body that is negatively affected. The soul is enriched and empowered by the experience.

"You may also be surprised to know that many, many souls voluntarily choose to incarnate into bodies that will be born deformed or handicapped, or will become handicapped due to accident or disease at some point during life. There is literally a waiting list of souls offering their love and energy to the experience itself, or to helping others in the experience. In view of the challenge, the opportunity for spiritual growth and development can be significant, not only for those handicapped but also for the parents, siblings, and caregivers."

My mind was bursting with new questions and ideas. I was about to ask yet another question on the relationship between guides and their loved ones, when my alarm-radio clicked on so abruptly it jolted me into a sitting position in my bed. Frustrated, I got up to start my day.

I was astonished at some of the information and concepts Meldor had shared with me. Even though I had read a few books that tried to explain how things worked on the Other Side, I had never given them much credence. Now it was different. Meldor had planted a seed in my mind. I began to realize how little I knew about myself and everyone else around me.

10

Exploration

Autumn of 1994 brought even more dramatic change to my life when I was elected mayor of our city. At the time, I had no idea how much this new duty would affect my life. While still operating my own business, the additional commitment left little time for leisure or family. My days were long and tiring. More often than not I would arrive home late and exhausted.

As the hectic pace of my life sped up, contact with Meldor and the spirit world waned. There weren't enough hours in the day. It became a rare occasion when I could slow my mind and body sufficiently to achieve a working altered state.

Inexorably, life's continuing demands relegated my quest for spiritual connection to the realm of dreams. On occasion, Meldor would visit me in my sleep, but dreams being what they are, most left me with only fleeting impressions. After more than a year of this maddening pace, I desperately needed a holiday to relax, and I couldn't think of a better place than Virginia.

Almost on cue, a letter arrived from The Monroe Institute inviting me to a newly developed program they called "Exploration 27." Designed to carry participants to new levels of consciousness, up to and beyond the Park, it was just what the doctor ordered. As its name suggested, the program's goal was to explore new levels of consciousness to find and identify what they contained. It sounded too good to be true. I signed up for the first available seminar.

After a chilly midwest winter, the unseasonable warmth of the Virginia air was a welcome relief. The beautiful, serene surroundings and familiar rustic buildings of The Monroe Institute welcomed me like an old friend. It was good to be back.

Our explorer group consisted of seasoned veterans of the Institute's programs and research. There were new faces as well as old friends. Flocking around the trainers, we coyly probed for previews of what awaited us. However, in traditional Institute solidarity, they deflected our probing with a standard Bob Monroe response. "You'll just have to wait and see for yourself."

The first day of the program was a familiar reconditioning to the numerous levels of Hemi-Sync. The process never ceased to amaze me. I loved the sensations the frequencies generated and quickly settled into the routine. Lying in bed, I took note of the changes slowly creeping through my body. It always seemed to start in my legs with an intense vibration tickling the soles of my feet. From there it would slowly move up through my ankles and into my calves. The electrical sensation riding the front of this wave always seemed to trigger small jolts and spasms in my larger muscles as it moved along. In its wake, a peculiar numbness and rigidity took hold. I would feel my muscles tightening, becoming immobile, and within a few moments all physical feeling would cease. The process usually took about ten minutes to work its way through to the top of my head. My body finally asleep, my mind would remain awake and alert.

As it turned out, that first morning was not exceptional. I slid smoothly into a relaxed altered state, but nothing more happened. Through several sessions I just lay in the womblike darkness trying to guide myself into some meaningful experience, but to no avail. I called on Meldor and any-one else who might be around to lend a hand, but still nothing happened.

Perhaps I was trying too hard. This had happened many times before, and it was frustrating. I took note of the incessant chatter going on in my mind. It was that little voice we all have, the one that originates within the left hemisphere of the brain, trying to analyze the hell out of everything. I would have to figure out how to shut off all the mental noise.

By the last session of the day I was becoming perturbed. Finally, I decided to let go of the wanting. I quit trying to control the process and allowed my mind to drift to wherever it would take me. Fifteen minutes into the session, I started clicking in and out of consciousness, my mind finally free.

Drifting closer to the edge of sleep, I felt a sudden falling sensation in the pit of my stomach. After a few moments the motion stopped and I found myself floating in a deep void. Enveloped in darkness, I hadn't the slightest inkling of where I was. Well, if we're supposed to be here for exploration, I thought, I'd better check this place out.

Pushing forward through the blackness, I strained my senses trying to perceive whatever lay ahead. Minute after minute I continued on, but there seemed to be nothing, no sights and no sounds, only darkness.

Suddenly, from out of nowhere, the wrinkled face of a gray, long-haired old man popped up in front of me. "BOO!" he screamed. And then waiting just long enough to see my startled reaction, he disappeared, howling with laughter.

I'm sure my heart quit.

The old guy, however, was practically splitting his gut. It sounded like he was rolling around on the floor.

"That'll sure git yer heart a-goin'," he yelped, sounding every bit like Gabby Hayes in an old Western.

I was so shaken it took me a few moments to get my wits back. Meantime, the old boy continued to howl like it was the funniest thing he had ever seen. Listening to his infectious giggling, I couldn't help but laugh myself. When he finally began to move away, I could still hear him cackling as he headed off into the distance.

"You crazy old bastard!" I yelled after him. "If I catch you, I'll kick your wrinkled old ass!" This only brought new howls of laughter as he continued his invisible retreat. Eventually his cackling faded out, and I was left chuckling to myself.

I couldn't believe what had happened. Here I was, hovering in the middle of God-knows-where, it was blacker than the ace of spades, and some old guy's spirit had just earned a great laugh at my expense. I looked around warily, but couldn't perceive a thing. After a couple more minutes, I decided that it would probably be wise to get my butt out of there before somebody else showed up for a laugh. Focusing on my body, I felt a flurry of movement and a moment later I was back in my bed.

Before I could get the headphones off I was laughing. The crazy old bugger had practically scared the snot out of me. I wished I knew where I had been. Who was that crazy old devil? And why was he the only person I had encountered? I began to wonder if Meldor had anything to do with it. I wouldn't have put it past him.

The following day saw a big improvement in my perceptual abilities, and I could feel the energy building inside me. We were being introduced to new frequencies that would take us beyond the Park into a special meeting place. The routine was the same for each excursion. We would all try to home in on a certain area of the Park, gathering there, before heading off individually to explore other areas and levels of consciousness.

During the first few sessions I was having difficulty connecting with the other members of the group. I wasn't, however, the only one having a problem, so I didn't worry about it. We would be naturally drawn to wherever it was that our spirits needed to go. Sometimes some of us didn't seem to go anywhere at all.

Although I occasionally sensed his energy, I hadn't yet met up with Meldor. I wasn't particularly concerned because I knew that he would be there whenever I really needed him.

During one of the morning sessions, I was having a great deal of difficulty staying focused on our destination. Believe me, during an altered state, this can be a significant problem. The spirit-mind has the ability to move so quickly, but it can also become bored when nothing is happening. You can sometimes find yourself heading off in unwanted directions, triggered by a mere thought.

Stretched out in bed, I tried concentrating on the meeting place, but with little success. My mind kept wandering. I thought about home and some silly little joke my son, Dave, had told me. Wondering how he was doing with his school project, I unexpectedly found myself hovering over the street in front of his school, some three thousand miles away.

A group of kids were heading in through the front doors, but my attention was drawn to one blond-haired boy. Even though he faced away from me, I knew it was Dave. But he was wearing a jacket I hadn't seen before. Striped in blue, green, and purple, it had the strangest combination of colors. I thought, Well, maybe it's not Dave. He wouldn't wear such an ugly jacket. A moment later, I was back in my body in Virginia.

I hadn't the time, though, to give much more than a passing thought to what I'd just witnessed. Steady vibrations rippled through my body, and I was set to head off on another adventure.

There was an abrupt spinning motion, and seconds later I found myself standing in front of an enormous building. It looked like something out of ancient Rome or Greece. Built of marble or granite, it must have been at least fifty feet high. Huge pillars spanned the front of the imposing structure and an immense stairway led up to a large arched entry. Throngs of people moved in and out of the building while a boisterous group of children played on the steps. I noticed that only two or three of the children were dressed in modern clothing. The rest wore plain, loose-fitting toga-style robes. A sudden pang of paranoia gripped me, and for a moment I panicked. Quickly glancing down to make sure I hadn't shown up in my birthday suit, I let out a sigh of relief. Thankfully I was clothed in the same tan-colored robe I usually traveled in.

Feeling more secure, I clambered up the wide steps to the massive landing. Everyone seemed happy. Small clusters of adults cheerfully greeted me as I made my way through the arched entrance and into the foyer.

The beauty of the interior was breathtaking. Ornate pillars drew my eyes upwards to astonishing domed ceilings. Flawlessly painted in flowing murals, the intricate images were stunning. Perhaps this was where Michelangelo perfected his art. The paintings seemed to move and flow with a life of their own. I had never seen anything so exquisite. But, somehow, it all seemed oddly familiar, like I had been there before.

I was so entranced, I hardly noticed a woman clearing her throat in front of me. She had been patiently trying to get my attention. Lowering my eyes from the ceiling I realized that my mouth was hanging open.

"Hi, Paul. My name is Larissa," she warmly greeted me. "We've been waiting for you."

She was a tall, elegant woman in her mid-thirties. Her long dark hair was swept back from her face, revealing a soft creamy complexion and the most extraordinary blue green eyes. A white braided sash tied around her waist accented a loose fitting, light blue, floor-length gown. She emanated a wonderful air of happiness and love.

"You've been waiting for me?" I stuttered.

"Oh, most certainly," she smiled. "We knew you'd be arriving and you're right on time. Come, I'll show you around."

"What is this place?" I asked.

"This is our library and Hall of Records," she responded as we began walking along a huge corridor. On either side were row after row of shelves filled with books and odd cylinders. It occurred to me that the cylinders might contain scrolls.

"Yes, you're right." She read my thoughts. "We have every mode of communication stored here. There are other beautiful libraries on this level, but this one contains the life records of all incarnated souls. Energy imprints of all sentient beings are constantly gathered and recorded here. Nothing is ever missed. You could, I suppose, call this a living library. It's constantly growing, changing, and evolving."

As Larissa spoke, a strong feeling of déjà vu came over me. Somehow, this felt uncannily familiar. "Have I been here before?" I asked.

"Oh, yes. Many times," she laughed. "You come here often between lives to study the records, to review what you've learned, and to plan for your next incarnation. Everybody does. This is an important step in your continuing development."

As we continued wandering through the aisles I noticed for the first time that my charming guide wasn't wearing shoes. I'm not sure why this struck me as odd, but looking around I realized that nobody else wore shoes, and neither did I.

The building was massive and appeared much larger inside than out. As we passed through the maze of shelves, aisles, and adjacent reading rooms, I caught sight of two other members of our group. My friend

Bruce was leaning over a desk in a tiny alcove chatting with a guide, while Robyn, a most wonderful, gentle soul, scanned the titles of several books at the end of the row. Noticing me, she smiled in recognition. I was thrilled to see them. It would be great to compare notes later to verify that we had shared the same experience.

"Would you like to see your book?" Larissa's soft voice interrupted my contemplation.

"My book . . . ?" I asked. "Yes, I guess so." For some reason I felt apprehensive. What would the book reveal? What would it say about me? Who had written it? I wasn't so sure I wanted to know.

"Oh, please don't worry," she whispered with a reassuring smile. "You wrote every bit of it yourself. You didn't sit down and write actual words for it, but you provided all the details through the energy of your existence. Everything that you do, say, feel, or even think is an exchange of energy. These life-force imprints are recorded and stored at this level so you can track them and learn from your experience. Every nuance of energy exchange in the astral and lower vibrations is stored here. There are also many higher levels of vibration, but they have their own repositories to record and store their energy impressions.

"Aahh, here we are." Larissa stopped near the end of an aisle, reached up and withdrew a book from the shelf. The manuscript itself seemed fairly thick as books go, but I couldn't imagine how it could possibly hold all the details of my life.

"Oh, it doesn't just contain the information from your present life," she said. "It holds the story of every incarnation you've experienced on this level, and there are many hundreds of them. It also details your time between lives. It's all here."

With that, Larissa led me to a nearby alcove. Inviting me to take a chair, she placed the book on a pedestal in the center of a small round table, and randomly opened it near the middle. Soon a shimmering, tubular beam of light appeared above the pages. Although transparent, the light—or energy field—had a bluish tinge to it. It reminded me of a miniature version of the transporter beam from *Star Trek*. The field was about 16 inches in diameter and about three feet high.

Amazed, I watched closely as a lifelike, three-dimensional moving image took shape inside the field. A dark-skinned, dark-haired woman, clothed in hardly more than animal skins, sat cross-legged in front of a small shelter nursing a newborn baby. Somehow, I knew I was that baby.

I felt the power of that moment, the peaceful, intimate connection, the soothing warmth of my mother. Emotions and feelings swirled through my mind like a long forgotten memory.

I would have continued the experience indefinitely, but the light touch of Larissa's hand on my shoulder brought me back to the present. Looking up at her smiling face, I saw in those beautiful eyes the reflection of my own delight and amazement in the timeless splendor of our existence. Flashing a warm, understanding smile, she flipped the pages to another section.

I returned my attention to the energy field. The image of a dirty, white-skinned young man with a filthy mop of long brown hair began to take shape. He lay shivering under a small dirty blanket and heaps of rubbish in what appeared to be a dark, dank corner of some old abandoned building. As I looked more closely it appeared that he was quite young, possibly only 13 or 14. Coughing violently, he seemed to be burning with fever. Slowly, sad recognition came over me. I knew he was dying, and I knew this boy was me, in another lifetime, another place.

I didn't want to become involved in the scene I was witnessing. I didn't want to feel the resignation and grief already weighing on me. Turning away from the images, I wished Larissa would flip to a new page. Again I felt her hand on my shoulder, but this time it was to comfort and soothe. With her other hand, she closed the book and withdrew it from the pedestal. The energy field immediately dissolved, leaving me sitting in contemplation. After several moments, Larissa gently interrupted my reverie. "It's time to go now," she whispered. "You can come back any time you like."

Smiling sweetly, she led me from the table. Hand-in-hand, we walked back to the shelf where she returned the book to its place. As we strolled along, I began to feel a tug on my awareness. The familiar pull of the session-ending beta tones became more pronounced. Larissa clasped my hand between both of hers. "It was so nice to see you again," she offered cheerily. "I look forward to the next time." I felt a small jolt to my consciousness and her image began to fade. Although I fought to stay focused, it was a losing battle. The next thing I knew, I was back in my body.

Sitting up, I removed the headphones. The room seemed intensely hot, and I was sweating profusely. This had never happened before. If anything, I usually felt a bit chilly after a session. Worried that I might be coming down with something, I headed to the bathroom to wash my face. By the time I returned, my body heat had normalized, and the temperature in the room had subsided. I struggled for an explanation. Could this have been a side effect of watching myself burning with fever as a boy in a past existence?

Replaying the vivid scenes in my mind, I sat on the edge of my bed making notes. The skeptical, analytical part of me still wanted to put everything in order. I tried to determine the culture and time period of the image of myself as a baby. My mother's skin color had been dark. The large leafed branches covering the shelter seemed tropical. I settled on Polynesian or Philippine culture, but hadn't a clue about the era.

The images of myself as a boy slowly succumbing to death, also returned to my mind. The boy's fair skin, along with the musty, old, decaying stone walls, reminded me of Europe. England, I thought. Perhaps Scotland. Maybe Ireland. Here again, I had no idea what time period this might have been. Finishing up my notes, I headed downstairs to join the group for debriefing.

Some of my fellow participants had also enjoyed vivid, powerful experiences in the same library-type building. A few had visited other places of note, while some hadn't had any luck at all. Most important for me, however, was the unsolicited confirmation by Robyn. She had indeed seen me in the library. As I walked into the debriefing room, she was already seated. With a mischievous smile, she winked at me. "Hey Paul, who was the good-looking woman with you in the library?" Bruce, on the other hand, couldn't recall having seen me, but he and Robyn had seen each other. The validation was both interesting and reassuring.

Success during the remaining sessions continued to be a hit and miss proposition. Sometimes I would fall asleep or end up spending my time staring into the darkness. Then, in the next one, I'd be off on a new adventure. There didn't seem to be any rhyme or reason to it.

I was beginning to wonder about Meldor. Three days had gone by and I hadn't seen him. Hoping that he wasn't off on vacation, I vowed that at the next opportunity I would try to find him.

When the late afternoon session began, I plunged rapidly through the threshold into an altered state. As the energy in my body began to oscillate, I deliberated whether to send out a call for Meldor to join me or to attempt to travel to him. Deciding that it might be fun to track him down for a surprise visit, I concentrated on his familiar vibration. Almost instantly a wave of energy plowed through my body. In a heartbeat I was standing in front of him.

I couldn't believe my eyes. I was standing on the peak of a high, desolate mountain. Meldor sat before me in an oversized chair, like the kind we sometimes saw in hotel lobbies years ago. It was so large, his feet hardly reached the front of the cushion. He looked every bit like a three-year-old in an adult chair. A childlike scowl knitted his bearded face, and with hands clasped across his lap he vigorously twirled his thumbs.

"What took you so long?" he snapped.

I didn't know what to think. He looked annoyed, but at the same time hilariously silly in the gigantic chair. I had no idea whether he was serious or not. Nervously I began to search for words. "Well, I aahh . . . I thought that . . . aahh . . ."

"Ha, ha," he interrupted. And in the wee small voice of a three-year-old, he taunted, "Bet you can't sneak up on me."

Eyes twinkling, an impish smile spread across Meldor's face. He swung his legs over the edge of the chair and slid to the ground.

"Jeez, Meldor," I stammered. "You are some piece of work."

"Hey, my boy, you gotta lighten up. This is funny stuff," he chortled, reaching out to hug me. "You should've seen the look on your face."

"It's good to see you," I grinned, returning his embrace.

What a comedian, I thought, looking around. The wind-blown rocky terrain, wisps of cloud floating by in the thin air, and this huge chair on a mountain peak in the middle of nowhere. The guy had style!

"What on earth are you doing out here on a mountain?" I asked.

"Oh, just waiting for you," he grinned. Then, pointing to the picturesque surrounding valley, his tone softened, becoming reflective, appreciative. "Isn't it a great view? A perfect place for contemplation, don't you think?"

He was right. The ambiance of the landscape was exhilarating, yet peaceful. The only thing out of place was the chair.

"What's with the big old chair?" I asked.

"What chair?" Meldor's eyes were beaming.

I turned to look, but there was nothing behind us but the barren mountaintop.

"The chair was just a creation for your amusement," Meldor explained. "It was a manifestation of my thoughts. I put it there to show you that in the realms of pure energy, a thought can be real and easily manifested."

"I've been wondering about that," I admitted. "I've seen so many things in different realms. Sometimes it's hard to tell what's real and what isn't."

"In a sense it's all real," Meldor responded. "In the spirit realm, a person can create their own reality, including what you would perceive to be actual physical matter. It is the density of the matter and the rate of vibration that is relative to one's perception. On the Earth plane, where matter is extremely dense and the rate of vibration is slow, physical beings have a comparative perception of reality. A rock is real. It's hard, heavy, and relatively unchanging in terms of Earth time. So from a human perspective it's easy to form concepts that material things are permanent and immutable. But in the spirit realms, the concept of permanence is much different."

"I'm not sure I understand what you mean," I said, looking for a place to sit. I chose a bare outcropping of rock. Meldor found a place beside me and continued his explanation.

"Take, for example, the chair I was enjoying when you arrived," he said. "It was completely real to your perception, was it not? You could have crawled onto it and sat as I did. It was very real, but at the same time it was only a temporary construction of my mind; whereas the library building you visited yesterday was much more permanent and substantial. It too, however, was created by thought. But, it is reinforced by the conscious energy of billions of souls. Each and every visitor to the building maintains and perpetually reinforces the reality of the structure."

"You knew I was at the Records Hall?" I asked.

"Yes, of course. I was there with you."

"But I didn't see you. Why didn't you let me know you were there?"

"It was better for you to have the experience by yourself, without my influence or interpretation. Your evolution is more complete through different perspectives."

"The building was phenomenal," I recalled. "It reminded me of pictures I've seen of some of the ancient buildings in Rome and Greece."

"A good comparison," Meldor agreed. "It's one of the places from which the builders and architects of your ancient civilizations developed their skills. They built these beautiful structures in the spirit realm before they returned to build them on Earth. It is often in the spirit realm that creation and construction concepts are developed and honed to perfection. But it is a much greater challenge to create and build on the dense Earth plane.

"As you know, in the lower vibrations, thoughts, in and of themselves, are not so easily manifested without the necessary physical actions needed to bring ideas into reality. On Earth, for example, before a builder of stone is able to bring his creative concepts into reality, he must first create the tools with which to shape the stone as well as bring together the proper mixture of available raw materials to create the mortar."

As Meldor spoke, I closed my eyes to absorb his message. In this manner his communication was more comprehensive and thorough. He spoke directly from his mind to mine.

"There are many millions of talented spirits with such an intense love of design and innovation, they constantly work at improving their creations both in the spirit realm and in the physical worlds. While in the spirit plane, they continue their endeavors, developing new ideas, solutions and inventions. It's much easier for them to work from this level where thoughts can be manifested instantly. The more difficult part is in transferring their ideas and knowledge to the physical planes. Many accomplish this through the slower process of reincarnation.

"But there are countless souls who choose instead to transmit their ideas and inventions directly to the minds of receptive physical beings. There are great numbers of creative people on Earth who make these connections, receiving inspiration during sleep or in altered states. They may not remember, or even be aware of their journeys, but the impressions stay with them. This is one reason why people in different parts of the world often seem to come up with the same ideas or patents at virtually the same time. They have been guided."

Meldor's revelations made a great deal of sense to me. In my travels to the Other Side I had witnessed many amazing things and was slowly beginning to understand the larger picture. There was no question. We are all connected.

I sat quietly for a few moments before opening my eyes. With the exception of the valleys far below, the mountain on which we sat was relatively barren. I wondered where we were.

Meldor broke into my thoughts. "I believe you would call it the Himalayas."

"You mean we're on the Earth plane?" I asked. "How did you make the chair appear in the physical world? I didn't think that was possible."

"Oh, it's certainly possible," Meldor replied. "But don't forget, at this moment you are not in your physical body. You're in an elevated level of consciousness where these manifestations are visible and real."

For a few moments Meldor sat quietly, reflecting. "I still come here occasionally," he mused. "This used to be a favorite place of mine on a couple of previous incarnations. I always found the energy here very relaxing."

I was on the verge of asking Meldor to tell me about his lifetimes on Earth when, without warning, I slammed back into my body. I couldn't imagine what had happened.

A sharp, heavy object was pressing into my left temple. Somewhat disoriented, it took me a few moments to figure it out. Before the session began, I had been resting in bed reading a book. When we were ready to begin, I had simply set the book aside on an extra pillow beside my head. Somehow, it had slipped off the pillow, and banging into my face, jolted me out of my altered state.

Although the session was still underway, I didn't think I'd be able to reconnect with my guide, so I removed my headphones and stretched out. I thought about Meldor's explanations of the creation of buildings and structures on the Other Side, and their relationship to our physical world. The structures that I had seen, such as the library, seemed absolutely real. The stone steps leading to the front entry were as solid as anything I had experienced. Inside the building, I had felt the smooth hardness of the beautiful marble floor beneath my feet. I had touched the solid ornate pillars. I had sat upon the bench with my elbows resting on a firm table as I watched the past life images in the energy field. These things were real, perhaps more real than the structures I was used to on Earth.

As I lay in my bunk pondering the creative possibilities in the spirit realms, a pressure began to build in the center of my forehead. I was again falling into an altered state.

Focusing my attention on the spot between my eyes, I concentrated on opening the portal. Soon a small pinpoint of light appeared. But, before I could even react, the aperture flashed open and a moment later I found myself peering down the hallway of what seemed to be a very long building. Numerous doorways led off to both sides of a wide corridor. The walls themselves emanated a soft, warm green light. White tile floors reflected spotlessly. It had the feel of a hospital.

To my left, a wide-open doorway displayed the number 17 above it. I wondered if there was any significance attached to the number, but more importantly, I questioned why I had been drawn to this particular place. It occurred to me that perhaps this was the kind of hospital room my mother had arrived in after making her way to the Other Side. Moving anxiously through the doorway, I half expected to see my mother sitting up in bed waiting for me. To my disappointment, there was no one there. Feeling a small twinge of loneliness, I slowly surveyed the room. It was indeed a hospital.

The whole room was bathed in a soft, warm light. Against an adjacent wall stood a standard hospital-type bed, made up in soft white linens. A couple of white chairs had been placed on either side of the bed. What struck me as odd, though, was the absence of any medical equipment. But when I thought about it, it seemed reasonable. There was no need for medical equipment here. There were no physical bodies to heal. Hospitals in this realm served only to provide a comfortable transition for those souls who may have died in an earthly hospital environment. This was a natural, peaceful place for newly arrived souls to restore their energy until they were reoriented to the Other Side.

On the right side of the bed, a vase filled with beautiful flowers adorned a small round table. Exotic and vibrant, the flowers filled the room with a wonderful fragrance. Enthralled by their form and texture, I carefully examined several of them. They were like nothing I had seen before.

A warm breeze drew my attention to a large, partially opened window. Moving across the floor, I peered out. Immediately outside the room was a beautiful garden overflowing with flowers and plants so vibrantly colorful they defied description. The plot extended for what seemed like hundreds of yards, finally giving way to the rich green grass of a large valley. A small blue stream meandered through the gorge into a background of bright green forest crowned with snow-covered mountain peaks. I knew this had to be an area of the Park.

With a sigh of appreciation, I finally withdrew from the window and turned back into the room. I could certainly understand how wonderful and peaceful it would be to wake up in this environment.

I wondered about the rest of the building, and whether there might be other buildings in the area. Heading for the doorway, I felt a swirl of energy as I passed through the opening. A moment later I was standing in a beautiful, high-walled, cathedral-style building.

It was massive. At first impression, it seemed like a cathedral, but it was different from any church I remembered. "Remembered" was the key word. As I stood, absorbing the images, a distinct feeling of recognition came over me. I had definitely been there before. Intuitively I knew that this structure was for revitalizing and tuning soul energy.

Although enclosed by high, sturdy, perimeter walls, there didn't appear to be a ceiling over the main structure. Throughout the long, open, marble corridors there were an inestimable number of pillared structures looking a lot like tall gazebos. Approximately 12 feet in diameter and 20 feet high, they consisted of six marble pillars placed in a circle, supporting a beautiful domed ceiling.

The center of each dome contained a massive multifaceted crystal at its peak. Having the appearance of a perfectly cut diamond, each one was at least four feet in diameter. In the shape of a child's toy top, they had been set upside-down into the roof structure. The crystal peaks protruded through the tops of the domes, while their convex bottoms formed the center of the inner ceiling. The crystals, or whatever they were, were dazzling. Every one of the hundreds of facets seemed to reflect a different color and vibration. On the floor directly below each crystal stood a large round bed, about two feet high and eight feet in diameter.

From my position about 20 feet from one of these structures, I noticed three spirits approaching. A middle-aged man and woman seemed to be giving instructions to a younger man of about 20. I watched intently as the youth, dressed in blue jeans and t-shirt, crawled to the center of the bed and lay down. I could sense his uncertainty as he cautiously prayed to God for healing energy and then nervously prepared himself to receive. Within moments, a dazzling field of shimmering, multicolored energy cascaded from the crystal, flooding the area below, permeating his body.

With a look of surprise and relief the young man appeared nearly overwhelmed in the bliss of the experience. So intense was the energy infusion, that after a minute or so in ecstasy he floated off the bed. His body began to shimmer and fade from view until only an energy outline remained. Within the form of his now translucent body I began to notice a row of bright, glowing spheres of light. About the size of tennis balls, they seemed to radiate a swirling power. Could these be the chakras, I wondered? Were these the energy centers that are supposedly contained in every living body? Ever so slowly, the luminous orbs continued to intensify and expand until they finally enveloped each other, becoming a single, glowing oval of energy.

The entire spectacle was mesmerizing. The beam from the crystal had begun a process of shifting colors and intensity. Every thirty seconds or so it would blend from one color to another until it had gone through every hue of the rainbow. Finally, having made its way through the color spectrum, the beam subsided, softening to a warm golden hue. The young man's body, now a radiant sphere of energy, slowly descended to the bed below.

I had been so engrossed in the scene that I hadn't noticed that the middle-aged couple had left. I glanced around but couldn't see them anywhere.

With the process apparently now complete, the crystal energy began to fade and then disappear. The rejuvenated soul lifted off the bed and floated gently to the marble floor. As he landed, he was joined by two other light-beings who appeared out of nowhere. A moment later, all three vanished.

Fascinated, I wanted badly to give the crystal a try. However, not being so sure of the effects it might have on someone still occupying a physical body, I decided to let it go for the time being. Perhaps, I thought, Meldor might be able to advise me on it later.

I had no idea how much time had passed back in the physical world. I remembered that I had removed my headphones, so there was no way to know if the session was over. I decided I'd better get back into my body, and a moment later I was.

The speakers were silent. The session had ended. I got up, made a few notes in my journal and headed downstairs. The debriefing session had long since broken up. Most of my fellow explorers were already gathering for dinner.

As the last day of the program wound down, a group of us had been discussing the various forms of communication employed on the Other Side. I had already experienced several of these methods. When I first met my guides, it seemed that our conversation was completely normal in the physical sense. Their lips moved, and I heard their voices just as I would in everyday conversation. I have since learned, however, that the sound of their voices was perceived only in my mind.

I had also experienced the speedier process of communicating by thought transference alone. I simply projected my questions or comments and received a telepathic response, hearing and feeling the other person's thoughts in my mind.

The most powerful means of communication, though, was the method my mother had shown me. I heard, felt, and saw everything she had experienced. It was a process of thought transference containing a great deal of information all at once. Robert Monroe referred to this type of telepathic communication as a "rote" or a "thought ball."

It seemed to me, however, that I still had some major unanswered questions regarding communication in the spirit realm. Knowing that people of all cultures and languages were able to communicate on the Other Side, I wondered about the process that allows for this apparent translation of languages. I was aware that whenever I thought about something, my thoughts were in English. But, there had to be thousands of different languages and dialects on our planet alone. How, for example, could a Spanish-speaking spirit understand what I was talking about? I resolved that the next time I connected with Meldor, I would ask him.

As we settled in for our final session of the week, I hoped to connect with my guide. Within just a few minutes, my racing mind had dropped through the threshold of normal consciousness into a peaceful altered state. Projecting a mental message to Meldor, I asked him to join me, and then waited. Several minutes passed. I repeated the message a number of times, but still there was nothing but darkness. Quickly becoming bored, I found myself drifting towards sleep. All of a sudden, a loud commanding voice startled me into awareness. "Go deeper!" It was Meldor.

I concentrated again on following the Hemi-Sync signals into a lower level of consciousness. But it felt like I was already in synch with the frequency, and it was at its maximum. How could I go deeper? The only solution, I thought, was to leave it in Meldor's hands. Carefully, I turned off the headphones and relaxed into the silence.

Minutes passed, and ever so gently I started to feel an unfamiliar energy building within me. Soon, I began to experience a duality of sorts. Still acutely aware of being in my body, I felt as if I was experiencing myself in an abstract manner from another place or dimension. Brief flashes of images and colors began to pierce my awareness, too brief, however, for me to make any sense of them. I could feel my energy changing, evolving to something I had never before experienced. I knew I was entering a new field of consciousness.

"In order to provide meaningful answers to your questions," Meldor's voice jolted me to attention, "my assistants and I have decided to bring your perception to a higher level than you are accustomed to. It is from this perspective, while your consciousness is still within your physical body, that we hope to be able to explain and show you the sometimes difficult-to-understand concepts of all-knowing awareness.

"As we have relayed to you previously, the energy of all consciousness is connected. Separateness is merely an illusion of the human experience. In the higher realms, there are no barriers to the communication of sentient consciousness. From infinite collections of like-minded souls, through numerous levels of expanded awareness, to the ultimate level of God-Realized beings, the energy of thought is the same for all.

"At its purest level, thought is merely directed conceptual emotion. Interpretation or translation is not necessary because in the spirit realms it is universal and automatic. In as much as the principals of mathematics are universal and applicable to all matter and energy, so too is the relationship of consciousness between sentient beings. Pure communication is, in a sense, an expression of the mathematics of conscious awareness."

Meldor's words burnt into my mind, but I wasn't at all sure that I understood their meaning. In my physical world, I was far from academically astute, and when it came to mathematics—I had spent my entire life severely handicapped. Engrossed in Meldor's dissertation, I lacked the presence of mind to ask a question or to even respond. I knew this was important information, but I could only hope to remember half of it when I returned to physical awareness.

"The communication of consciousness," Meldor continued, "in its more universal application, is the creative expression of the energy of light and the vibration of sound. It is pure energy, and therefore embodies the elements of wave and frequency. Through these constant principles, beings of all planets and universes are able to communicate at higher levels without confusion. We are all connected and related to each other."

The realization of what Meldor was saying gripped my attention like a vice. Had I heard right? Had he actually said there were intelligent beings on other planets and universes? I didn't have to phrase the question; Meldor had picked up my thoughts.

"Most certainly," he responded. "There are infinitely more sentient beings throughout the cosmos than your world can even imagine. But, as we have discussed before, we are all part of the same collective consciousness."

My mind raced with the possibilities. I'm not sure why this was having such a profound effect on me. I had always believed there had to be other intelligent beings in our universe. But now Meldor's confirmation made it all the more plausible and real. Trying to put this all together in my mind, it occurred to me that if all beings throughout the cosmos were part of the collective consciousness, then I should be changing my perception of God to an infinitely more awesome power. Again, Meldor knew my thoughts and responded.

"The power of *The All* is beyond ordinary comprehension or imagination. Only God-Realized beings can truly know the magnitude of the massive collective energy that is *The All*."

Getting back to his original message, Meldor continued. "Although, in your present state you may not fully grasp the potential or complexity of this higher form of communication, we feel that you may benefit from a new experience."

Until this point, I had been in darkness, earnestly listening to Meldor's words. But now, a small, single point of blue light appeared in the upper left hand corner of the dark space in front of me. As I watched, the speck of light began to oscillate and started moving across my field of vision towards the right. Like a fine laser, it flowed in a slow wave motion, tracing its path with a continuous trail of light. Soon, a purple beam appeared just below the first, beginning its flowing journey across the darkness. Almost immediately, the two lasers were joined by one after another, each a different color, until the space before me was filled with wave upon wave of beautiful, oscillating colors.

As I watched in fascination, the whole thing started over again at the top, working its way down. But this time each wave of color came accompanied by a sound, a distinct pure tone. Every color vibrated its own tone. In increasing succession, wave after wave of light and sound were flawlessly added to the mixture, every tone in harmony with the previous one.

To my increasing delight, each tone seemed to elicit a different feeling and vibration in my body. Within moments, the area around me was filled with a gyrating spectacle of light, sound, and vibration. As I grew more absorbed, it increased in complexity and richness. Before long it had built into a living symphony for the senses. For some reason I couldn't help thinking about the spaceship communication scene from *Close Encounters of the Third Kind.*

I had no idea what it all meant or why it was affecting me so dramatically. I felt like I was riding on an emotional roller coaster. Depending on the color, sound, and speed at which it moved I could be carried from absolute joy to deep emotional sadness. As I delighted in flowing with the vibrations, colors, and emotions, time passed unnoticed, until the montage came to an abrupt stop and I found myself in the silent darkness of my CHEC unit. Meldor was gone. The vibrations were gone. The session had ended.

I lay in my bunk for at least another twenty minutes, going over the things I had seen and heard. It had been another remarkable week. I had learned a great deal more about who we are and where we came from. Silently, I offered a prayer of thanks for the wonderful gifts I had been given. And I thanked Meldor for his love and guidance.

The trip home was long and uneventful, but it gave me time to contemplate the new knowledge I'd absorbed. More importantly, it gave me time to wind down my energy before I plunged back into the demanding world of business and politics.

When I finally arrived home, Candace and I sat at our kitchen table as I filled her in on the great experiences I'd had. Listening intently, she eagerly asked questions while I recalled the significant events. I almost forgot to mention, though, that I had zipped home one day while out-of-body and watched a boy I thought was Dave heading into the school. I allowed however, that it might not have been Dave because this kid was wearing a weird-colored jacket I hadn't seen before.

With an incredulous look on her face, Candace asked what the jacket looked like. I described it as best I could. Without saying a word, she abruptly got up from the table and left the room. A few moments later she reappeared from the back closet carrying a jacket. "Is this it?" she asked. I didn't have to say a word; the look on my face said it all. Without a doubt it was the same ugly jacket. Shaking her head in amazement she added, "We bought it while you were gone."

11

Our Journey Together

Some of the strangest mysteries in life are oftentimes those fleeting, innocuous synchronicities that seem to be just beyond our grasp and understanding. For example, how is it that we may be meeting someone for the first time, yet feel as though we had known him or her before? Isn't it odd how, on occasion, we can be instantly attracted to some people and inexplicably repulsed by others? Could it be that we have, in fact, known them before, in another time and place?

Like most everyone else, I occasionally noticed these anomalies, but usually didn't give them more than a passing thought. Given what I have learned about the reality of reincarnation, these intuitive recognitions of other people now make a lot more sense. If most of us have lived hundreds of lives, chances are we'll run into people we've known previously, some who have affected us positively and others negatively. Although I was gaining a clearer understanding of how things really worked, my next contact with Meldor would open my mind to the intriguing realities of the tremendous support group we all have on the Other Side.

Several weeks following my return from Virginia, I had gone to bed earlier than usual to get a good rest before an intense series of meetings the following day. As I approached the borderland of sleep, a distinct popping sound captured my attention. I could feel the presence of someone else in the room. Expecting to see my wife sleepily trudging to the bathroom, when I opened my eyes, I was surprised to see Meldor floating quietly beside the bed. Sitting with his legs crossed lotus style, he was hovering about three feet off the floor, looking like the Dalai Lama in meditation. Intrigued, I watched in silence as he continued to hover without opening his eyes or saying a word. After a couple of long minutes, I could no longer stand the suspense. I had to find out what he was doing.

"Pssst, Meldor," I whispered. "What are you doing?"

Opening one eye, he looked at me briefly and then closed it again. Another few moments passed. Then, as if resigned to the interruption, he sighed and opened his eyes. A smile spread across his face.

"Just floated in for a visit," he whispered. "I haven't heard from you in a while, and there are some things I want to share with you."

"That's great," I whispered back. "I'm really happy to see you, but I can't visit for too long. I have to get some sleep. Tomorrow's a busy day."

"Don't worry," Meldor laughed. "You'll be just fine." And then with a curious look on his face, he asked, "By the way, why are we whispering?"

"I don't want to wake up Candi," I replied.

"But she can't hear us!" Meldor looked mildly perplexed. "We aren't using physical voices."

For a moment I didn't grasp what he was saying. I could have sworn I was still grounded in my body and very much physically awake. There was no doubt in my mind that I was speaking with my normal physical voice.

Meldor just smiled knowingly. Slowly unfolding his legs, he straightened his body until he was standing upright on the bedroom floor. "Come," he said, reaching for my wrist, "take a look for yourself."

Grasping his arm, I pulled myself to a sitting position, dropped my feet over the edge of the bed and stood up. Turning back towards the bed, I was in for a bit of a shock. There, still under the covers, sleeping peacefully was my body. The transition out of my physical form had been so smooth and effortless I couldn't believe I had simply sat up and walked away from it. Meldor was right. We didn't have to whisper.

"So, where are we going tonight?" I asked.

Meldor's eyes twinkled. "How about to the heart of your soul?"

"The heart of my soul?" I questioned. "Am I not the heart of my soul? Where else could it be?"

"The reality of your soul and who you really are is much more complex than you realize, or rather I should say, remember. There are many aspects to the reality of every soul. Your reality is a combination of what you experience personally as well as the experiences you share with others."

With that Meldor sat on the foot of the bed, motioning for me to join him. Being careful to avoid sitting on my own body, I selected a spot beside him and sat down. Reaching out, he placed his hand on top of mine and quickly got into the heavy stuff.

"In order for you to better understand the realities of your existence, it is important for you to know the context of your creation and origin. My teachers tell me that when the Creator first manifested the individuated aspects of *The All*, they were created by pure thought in the form of energy, light, and vibration. Each unit of energy, being part of the Creator, carried with it an aspect of the Deity's consciousness.

"As we've discussed before, these individual aspects of God formed part of the Creator's wish to experience itself. The design and intent of the intricate light-beings thus created was and is a manifestation of perfect love. It is in this manner that we have all been created from the energy and likeness of God.

"In order to instill an innate yearning for reunion and completion, as well as diversity of experience, each of these energy manifestations was further split into two individuated beings. In much the same manner as the nucleus of a fertilized egg begins its life experience by first growing into two individual cells, so too do these identical aspects of God begin their conscious existence. Although identical in source and vibration, they develop their own realities through differing experience.

"The two souls thus created are never far apart in their thoughts and vibration. Attracting each other like magnets, they interact continuously in the spirit realms, and if they have chosen to incarnate, they may be together in the physical world as well. Their bond is strong and eternal."

"So the talk about soul mates is actually true?" I breathed. But it was more a statement than a question. The revelation astounded me. I had often heard people using the term, but to me it always seemed nothing more than a wishful romantic notion. Now I had to consider that there might be more to it than I'd previously been willing to believe.

"The term 'soul mates,' is actually an appropriate description." Meldor had obviously read my thoughts. "Although, I think it has become something of an overused term in the reality of the world today."

A question arose in my mind. "Meldor, you said that they *may* be together in the physical world. Wouldn't soul mates *always* want to be together?"

"Actually," Meldor replied, "it's not as common as people would like to believe. Most incarnates spend occasional physical lives with their soul mates in various relationships, but most of their time together is spent in the spirit realms. You should understand that if it were common practice, it could seriously hinder the development of a soul who most often seeks to learn and evolve by challenge and diversity. Repeating life after life with the same soul would not provide the diversity of experience conducive to spiritual development."

Another question popped into my mind and I couldn't resist asking. "Is my soul mate in the physical world right now? Have I met her?"

"To begin with," Meldor chuckled, "it might be unwise to assume that your soul mate is someone of the opposite sex. Secondly, although I understand your curiosity, it would not be appropriate for me to provide an answer to your questions. It is your life to live as you have chosen. We may help and guide you toward your intended direction, but we would never short-circuit your desired path. Suffice it to say that everything will eventually be revealed to you.

"You should also know," Meldor added, "that there are many other levels of soul interaction that are just as important to our development, if not even more so. In our quest to grow and develop from experience, we also find that there are other souls whose vibrations and energy resonate in almost perfect harmony with ours. The attraction amongst these harmonious like-minded souls is formidably strong and nurturing, resulting in a very special bond and relationship. In seeking ultimate perfection and unity, these groups of souls may bond together as powerful units of energy, essentially becoming a single larger and more powerful entity. They work together so harmoniously that their combined energies vibrate as one."

I had also heard various theories about "soul groups" or "soul clusters," but the descriptions given were mostly vague and speculative. A number of questions and doubts came to mind.

"Meldor," I asked, "when you talk about these groups of souls, are you talking in terms of a family? For example, would members of my family here on Earth be from my soul group?"

"Usually that is not the case," Meldor replied. "Although members of a group may incarnate into the same family, it usually doesn't involve more than a couple of members in one family at the same time. The reason for this is that members of the same soul group would not have as much to gain by continuously incarnating with each other. Their bond and love for each other may override the challenge and intensity of the lessons that were intended. For this reason, among others, members of the same soul group do not normally incarnate together."

"So, then," I asked, "what is the purpose of souls spending time in groups?"

"As you know," Meldor explained, "the main goal of a soul's journey is to attain the perfection of unlimited love through the accumulation of knowledge by experience. Most soul groups accomplish this through a cycle of incarnations, challenging themselves, and working to overcome the obstacles. Every entity in the cluster adds to the experience, knowledge, and energy of the group. Although each soul has its own plan and life blueprint, it is loved, encouraged, and supported unconditionally by the entire group.

"The life experience of every member of the group contributes immeasurably to the strength of the whole. This is a very important aspect of the soul group. As the entire cluster of souls vibrates as one, the individual life experience of any single member becomes an experience shared by the rest of the group. This is of tremendous benefit to the advancement of the entire group. With several members of the group incarnated at the same time, the process of learning and accumulating experience is significantly improved. As the combined experience of the cluster grows, so does the power of its overall spiritual vibration. This acceleration of the developmental process allows the group to move more quickly to higher levels of understanding and vibration."

Meldor's statements intrigued me. "So, are you saying that other members of my soul group are able to share the experience of the life I'm now living?"

"Yes, precisely," he replied. "If you could have the experience of several lives simultaneously, would it not accelerate your understanding and accumulation of knowledge?"

I began to wonder about possible connections with my own group, if in fact I was part of one. How many souls were in my group? Was there a set number, or could it vary? Why hadn't I met any of them in my spiritual journeys? Or had I, and just didn't realize it?

Meldor read my thoughts and responded. "Yes, most certainly. You are a valuable part of your group's activities and experiences. There are 14 individual aspects in your present group, which seems to be a bit smaller than average. There are groups that have as few as three or four, but there are also others that contain many more souls. While you may not be consciously aware of other members of your group, you do often join them during sleep. Although you had no way of knowing it, some of the faces you have seen through your mind's eye are theirs."

"Are any of my group living on Earth right now?" I asked.

"Yes," Meldor responded. "Besides you, there are currently four other aspects of your group involved in a life experience."

"Do I know them?" I asked. "Have I met any of them?"

"No, not in the physical world, but you have interacted with one of them briefly during an altered state."

This was a complete surprise to me. I couldn't recall anything that would lead me to believe I had been in contact with a member of my soul group.

I felt a surge in vibration and knew that Meldor was retrieving an energy imprint that would help me remember. Within a few short moments the forgotten experience began to play in my mind. I recognized it immediately.

About four months earlier I had awakened one morning and was drifting in and out of sleep, when a subtle vibrational change swept through me. The next thing I knew I was riding in the back of a pickup truck in some unfamiliar place. The truck was traveling down a paved road past a cluster of large, high-roofed buildings resembling warehouses. With me in the back of the truck were a number of orange road pylons and what appeared to be a collection of ropes and pulleys.

Puzzled, at first I couldn't imagine where I was. But as we rode along, the strangest thoughts began surfacing in my mind. I somehow knew that we were in the midst of a large property containing numerous film studios and soundstages. Fatigued, I found myself looking at a wristwatch I didn't recognize, thinking, "Shit, it's only 7:00 A.M. and I'm already wiped."

As the truck turned a corner and pulled through a large overhead door into one of the warehouses, I was thinking about the upcoming week when I would actually get to do a couple of car crashes. All of a sudden, my surroundings began to fade, and a moment later I was back in my own body.

The whole incident was so curious and confusing I had simply discarded it as a weird anomaly or vivid dream. Now Meldor was telling me that this wasn't just a dream, it had actually happened.

The concept was entirely new to me. I remembered the confusion I experienced at the time. Although it felt like I was in my own body, the mental process was perplexing. I could identify my own thoughts as I sat in the back of the truck trying to make sense of what was happening, yet I seemed to be simultaneously experiencing someone else's thoughts. I wondered if this other person had been aware of my intrusion. Was he as confused as I was? Perhaps, if I had gotten out of bed immediately following the experience, I could have examined it more closely and come to some conclusion. Instead, I had simply rolled over and gone back to sleep. When I finally awoke, my memory of the episode was hazy and dreamlike.

"The vibration of your two energies is so similar," Meldor broke into my thoughts, "it is understandable that you may not have realized that you were interacting with the physical body of another soul."

My mind spun. There were so many things I wanted to know.

What was this person like? Was he like me? Who was he? Where did he live?

"Your curiosity is certainly understandable," Meldor smiled in sympathy, "but the information you seek cannot be shared with you at this time. It could only serve to alter the individual paths that both of you are following. You will, at the appropriate time, know and remember."

"Yeah, I suppose you're right," I acknowledged. "But it would sure be neat to meet him while we're still on Earth. I am curious, though; can you tell me why or how this happened? Could it happen again?"

"Yes, I can do that," Meldor confided. "It is actually a fairly common experience for incarnated souls. Because of the extremely close ties among members of a group, various personalities may spend a great deal of time with each other individually or within the overall group consciousness. As I have mentioned, incarnated souls often rejoin their soul groups for short periods of time while their bodies sleep. As this is a very powerful relationship, many souls do in fact find themselves connecting in the same manner that you did, but most often it is remembered only as a dream."

We sat in silence for a few moments as I contemplated these astonishing revelations. I couldn't come up with any new questions, and I wasn't so sure I even wanted to. I knew that everything would work out exactly as it was supposed to. And then I began to wonder, as I had so often in the past—why me? Why were these things happening to me? And what about this latest experience? Why was Meldor bringing it to my attention? Where was this supposed to lead?

"This is your wish," Meldor's gentle voice broke into my thoughts. "This is the challenge and goal of your experience. There is a definite plan and a specific purpose to all things. This is the path that you have chosen. *Remember, it's the journey that's important, not the destination.* You are beginning to understand that it is impossible to not reach your destination. It will always be the same for everyone."

With a warm smile, Meldor then placed his hand over my heart. "Now it's time for me to leave," he whispered. "Until next time, know that you are loved." For just a brief moment I seemed to lose consciousness. A second later, I was back in my body.

In a sleepy state, I lay thinking about the possibilities that seemed to inhabit our lives. Again, I had learned something new, yet it seemed I was barely scratching the surface.

⊗

In my busy world, time passed quickly, and several weeks went by without any significant spiritual activity. Then out of the blue I was presented with another intriguing experience that would eventually have a remarkable impact on my perception of life.

I awoke early one morning from a long and restful sleep. Not ready to rise, I decided to snooze for a while, and settled into a meditative state. A montage of dreamlike images had just begun to waft through my mind, when I seemed to lose consciousness. A moment later I found myself walking along the concrete floor of a long corridor in what appeared to be a large stadium. "Hmm," I thought. "This is interesting. I wonder where I am this time?" Its concrete walls painted a light shade of green, the hallway was about ten feet wide with a well-worn path down the middle of the floor.

As I approached a corner, I found myself thinking that it had been a good concert. There had been a couple of screw-ups, but overall everything had gone well. The adrenalin was still pumping, and I was feeling pretty good.

Suddenly it dawned on me that these could not be my own thoughts. They had to be someone else's. Although comfortable and completely at ease with the circumstance, I was, nonetheless, more than a little confused.

Turning right, I continued down an adjacent hallway before reaching the doorway to a dressing room that I knew was mine. Opening the door, I crossed the floor to a chair and makeup table in front of a large mirror. As I lowered myself into the chair and looked up into the mirror, I was in for a shock.

It wasn't me! The face staring back from the mirror wasn't mine. The surprise jolted me so badly, I instantly slammed back into my body.

I couldn't believe it. For a second time I had somehow ended up in someone else's body. This time I had actually seen his face. He appeared to be much younger than me, perhaps in his early twenties.

A good-looking young man, he had long jet-black hair and stunning blue eyes. Mesmerized by the intensity of his eyes, the image burned its way into my mind and soul.

From the brief moments when I shared his thoughts, I knew that he was a musician or a singer. Probably, I decided, just one of millions of young musicians in the world, struggling to make his way. Could he, I wondered, be another member of my soul group?

The powerful images of this experience stayed with me for a long time. I often found myself returning to them in my quiet moments. On a couple of occasions I even dreamed about the young man, but in the morning couldn't recall any more than vague impressions. Eventually, as with all things, time and life took their toll, and the incident faded into the recesses of my mind.

❦

I love sleeping in on weekends. To me, there are no finer moments than lounging in bed after a long sleep, dozing and dreaming. A couple of months had gone by since my last contact with Meldor, when one of those glorious, lazy Saturday morning opportunities arrived. Relaxing in bed, I enjoyed the luxury of a do-nothing-day, drifting in and out of consciousness. All of a sudden, the sound of a voice jolted me to attention. "Knock, knock."

It was Meldor.

With unreserved delight, I immediately locked in on his vibration, laughing to myself, "Oh no, not a dumb knock-knock joke." I was about to play the straight man with the inevitable "Who's there?" when a wave of vibration swept through me. A moment later I was floating in a void.

"Oh, just me." Meldor's amused voice came from behind me. "Why—you were expecting someone else?"

Anticipating his usual robed appearance, when I turned around, I was surprised to behold a shimmering sphere of energy. I had never seen Meldor without a physical form. For just a moment, I felt a twinge of anxiety. Recognizing my uncertainty, he began to radiate a subtle shade of violet light. Warmth and love permeated my being. "If you prefer," he said, "I can revert to the human projection of my body."

"No, it's quite all right," I stammered. "It just caught me by surprise. It seems strange though. I don't know how to describe it, but it's like I can feel or sense your body in the same way as before. Even though you don't look the same, you still feel the same."

"The feeling that you're experiencing," Meldor explained, "is due in part to your recognition of my vibration, as well as the imprint that my physical appearance has left in your mind. As we have discussed, the vibration of every soul is unique. It is our true and indisputable identity. You would know me even if I was here with only a small part of my energy."

"What do you mean?" I asked. "How could you be here with anything less than your total self? Are you saying that you can be in more than one place at a time?"

"Aren't you?" I could sense Meldor grinning. "Aren't you here talking to me while your physical body is somewhere else?"

"Jeez, I guess so. Good point," I sheepishly conceded. "You would think I should have learned by now to take you at your word."

My curiosity had been piqued. I just had to ask. "So, right now, are you here with all your energy, or is part of you somewhere else too?"

"Well, right at this moment, as you perceive time, the complete focus of my attention is with you. But there are often times when I am with you, and part of me is elsewhere."

"But, where would you go?" I asked. "You don't have a physical body to maintain in another place."

"That is true," Meldor acknowledged. "But I do have responsibilities and commitments in other places. Often while I am in this plane, part of my energy is in another level, learning and studying. Besides my commitment to you, I help to train other souls to become guides, and I am also working with a wonderful group learning to control and transmute emotional energy. The work we do is very important in helping returning souls shed or transform some of the intense emotional baggage they often bring with them."

"That sounds like a lot of work," I interjected. "I had no idea. Does everyone keep so busy in your level?"

"No. But a great many are even more involved than I am. You must understand that there is no requirement or pressure on anyone to become involved. But everyone, at some point, happily donates their efforts and skills for the betterment of all."

As we chatted, I looked around, but there was absolutely nothing to see. I perceived only an endless, dark void. There was something foreboding about it. It seemed to exude an atmosphere of depression and negativity, and it was beginning to bother me. Increasingly curious, I finally asked, "Where on earth are we?"

"Well, we're definitely not on Earth," Meldor sighed. "We are in the void between the physical world and the astral realms. More correctly, this is actually *part* of the astral realm. It is the lowest vibration of the first spirit levels."

"But there's nothing here," I observed, wondering why he had brought me to this place.

"On the contrary," Meldor corrected me. "There are, unfortunately, a great number of souls in this realm. They are cloistered here by their own actions and intentions. The souls in this territory have been severely affected by the negativity and despair they brought on themselves during their last incarnations. This is the result of guilt, along with self-imposed punishment and confinement. This is the level of consciousness closest to the human concept of Hell."

"So that's why I've been feeling so anxious," I mused. "I don't like the vibrations. It's really quite uncomfortable, like something's eating away at me."

"Yes, I understand. Due to the tremendous emotional energy given off by the souls isolated here, the atmosphere in this realm can be very menacing.

"As you know," Meldor continued, "none of these souls are forced to be here. No one is preventing them from leaving. They have not been judged or punished by God or anyone else. *The All* manifests only love and compassion; it does not judge or punish.

"You will remember from your recent experience of a life review, how you felt upon reliving the memory of some of the uncomfortable moments. All of your actions and thoughts were clear and transparent. Nothing was hidden or shielded. No one had to tell you what was negative or positive. You knew and judged yourself accordingly. Suppose that during your life you had committed seemingly vile, unforgivable acts; you would certainly feel the intensity of the impact you had on others. Depending on your mental state and level of consciousness, you may become so despondent and distressed that you might put yourself into a deep state of tormented contemplation and self-review. This is the state of the souls in this level. They have closed themselves off from everything while they deal with the internalized misery they have inflicted on themselves and others."

"But they do eventually get out, don't they?" I asked.

"Oh yes," Meldor replied. "With the assistance of loving spirits, eventually all of them are brought along through the reorientation process.

"The cycle of numerous incarnations can be very difficult, and most souls, through one life or another, will spend some time in this state. As we have discussed before, the development of each and every soul is of great importance to the rest, and we all want to help. All are loved and nurtured through the many levels, until they reach the goal of God-Realization."

Perhaps it was due to concerns with my own ego, and I wasn't so sure if I really wanted to know, but I just had to ask, "Have I spent any time here?"

"More than once," Meldor laughed. "So you see, there is certainly hope for everyone."

I tried to laugh along with him, but I couldn't hide the disappointment in myself. My all-too-human ego was a bit bruised. I began to wonder what kind of despair and confusion it would take to close oneself off so completely. I wondered what I could have done to put myself into a self-imposed Hell.

Meldor broke into my thoughts. "But there is another reason I brought you here. There is something special I want you to experience and remember. There are some very powerful light-beings that have attained the ultimate goal of God-Realization. Although immersed in the massive consciousness of *The All*, they continue to dedicate their existence to serving humanity. Their knowledge and awareness is virtually incomprehensible to any entity that is not itself God-Realized. Truly they embody the greatest love of all, giving freely of their love and compassion. They are perfected souls, the greatest manifestations of God.

"These special light-beings are able to manifest on any level at any time, or indeed on all levels at the same time if that is their desire.

However, it is to the souls in this lower vibration that they dedicate much of their energy. The radiation of their love is so immense that often it is the only power that can penetrate the cloistered consciousness of these tormented souls. It is here that these marvelous deities perform their greatest service. And it is this power that you are about to experience."

Not knowing what to expect, I was becoming more anxious with each passing moment. Meldor had used the word "deities," and called them "the greatest manifestations of God." What would their energy be like? Who was I to be experiencing a manifestation of God?

Sensing my growing anxiety, Meldor reassured me, "There's no reason to be concerned. I'm sure you will find the experience very enlightening."

Silently we waited in the darkness. After two or three minutes passed with agonizing apprehension, I began to feel a warm tingling sensation in the center of my chest. Ever so slowly the sensation grew stronger and stronger until every particle of my being was vibrating with overwhelming emotion. And then it appeared—a blinding white light, radiating energy from its center, growing in intensity as it approached. I could not even begin to grasp the size or magnitude of this light-being as it moved slowly by. My sense of relative space seemed inadequate and delusional. My perception reaching overload, I closed my eyes.

To this day I struggle to describe the feelings and emotions that permeated my being. My words seem frustratingly inadequate.

Eyes closed, my consciousness was flooded with a wonderful feeling of tenderness and love. All tension and uncertainty drifted away, leaving me with a peaceful, undisturbed clarity of mind. It seemed as if I had been reduced to a state of childlike trust and wonder. It was simply blissful. Loved and accepted, I wanted nothing more than to become one with this vibration.

As I floated in euphoria, a sudden surge of vibration forced me to open my eyes. To my astonishment, the likeness of Jesus Christ materialized before me. Obviously choosing to appear in a form I would recognize, he looked every bit like the painting of Christ my mother kept on a kitchen wall when I was a child. Manifesting as a most wonderful, kind-looking man in his thirties, he had a light brown beard and shoulder-length hair. His eyes beaming the very essence of love, he quietly smiled in acknowledgment, and then faded into the darkness. As quickly as that, it was over.

"A powerful presence, don't you think?" Meldor's voice cut the silence.

"Wow!" I exclaimed. "That was incredible!" I could think of nothing else to say. It would take a few minutes to center my thoughts.

"As you can see," Meldor continued, "the energy of a perfected light-being is awesome to behold. Because of their pervasive power, these deities are able to break through to the despondent consciousness of the souls in this realm when they are finally ready for healing."

As Meldor spoke, I wondered if other beings of the stature of Christ visited this plane.

"Yes, most certainly," Meldor answered. "Having been raised in the Christian faith, you are naturally more familiar with the Christ Consciousness. There are, however, many other perfected light-beings that assist the souls in this level. Due to their perceived affiliation with major Earth religions, the better-known deities and masters such as Muhammad, the Buddha, Krishna, and Christ undoubtedly spend more time in this realm.

"These perfected souls continue to be guiding lights as they were during their Earthly incarnations. Considering the awesome power and awareness they possess, it was with great sacrifice and love that they voluntarily reincarnated into the gross vibration of the physical form, entirely for the benefit of humanity. Even though man has misconstrued their messages into differing religious dogmas, these Masters are one and the same in *The All*. As I have said before, they are the highest manifestation of God."

"But some of these other weird religions can't be right?" I reasoned. It was an old thought, a relic from my past, but ever so fleetingly, it surfaced in my consciousness. Meldor picked up on it immediately, and although I felt a bit foolish for even thinking such a thing, later I was glad that I had.

"The answer to your question is a paradox," he said. "They are all correct and yet none are correct. All of the major religions are correct in that they teach about the love of God in all things, but their individual dogmas are the construct of human minds and have little significance to God.

"God is not Catholic or Muslim or Hindu. Nor is God associated with any other man-made belief system. Within *The All* there is only one universal precept, and that is *love*. God commands nothing, but only gives and asks for love. If this one universal principle were adhered to, all the "shalt nots" of man-made religions would be rendered redundant. Any soul seeking the perfection of God-Realization needs only to perfect its love through every expression and manifestation. As you know, from the perception of an incarnate, this may sound simple in theory, but in practice it is not."

"No kidding!" I was wrapped up in Meldor's observations. Everything was beginning to make a lot more sense. Even for those souls trapped in their own self-imposed Hell, there was hope. I knew that there was no place anywhere where God did not exist.

Meldor interrupted my thoughts. "The time has come to return to your body. The negative vibrations of this realm can have a disturbing effect on one's vitality. You may need to restore the balance of your energy. As always, it is a pleasure to assist you on your journey. Until we meet again, remember, my love for you is eternal."

With those last words echoing in my mind, I felt a sudden swirling motion, my consciousness faded, and a moment later I was restored to my body.

After working a small kink out of my neck, I propped up a couple of pillows and settled into a light meditation. I certainly had a lot to think about. Contemplating how enlightening the experience had been, I chuckled to myself. The irony of it all. An enlightening experience—I had literally been to Hell and back. And apparently it wasn't the first time.

Considering the task it would be to reach the point of spiritual perfection, I thought about my continuing struggle to overcome my own intolerance and impatience with others. Could I ever hope to love without condition and expectation? Could I learn to love and accept others for who and what they were? Perhaps more importantly, could I learn to love and accept myself for who and what I was? It sure seemed like an awfully long road ahead.

This particular Saturday morning experience has always remained a special memory for me. I am unable to recall it without strong emotion and nostalgia. Not only because of the lessons learned or the experience with the Christ Consciousness, but more significantly, because it turned out to be the last conscious meeting I would have with my cherished guide, Meldor. Although it marked the climax of an important phase in my journey of self-discovery, it also established a solid base to prepare me for what was still to come.

12

Removing Walls

Sometimes there doesn't seem to be enough time to stop and smell the roses. There's always another deadline, another commitment, another fire to put out. Regardless of all good intentions, for me, life's busy wheels kept on turning.

Maintaining two jobs, raising a family, and trying to stay ahead of the game, my life became increasingly convoluted and demanding. Working 12- and 14-hour days, the weeks and months rolled by in numbing succession. Each day, I was drawn deeper into the dense vibrations of the physical world and further away from the spiritual yearnings of my heart.

While at one time, hardly a day would go by without some contact with my guides, my connections to the spirit world had all but vanished. When I did find time to attempt out-of-body travel or contact with Meldor, I often fell asleep. Or, after hours of staring into the darkness, I would give up in frustration. Eventually, I quit trying.

After nearly two years with precious little spiritual activity, I was beginning to feel a great void in my life. I missed the wonderful excitement and connectedness I had once cherished. I'd read somewhere that our guides can change at different stages of our lives. I wondered if Meldor had perhaps moved on and been replaced by new guides whose vibration I couldn't perceive. In my more despondent moments, I wondered if I had been left entirely on my own. Although my physical life had never been more active, I had never felt more lost and abandoned.

I could not shake the loneliness. More often than not, before going to bed at night, I would end up in the quiet of my backyard, absorbed in the beauty of the star-studded prairie skies. Often, tears would fill my eyes as I struggled to stem the flood of emotions that threatened to overcome me. My heart was breaking, and I didn't know why.

I needed to get away from the rat race to recharge my energy and restore my soul. The best place for this was The Monroe Institute. It was the only place that could provide the peace and relaxation I needed to reconnect. Hoping to get into the first available "Guidelines Program," I called the Institute in the spring of 1999. To my disappointment, I was told that there were no seminars available until mid-July. Although longer than I thought I could possibly wait, I eagerly grabbed one of the last openings.

Waiting was difficult. The stress of my spiritually barren existence was becoming unbearable, but the day finally came. For me, there couldn't have been a more welcome feeling in the world than when I arrived at the front doors of the Institute. Stepping through the threshold, I could feel a great weight lifting from my soul. The anticipation was thrilling. But even in my wildest dreams, I could not have imagined what lay in store for me during the coming week.

After stowing my luggage, I headed off to the dining hall where most of the participants were gathering. Scanning for familiar faces, I didn't see anyone I knew. I was, however, struck by the presence of an attractive, blond-haired woman sitting at one of the tables. From across the room, I watched her for a few moments. I didn't know what it was, but there was something about her that seemed hauntingly familiar. Deciding that she probably just reminded me of someone else, I shrugged off the notion, and moved on to meet some of the others.

Later that evening we all met in the lecture hall for formal introductions and the usual preliminary briefing. To facilitate breaking the ice, the trainers decided to partner each of us with another participant. Each person would interview the other, learning all they could about their background before introducing their new friend to the group.

I thought this novel idea might be fun. When we were told to select a partner, I was about to turn in my chair to check out the people milling around, when from behind me came a cheery female voice. "Hi! Can I be your partner?"

Turning, I found myself face-to-face with the pretty lady I had noticed in the dining room. "Hi. I'm Patricia. Can I be your partner?" she softly repeated, extending her hand to greet me.

"Hi. I'm Paul," I stood quickly, returning her smile as I reached out to shake her hand. "It would be my pleasure."

Our hands touched and, as I looked into her eyes, I'm sure my heart skipped a beat. In an instant, I was rocked by an electrical vibration that swept from her hand into my body like a wave of warm water. As our eyes met, it was as if some powerful energy had reached deep into my chest and squeezed my heart. It took my breath away. My knees suddenly weak, I dizzily returned to my chair.

I had no idea what had just happened to me. I was trying not to let it show, but I'm certain the bewilderment must have been clearly visible on my face. I was having trouble thinking, much less speaking.

When I finally recovered enough to continue, we began, as instructed, to interview each other for our later introductions. Patricia, I learned, had been born and raised in the mountains of Oregon. Throughout her life, even as a child, she had been able to see and hear things that other people couldn't. She had always experienced intuitive flashes, but until she was a teenager, she thought that everyone had the same experiences. She described herself as someone searching for truth. She loved The Monroe Institute, and thought it was a great place to further her search.

Although virtually mesmerized, I managed to stumble through a quick review of my life and background. Patricia smiled in understanding as she made her notes.

The nine teams finally began their introductions. It was a fascinating process. At the end of the introduction, each partner was supposed to provide a teaser, an intriguing little insight about their new friend that would impel the rest of the group to want to get to know them too.

When it came to our turn, Patricia began. She eloquently recounted my background and keen interest in the spirit world. Then she made an astonishing announcement. In a quiet, almost blushing fashion, she said she just knew I was a kind and gentle person with a warm heart, but the most intriguing thing about me, she said, were my eyes.

With a perplexed look on her face, she said, "He has the most amazing eyes. They're like a painting. You can lose yourself in them. It's as if you're drawn right into his soul."

A huge lump quickly formed in my throat; my eyes began to sting.

It was my turn to speak next. I swallowed hard. Glassy-eyed, I glanced at my notes, trying to pull my thoughts together, hoping that nobody, including Patricia, would notice the emotional turmoil I was in.

After clearing my throat, I shakily began. I hardly heard my own words or knew what I was saying. To hide my nervousness, I tried to lighten the situation by making a couple of funny remarks, but failed miserably. Soon I was at the end of the introduction and couldn't think of anything more to say.

I was relieved when the group's focus finally moved on to the next pair of introductions. Glancing at Patricia, I found her staring at me with wide glistening eyes, a bewildered smile on her face. Finally, lowering her eyes, she shyly looked away.

Introductions concluded, we spent the rest of the evening chatting with other members of the group, talking at length about other programs and experiences. Throughout the many conversations, my thoughts often returned to the rush I had felt upon first touching Patricia's hand and looking into her eyes. I had never experienced anything like it before, and didn't know what to make of it. She *must* have felt something too, I thought. The look on her face, the way she introduced me, the things she said.

As the evening wore on, Patricia and I occasionally found ourselves in idle, if not uncomfortable, conversation. I was becoming certain that she had also felt something unusual, but I was too afraid to even talk about it. Finally, along with everyone else, we said our good nights and headed off to bed.

The next morning, I awoke eager to get into the program. Of the various seminars I had attended at the Institute, "Guidelines" had been my favorite. It was during Guidelines that I had first met Meldor, and I was desperate to reestablish our connection.

It came as no surprise to me when the first sessions yielded little in the way of experience or insight. I had come to expect it. Whether it was jetlag or just my need to unwind and relax, it proved a pretty normal start to the week. I spent most of my time either sleeping or staring into the darkness of my CHEC unit. It didn't matter to me. I was thrilled just to be back in peaceful surroundings.

Although I tried to put the introduction experience with Patricia out of my mind, it was easier said than done. Whenever I saw her between sessions, I would feel a strange vibration in my chest. Occasionally during the group discussions, I could sense her energy and when I looked up I would find her staring at me. Without realizing it, I often found myself doing the same thing. Something about her was so compelling it attracted me like a magnet.

Later that evening, I was relaxing at a picnic table in the yard, when I spotted her timidly approaching. Following an exchange of pleasantries, I invited her to sit and chat. It turned out to be a lengthy conversation that would have a profound effect on my life.

Patricia acknowledged that she too felt a strange sensation when she first saw me. It became even more intense when she touched my hand or looked into my eyes. She felt as if she had somehow known me before. I suggested that it was perhaps from another lifetime. She countered that she really wasn't sold on reincarnation, but had no explanation for the familiarity we both felt.

Although Patricia had grown up in the mountains and I on the prairies, our experiences and values were strikingly similar. She too had endured a difficult upbringing. Her mother had died while she was still very young, and she and her little brother had been raised by their father. Actually, if the truth were known, the raising of her brother had been Patricia's responsibility. No time to play or to just be a kid, there was only hard work and responsibility. In addition to looking after the house and her brother, she could not remember a time when she didn't have to work in her father's small lumber mill.

As Patricia talked about her childhood, so deeply did I identify with her feelings and emotions that I often felt a lump in my throat and a burning sensation in my eyes. Like me, Patricia had grown up with a constant yearning for something better. Other than attending school, she was rarely able to get away from home and, as a result, had very few childhood friends. At an early age she developed a great love for reading. But beyond schoolbooks, the only other reading material in her house was a set of 1937 encyclopedias and a Bible. She had read them all from cover to cover, voraciously consuming the knowledge they offered. When she turned 18, Patricia left the mill and the mountain, and never looked back.

As I listened to her story, my heart went out to her. It brought back a flood of my own childhood memories. I thought that I had had it tough, but I couldn't even imagine how hard it would be to grow up without a mother. It was apparent that, like me, Patricia had also learned to place a strong wall around her heart to keep from getting hurt.

Patricia confided that in the past couple of years, she had also been feeling listless and disconnected. There was something missing in her life. She loved to spend time at night looking into the starlit sky and she too felt a yearning and loneliness that plagued her.

As we continued to chat about everything from world affairs to the stock market, I became more amazed at her insight and intuition. She was without question one of the most intelligent and knowledgeable people I had ever met. Extremely well read, she seemed to have developed a near photographic memory.

Engrossed as we were in our conversation, the hours flew by. Finally, after midnight, we bid each other good night and headed off to bed. Sleep, however, did not come easily. I had become utterly intrigued by the connection I felt with this sweet, quiet soul. In all my life I had never felt such an extraordinary attraction, and I was unsure of how to deal with it. Finally, after what seemed like hours of tossing and turning, mercifully I fell asleep.

The next day, although suffering from lack of rest, I sensed a huge improvement in my psychic energy. The vibration within my body was steadily increasing as I became more relaxed. By midmorning, as we began the second session of the day, I felt confident that I was moving closer to a meaningful experience. I looked forward to finding answers to my questions about Meldor, but I could not have anticipated the strange encounter I was about to have.

As the Hemi-Sync signals lulled me into a deep altered state, I settled into my breathing rhythm, prayed for help, and mentally projected my questions into the ether. I asked if my feeling that Meldor was no longer with me was correct. I asked if new spirit guides had taken his place. And finally, I asked that if I did have new guides, they present themselves to me as soon as possible. I desperately needed to know.

Within seconds of sending out these thoughts, I felt a shift in vibration, and almost immediately the form of a male spirit appeared. He seemed to be about 40 feet away, and although he looked familiar, at that distance I couldn't get a clear picture of his face. Thanking the spirit for answering my call, I asked him to come closer. In one quick movement, he drew to within four feet of me and stopped.

I couldn't believe my eyes! The face staring back at me was my own! The spirit was me, or at least a good duplicate of me. For several moments, I stared at his features. It was as if I was looking into a mirror. The problem was that the person in the mirror was moving and acting independently of me. I began to wonder if this was just some mischievous spirit playing tricks on me. Picking up my thoughts, the other me looked directly into my eyes, smiled, and slowly shook his head in reply. I was about to ask who he was and what this was all about, when he abruptly vanished.

Talk about being confused. This was hardly an answer to my questions. Try as I may, I could not get the spirit to return or provide any other insights or answers. I became so perplexed I ended up breaking out of my trance. Moments later I was back to normal consciousness.

I didn't know what to make of this strange occurrence. Was this a message showing me that, I, myself, was the only one responsible for my guidance? Could this entity have been some aspect of my higher self, or did it mean that the answers I sought were actually within myself? For the life of me, I couldn't figure out what this was all supposed to mean.

On the fourth day of the program I could feel my vibrations increasing steadily throughout the morning sessions, but I was still falling asleep. There always seemed to be a lot of activity going on around me. I could feel subtle changes in vibration, but I just couldn't break through the veil.

Soon after the start of the first afternoon session I had fallen asleep yet again, when unexpectedly, I found myself jerking back into full awareness. To my surprise, I was locked in the grip of a wildly fluctuating vibration. My body tingled from head to toe as wave after wave of energy coursed through me. I began to sense a powerful presence, the unmistakable feeling that I was not alone.

I opened my eyes to a dazzling display of multicolored lights. Shimmering waves of blue and violet energy swirled around my body. I didn't know what was happening, but I didn't want it to stop; the vibration and feeling it created in me were exquisite. Every molecule of my body felt electrically supercharged.

Then I noticed them. At first, only a fleeting glimpse of a hand and arm moving in a circular motion above me became visible. But when I focused my attention, through the swirling haze I could make out the form of a woman. Although it was difficult to get a good look at her through the energy field, she appeared to be a rather petite lady in her early thirties. Her light blonde hair was swept back over her shoulders, seemingly blending into the material of her loose-fitting ivory-colored robe.

As the energy waves and swirling light continued, I became aware of another pair of hands, and then another. At the foot of the bed was a male form, and on my left, another female. I tried to get a better look at them, but the energy field was so thick, they were difficult to see. From what I could tell, the male and the second female were also wearing light-colored robes, but both had hoods drawn over their heads, partially concealing their features.

All three were busy with some sort of energy work. Their hands slowly circling at various distances above me, they seemed to be smoothing and shaping my aura while at the same time supercharging the energy in my body. Like strong electromagnetic fields sweeping in different directions, I could feel their power as each pair of hands moved over me. Every movement seemed to set off a new wave of energy crashing into the next, sending strong electrical currents spinning throughout my physical form. No words were spoken, and no messages were received. I simply lay quietly, relishing the wonderful feelings of warmth and love that permeated me.

Ever so slowly the urge to sleep began to overtake me. For some reason, even with the energy gyrations going on around me, I was having difficulty staying awake. In the presence of these three loving souls, completely safe and relaxed, I finally stopped resisting, allowing the energy to carry me into a deep sleep.

When I awoke, it felt like a huge weight had been lifted from me. But, I also felt a strange and haunting sadness. I was experiencing a sensation that could only be described as homesickness.

When I walked into the debriefing room, Patricia immediately noticed something different about me. Letting out a breath, she exclaimed, "Wow! What on earth happened to you? You should see your eyes."

"I'm not really sure," I smiled weakly, shrugging. "I think I might have just met some new guides."

Without taking her eyes off mine, Patricia reached out to give my hand a reassuring squeeze. As our fingers touched, I felt again that surprising flood of energy that jolted me when we first met.

Without saying a word, I placed my other hand over hers, and closing my eyes, I stood still, quietly absorbing her energy. A feeling of peace and tranquility came over me. I could practically feel my brain producing a flood of endorphins, soothing and relaxing. Mesmerized, I didn't want to let go, but I began to sense other people moving around us. With a sigh, I opened my eyes. Patricia stood in front of me, her eyes closed, eyelids twitching rapidly as if in a dream state.

Other people had begun filtering into the room for the debriefing. I cleared my throat to get Patricia's attention. Startled, she opened her eyes and stepped back, a puzzled look on her face. "Thank you!" She whispered and, as if slightly embarrassed, moved away, taking her place on the soft carpet.

While the other participants shared their experiences, I was practically oblivious to my surroundings. Absorbed in my own thoughts, I shifted back and forth between the experiences of the last session and the strange energy I felt whenever I was near Patricia. There was a lot to think about.

It wasn't long into the next session before I found myself clicking in and out of awareness. At some point, I felt a slight movement and knew I was about to separate from the physical. Prepared for the inevitable surge of vibration that usually precipitated my launch into the spirit world, I was surprised when nothing happened. Instead, my body began gently rocking from side to side. Within moments, I again sensed the presence of other beings in my room. Opening my eyes, I was greeted by the same three spirits from the last session. They were already at work sending energy through my body.

Visually, all three spirits appeared unchanged. But the energies they projected seemed more pronounced. As their hands passed rhythmically over me, their energy and vibration became more intense. Shimmering blue, green, and violet waves rolled through me, growing in power and magnitude, electrifying my body. Soon the energy flow expanded to such intensity that it enveloped all three spirits in one continuous field. Their combined radiance flooded the room and permeated every part of me. Vibrating into my body and soul, it filled me with incredible feelings of love.

Determined not to fall asleep again, I reached out with my senses to draw in any impressions I could get from the trio. Soon, myriad thoughts and images percolated into my mind. Scenes of gut-wrenching emotional pain began to surface; scenes of longing, rejection, and unrequited love. There was something so familiar about them: they felt more like memories. And then it dawned on me. They were indeed memories, memories of my own past lives, previous heartaches, past hurts. The message became startlingly clear. My fear of rejection, and the compulsion to put walls around my heart had a much longer history than this present life. I had spent previous lives literally afraid to fall in love.

To protect myself from hurt, I had long ago closed off my heart to deep and total love. I would not allow myself to risk again the possible pain and helplessness that love could bring. But now I felt the error of living in a shell. I understood that unless we open up our hearts to love, we will never know what it's like to truly live. To know the pain of a broken heart, however intense, is far better than never having loved at all. Having our hearts broken time and time again is still better than putting up walls to keep our love in, and others out. This, I somehow knew, was one of the main reasons we were here, to know and experience love.

The spirits' thoughts continued to flow through my mind. Nothing in our physical dimension is of any consequence or lasting reality. The only enduring reality is love. To live without opening our hearts denies the most beautiful and enabling aspect of the human experience.

Feeling the awesome power and compassion of these three wonderful beings, I began to sense a history of our companionship. It seemed like I had known them for a very long time, but couldn't place the context of our relationship. Were they angels? Spirit guides? Was there a difference between the two? I didn't know.

Raw with emotion, I thought about how much I missed Meldor. Why hadn't I been able to see or feel his presence for such a long time? Had I been too engrossed in the physical world? Or had he completed his task and moved on? Were these radiant beings my new guardians? If they were, why hadn't I seen them before? Recalling the pain of loss and abandonment and praying for an answer, I projected these thoughts into the room.

Almost instantly, it seemed as if the air pressure in my CHEC unit plummeted. I could feel my eardrums reacting like I was in a descending airplane. The shimmering waves of energy slowed and began to change, coalescing into a beautiful golden light, enveloping me with love and warmth. Radiating a powerful feminine aura, the sound of a woman's soft whispered voice filled my mind.

"We have always been with you. Although part of our energy has been changed to meet your needs, we would never leave you. Our beloved Meldor has completed his work with you on this level and has returned to his higher vibration. You must know in your heart that you will again be reunited with him.

"We have been with you throughout, and will continue to be. Even when your conscious mind becomes too dense and physical to perceive us, we are with you. We come to you in your sleep and when your body is resting or meditating. Your well-being, your evolvement, and the very essence of your soul are intricately bound to our energy. You are a wonderful part of our existence and we love you beyond measure."

As she spoke, I closed my eyes. Powerful images flooded my mind. Drawn from memory, I saw an old picture of footprints in the sand and I recalled the story of a man who was carried by the Lord during his darkest hours when he thought that he had been abandoned. The vision carried too much pain. Emotion overwhelmed me. Clinging to her every word, tears welled up in my eyes, trailing down my cheeks.

"In this physical world," she continued, "the greatest aspect of one's spiritual awareness has to do, not with the intellect, but with the heart. Although you have grown much in this respect, there is much more that you must learn. In order to fully assimilate the beauty of love, you must seek a greater balance to the masculine and feminine energies of your ego. We have been working with your energies to help dissolve the protective walls built around your heart. But in order to fully experience this reality, you must also open your heart to embrace the feminine aspects of your being."

Waves of energy rolled through me. From deep within I could feel emotion building, lodging in my throat, choking me. I couldn't speak; I could hardly even think. With eyes closed, I felt the warm loving arms of my angels drawing me close, embracing and comforting me. At first it was just a trickle. And then it felt as if a great dam had broken inside me. The walls finally gave way.

As emotion overcame me, I began to cry. Through deep wracking sobs, I released the pain of this lifetime and perhaps countless lifetimes before. I didn't know if it was for sadness or joy, but from the depths of my soul I wept. I cried for all the love I had been given, and for all the love I had lost by shielding myself from it. I cried until my mind was numb and I could cry no more. Finally I drifted into a deep healing sleep.

When I awoke, the session was over; the angels had disappeared, and I was left alone with the fading remnants of their energy, a light unburdened heart, and a clarity of consciousness I had never known.

As I sat up in bed, I could hardly contain my happiness and relief. It was as if I had been given a new lease on life. I hadn't a clue as to how this might affect me, but I knew it would be significant.

The debriefing session flew by. I couldn't seem to get the grin off my face. I'm sure I looked a bit daft, just sitting there, smiling at everyone. I couldn't even begin to explain what had happened to me, much less share my experience with the group. For the moment, at least, it was far too personal.

Following the debriefing and a late dinner, Patricia and I headed outdoors to enjoy the warm evening. We hadn't been able to talk since before the last session, and I was curious as to what she had experienced when we had clasped our hands earlier in the debriefing room. After a bit of pleasant chitchat, I broached the subject. I talked about the vibration and the peaceful feeling that came over me every time I touched her hand, and I asked if she had been feeling anything similar.

Reaching across the picnic table, she placed her hand in mine, covered it with her other hand, and closed her eyes. Quiet seconds passed, and then finally she began to speak. "When I'm holding your hand," she started slowly, searching for the right words, "I feel warmth and tenderness. I feel completely safe and protected. Nothing can hurt me."

Several moments passed as she sat motionless, and then without opening her eyes, she continued, "This is so strange. I don't know what to say. I've never felt anything like it before. It's like I've known you for a long time. It's wonderful, but I don't know what to think. Weird things are happening. This afternoon, before the other people came into the room, I had the strangest vision. When we were holding hands, I closed my eyes and all of a sudden I saw a beautiful silver locket, like the kind you see people wearing around their necks. It looked really old, like an heirloom. The two compartments opened up and in each side was a beautiful butterfly. They spread their wings and flew out into the air. They were so happy to see each other. They came together in the air, touched each other, and then they just disappeared."

Patricia opened her eyes. "It was really quite beautiful. What do you think it means?"

My mind was reeling. I struggled for words. "I don't know," I stammered. "You really saw that? That's incredible."

"I see a lot of things," she replied, "but usually it's when I'm meditating or really relaxed. I don't know why I saw butterflies, but it must have something to do with you and me. Maybe it's a symbolic thing."

I felt a swirling queasiness in my stomach. "Hey, maybe we did know each other in a past life," I quipped, trying to make light of the situation.

"Well, maybe," she smiled, "if you believe in that sort of thing."

"Yeah, if you believe in that sort of thing," I laughed, squeezing her hand.

She was such a wonderful paradox. How could she not believe in reincarnation? She was one of the most spiritually adept and knowledgeable people I had ever met, yet she questioned the possibility of other lifetimes.

As if reading my mind, she responded to my thoughts. "I'm not saying I don't believe in reincarnation. For all I know, it could be absolutely true. I just haven't experienced anything that would convince me. I guess I'll just have to keep my mind open to the possibility."

"Okay," I beamed back, "we'll just have to see if I can convince you."

At that point, several other group members gathered around the picnic table and we spent the rest of the evening visiting. It was after midnight when we finally said our goodnights and headed off to bed.

The following morning I awoke energized. Although I looked forward to what the day would bring, I was sad that we would soon be saying goodbye and heading home.

The two morning sessions flew by without any significant happenings. Although I tried to reconnect with my angels, it was not to be. Other than a few innocuous images, my time was spent staring into the darkness or dozing. I was having difficulty focusing, and it was becoming more and more frustrating.

The first session of the afternoon wasn't much better. Even though my energy had been building, I still found myself drifting off. To make matters worse, all of the pent-up energy was causing a peculiar reaction in my body. I was becoming aroused. This certainly wasn't making things any easier. Finally I tried to focus on suspending all feelings in my body. It worked too well—I fell asleep, and didn't wake up until the end of the session.

The next exercise started off a bit more promising. As I drew ever closer to the threshold of expanded awareness, an intense vibration permeated my body. That was usually a sign of good things to follow. As I focused on taking myself deeper, at some point I fell asleep. When I clicked back into awareness, to my frustration, I discovered that I had again become aroused. Determined not to let this distraction ruin another session, I began a mental struggle against the condition. I wasn't making much headway, though. Finally out of frustration I decided to allow myself to fall asleep, hoping that when I awoke the problem would be gone and forgotten. But just as I was drifting off, I was suddenly jolted back into awareness with the distinct feeling of someone kissing my lips.

The feeling was unmistakable, an intense physical sensation. There had to be someone in my CHEC unit. I opened my eyes. Instead of the usual darkness, the room was bathed in a warm golden light. To my amazement, floating beside me, just a few inches above the bed was a very pretty, scantily clad woman.

I couldn't believe what I was seeing. It was clear that this was not a physical person, but a full-bodied spirit. In instant panic reaction, I tried to pull away, but couldn't move a muscle. Immediately, as if in response to my fear, from out of nowhere, a feeling of warmth and love enveloped me, dissolving and washing away my anxiety.

As my shock subsided I tried to get my wits about me, but could do little more than lie there staring at her. There was something so familiar about her, it made my head spin.

Lying on her side, she was an angelic vision. Propped up on her left elbow, her long dark curls flowed past her rounded shoulders to the bed below. Dark eyes beaming brightly, she gazed intently into my eyes. It was as if she were looking for a sign, a recollection, perhaps a fond memory. As I stared back, I began to feel little sparks of recognition. Then all of a sudden it hit me. I knew where I had seen her before. She had been in my dreams.

As I lay on my back in disbelief, I drank in her image. She took my breath away. Invitingly open from her neck to her feet, a full-length creamy white gown hung loosely, caressing her body, accenting and revealing her sensuous form. She virtually radiated love and desire. Permeating my mind and body, her intense vibration filled the room with a raw sexual energy. Although I had seen her in my dreams, I could recall only fleeting glimpses. Something about her seemed hauntingly familiar, but I couldn't place her.

I lay speechless. Helpless in the aura of her intoxicating feminine energy, my desire was increasing by the moment. The sparkle in her eyes grew stronger, and a loving, understanding smile spread across her face. Ever so gently she reached out with her right hand to lightly touch my face, then slowly, sensuously, traced her fingers down my chest and across my stomach. As her hand moved lightly across my body, it created within me a surging vibration that rippled through my entire being. The power was so electrifying. I felt like I was lifting off the bed in response to her touch. It was as if I was being zapped by an electrical transformer. But the sensation was pleasurable beyond belief.

Tingling and shaking with the most intense desire I had ever experienced, I lay with the vibrations coursing through me, my mind practically numb from the rush of adrenaline. Moving her right leg across me, my celestial lover slowly positioned herself above me, straddling my aching body. Intense vibrations began to rocket through me. My heart was pounding, my brain begging for oxygen.

The feeling was so exquisite I felt like I was about to faint. Her eyes glistened like diamonds as she began to slowly lower her body to mine. Our lips met! For a brief moment I was aware of her breasts touching my chest. Then to my astonishment, her entire body seemed to dissolve, sinking into mine.

In panic, I found myself suffocating, fighting for air. It was, at the same time, one of the most terrifying yet exhilarating moments of my life. In just seconds, however, my thoughts carried me from fear and anxiety to surrender, and then to ecstatic passion. As our bodies flowed together, our energy and molecules seemingly occupying the same space, a growing heat began to vibrate in my heart. Quickly spreading to my stomach and genitals, it soon enveloped my whole body. With each moment the intensity increased, flowing, bubbling, and expanding until I thought I could take no more. Every particle of my being on fire with desire, I couldn't tell whether it was a physical sensation or a spiritual one.

As my breathing turned to short hyper bursts, my heart pumped wildly. With building intensity, a powerful contraction began to spread through my stomach, gripping and paralyzing me. My mind and body screamed for release.

Beginning at first as a low rumbling vibration, it hit me like a freight train. From deep within, a wave of tremendous orgasmic energy exploded through every cell in my body. Overwhelmed, I nearly lost consciousness. Almost immediately, my muscles contracted yet again and, from the center of my being, a second volcanic wave carried me to virtual oblivion. In a frenzy of ecstasy, I hung on for dear life.

Wave after wave of electrifying energy swept through my body, locking me in the throes of uncontrollable passion. Then, as if seeking relief from the intensity of the experience, my mind began to slip. Flashes of light and vibrant energy flowed into my awareness, and then everything turned quiet and peaceful.

I found myself looking out over a beautiful valley of green grass caressed by a warm morning sun. Sitting on a small grassy knoll, my lover's slim arms were wrapped around my waist. Against my back, I felt the warmth and comfort of her gentle embrace. Overflowing with unreserved love and passion, I could wish for nothing more. My life was complete. Love was all that mattered. Suddenly, my senses began to swirl and fade. Consciousness escaped me. A moment later I was back in my body, startled again by the light touch of tender lips on mine.

Opening my eyes, I watched in awe as the female spirit rose above me. In radiant elegance, she floated to a standing position at the foot of my bed. Slowly and sensuously she traced her left hand across her breast until it came to rest over her heart. Eyes glowing with warmth and affection, a gentle smile spread across her face. Then, without diverting her gaze, she quickly faded from view.

For several moments I stared into the unrevealing darkness. My heart only now beginning to return to a normal rhythm, a flood of questions arose in my mind. Who was this spirit? Why had she come to me? What had happened? Had I just experienced a sample of the spirit world's version of sex? Could I even *call* it sex? There was certainly nothing in the physical world to compare with it.

The last session was over, but I was in no hurry to join the others in the debriefing room. This had been a strange and amazing week. It occurred to me that, although I would normally have been traveling all over the place, during this seminar I had not once ventured out of my CHEC unit. I had, however, had some of the most incredible experiences of my life.

When I finally headed downstairs, Patricia was waiting for me. She'd had some extraordinary experiences of her own and wanted to share them with me. Knowing that this might be the last time we would ever see each other, we talked through the evening and into early morning. We were both amazed and intrigued by the familiarity we found in each other. Somehow, somewhere, we had known each other before, and now we promised to stay in touch.

When it finally came time to say goodnight, I drew her into a long heartfelt hug and, as her soothing vibrations flowed into the deepest recesses of my soul, sadness welled up in me. I knew from the glistening in her eyes that she was feeling the same. We were both happily married. Would it be possible to stay in touch? Would our spouses understand our friendship and connection? With a lump in my throat, I headed off to bed.

Morning, as usual, came too soon. I was always sad to leave the Institute, but this time my reluctance was even stronger. After saying our goodbyes to everyone else, the inevitable moment arrived. With tears in our eyes and sorrow in our hearts, Patricia and I quickly hugged each other and left for the airport.

As we made our way into the Virginia sky, I sat back, reflecting on the week's events. Every nuance of the trip had been intense and mystifying. From meeting Patricia to encountering my angel guides, it had been an emotional affair. The angels had said they were helping to tear down the walls I'd placed around my heart so I could learn to love again. I didn't know if it was the things they had done or the emotional circumstances of the week, but I was feeling completely raw and exposed. My heart ached and I didn't know why. But in some strange way, it felt good.

The first leg of my trip home took me to the Washington, D.C., airport for a two-hour layover. Plopping myself down into the most comfortable chair I could find, I pulled out a book to read. After just a few minutes, having difficulty concentrating on the words, I gave up. Setting the book aside, I closed my eyes to rest. Almost immediately I found myself sinking into an altered state. Shortly, I became aware of a subtle pressure building in my forehead. It had been some time since I had had a third eye vision, so I quickly focused my attention on the spot. The air around me began to change. The portal burst open, and a moment later I found myself looking at the front cover of a book.

What on earth is this? I wondered. This was not at all what I expected. The cover was fascinating: simple and striking, it bore the image of a beautiful, blue eye, containing the reflection of an angel's wings. It's title was *Eyes of an Angel*.

I had no idea what this was supposed to mean. Was this a book the angels wanted me to read? Scanning the cover for the author's name, I couldn't believe my eyes. At the top of the book was my own name.

"No way!" I instantly protested. "I'm not writing a book. Besides, what do I know about angels?"

This had been a long-standing argument of mine. A number of friends had previously suggested that I write a book about my spiritual experiences. And I had always resisted the notion. There were lots of good metaphysical books on the market. Most of the things I'd experienced had already been written about. I didn't feel I had anything new to offer.

In the previous two years, three different psychics had predicted that I would write a book. In fact, just two months earlier, I had become upset with a psychic who kept insisting that I was going to write a book. It was all she could talk about. She went on and on about a book, until I thought, "Look, lady, if you're not getting any messages, just admit it and let me out of here. Forget it! I'm not writing a book!"

Now, it appeared that even the spirit world was on my case.

I continued my mental protest. "No, I can't do it. I'm not a good writer. Where will I find the time or energy?"

I had hardly finished enunciating these thoughts when the book faded, and in its place appeared a blank sheet of paper. As I looked on, words began to form on the page, quickly flowing from line to line until the entire page was filled. While this was taking place, I heard a woman's whispered voice. "Don't worry. We'll help you."

With that, the vision disappeared, and I bolted to an upright position.

I couldn't believe what I'd been told. How could I write a book? I didn't have the time or, for that matter, the desire. And I certainly didn't feel I had the skills necessary for such an undertaking.

As I boarded the plane for the last leg of my flight home, I couldn't chase the images out of my mind. Me, write a book? It just didn't seem possible.

We hadn't been long in the air before I fell into a deep, dream-filled sleep. I recall fleeting images of butterflies and Patricia. I dreamed about grass-covered valleys, the ocean, and a dark-haired woman I seemed to have known so long ago. As the plane finally touched down, I awoke with a feeling that these two wonderful beings were somehow connected. Their energies felt so similar, so familiar.

13

Healing Hearts

Back from Virginia, I felt like I had returned from a lifetime away. Nothing seemed to be the same. I was having a great deal of difficulty picking up where I left off, and determining how I fit into the scheme of things. Everything around me seemed too harsh, too crowded, and too noisy. My biggest problem, though, was figuring out how I should be feeling. Completely open, emotional, and vulnerable, I wasn't so sure I liked it. Things that I previously held as important now seemed insignificant and petty. Each day I spent hours lost in thought, reviewing and reliving the experiences that had turned my world inside out.

The integration of feminine energy into my life was a lot tougher than I would have believed. When the angels first told me about it, I couldn't even imagine what it would be like, much less deal with the powerful effect it held over me. Through their ministrations and energy treatments, they had facilitated a change in my vibration. But most significantly, they had opened my heart to accept and embrace the feminine energies within my being.

Although worried about her reaction, I shared all of the week's experiences with Candace. From the meeting with Patricia, to the emotional reunion with my angels and the sensuous encounter with the female spirit, I told her everything. Her reaction was amazing. Although she admitted to a bit of jealousy, Candace found the account fascinating and intriguing. She thought it would be wonderful to meet someone with whom you felt a soul connection. She also thought that I should stay in touch with Patricia. I was sincerely grateful for her thoughtfulness and understanding.

As the days went by, I became obsessed with thoughts of Patricia. Wondering about the possible spiritual connections we shared, I yearned for answers. Why had I been so affected by her? Were there any special reasons for our meeting? The questions were endless and bewildering.

On top of problems focusing on work, at night I had difficulty sleeping. I would lie awake for hours, fighting the barrage of thoughts that often kept me awake until dawn.

Several nights after my return home, I settled into bed with the usual scattering of images cluttering my mind. As I began to drift into the twilight of sleep, thoughts of Patricia surfaced in my awareness. In frustration, more to myself than anyone else, I pleaded, "Why can't I get her out of my mind?" From out of nowhere came a distinct, whispered reply.

"Because she is a part of you."

The presence of my angel guides swept through me in a wave of energy. Although I heard their words clearly, I struggled to grasp the meaning. "She's a part of me? What's that supposed to mean?"

"You and she are of the same energy." The soft female voice was lucid and precise.

Puzzled, I asked, "The same energy?"

"You and she share the same soul energy. You are what some refer to as soul mates."

"Soul mates?" The words reverberated in my mind. I felt certain that Patricia and I had known each other in a previous existence, but I sure wasn't prepared for a soul mate connection. Even though Meldor had once described the concept to me, I gave it little consideration. Now I was stunned by the revelation.

"You and Patricia," the angel continued, "are part of the same individuated energy. The intense emotional pull that you feel is the memory of another part of you that is in harmony with the total vibration of your being. She is the balance of your energy. When two aspects of the same energy source meet in the physical world, the reaction can be powerful and unsettling. That is why you feel the way you do. Your reunion in this lifetime is not by accident or chance, but rather due to specific purpose and need. Through your heart, you will soon come to realize that need and purpose."

As the angel spoke, her voice began to fade, and I found myself struggling to stay awake. The more I fought to maintain consciousness, the further I sank into the heaviness of sleep. The next thing I knew, it was morning, and I was awakening from a dream of a hauntingly familiar classroom and a group of wonderful, loving, light-beings.

Throughout the day, I carried with me an odd feeling of homesickness. It left me perplexed. Which home was I missing?

Although the angelic message had brought me some relief as to the nature of my connection with Patricia, it created a multitude of new questions. The concept staggered me. Had I truly found a soul mate? But there was an even bigger question: "Now what?"

We had promised to keep in touch, and thanks to e-mail, we did. As the weeks sailed by, Patricia and I learned more about each other and we quickly became the best of friends.

Candace remained supportive and understanding throughout. Firmly believing that our meeting was not just a coincidence, she encouraged us to explore our spiritual connection.

While all of this unfolded, a strange mixture of feelings haunted me. It seemed that just about everything affected me in an overboard, emotional way. Where in the past I could suppress or ignore my emotional responses, I now found it impossible. I began to feel and internalize even the slightest bit of emotional pain in the people around me, especially my family and friends. The way I reacted or thought about things was changing dramatically, and there didn't seem to be a thing I could do about it.

Through the years of raising children, Candace and I never seemed to have had much time to just sit and talk. But following my return from Virginia, we would spend hours each day chatting about our goals, relationships, and spirituality.

I found that the connection with my new guides, or angels, was much more subtle than my previous associations with Meldor. Reaching their vibrational state seemed more difficult. I knew they were always with me, but their communication was mostly soft and gentle. I very seldom saw them, yet in times of need I would often hear their thoughts in my mind, always reassuring, always loving, and always feminine. Sometimes I had the impression that if something was in my best interests, they simply made it happen.

All of these things added to the raw emotion I was already experiencing. There was no question about it; the angels had certainly managed to open my heart, and I felt every ounce of the love and pain that came with it.

In the months that followed, I grew more and more homesick. Hoping it might provide some clues to my nostalgia, I reread my old notes, especially Meldor's discussion of soul mates and soul groups. The answers, however, were not apparent. With the persistent sadness continuing to weigh heavily, it became obvious I was going to have to work through it myself.

One night as I lay in meditation, I suddenly found myself floating in a bright, vibrant space. Before me, a massive, rotating sphere of energy began to materialize.

I had no idea what, or who, it was, but something about it was so familiar, it started a reaction within my body. Before I knew it, my own energy had begun to change. Within seconds, I was vibrating in harmony with what appeared to be a single colossal spirit.

Although it didn't seem rational, I had the urge to allow myself to become absorbed into its energy. Like a giant magnet, drawing me ever closer, it exerted a compelling power over me. But just as I was about to give in to the pull of this giant being, it began to soften and change in appearance. Soon I could discern a number of individual, swirling bright spots within its aura. As I drew closer, some of these oscillating energy clusters began to break away from the larger body. Within moments I was surrounded by a group of bright, shimmering forms. Then, one by one, they transformed into distinct physical beings. Faces appeared, male and female, smiling reassuringly, their loving radiance melting into my heart.

Slowly, feelings of recognition and longing came over me. Then suddenly I understood. This was the source of my homesickness. These were the members of my soul group—my classmates, my spiritual family. They knew me intimately, perhaps better than I knew myself, and they loved me unconditionally.

Overwhelmed with the emotional energy of their combined presence, I remained motionless, absorbed in the power of their vibrations, wishing I could stay. In the euphoria of their blissful energy, my awareness began slipping away, and momentarily I succumbed to sleep. An instant later, I was back in my body.

I didn't want the experience to be over. Fighting to maintain the connection, I struggled to hold onto their vibration. For a moment my third eye reopened to bright smiling faces. Then the vision faded and I was alone in the darkness of my bedroom. Tears flowed from my eyes. Whether from sadness or happiness, it was impossible to contain my emotions. Hugging my pillow, I cried until sleep again overcame me.

In the morning I awoke with vigor and renewed direction in my life. Reflecting on the significance of my soul group encounter, I understood they had come to support and encourage me. Awed by the reality of their existence, buoyed by their unconditional love, I felt immensely better. A burden had been lifted from my heart.

❦

Patricia and I continued our correspondence. The bond between us was too powerful to ignore. Anxious to see each other again, we came upon a solution—a spiritual conference in Utah. With my wife's encouragement, I agreed to go.

Candace never failed to amaze me. Although I'm sure she struggled with the possible risks this could present to our marriage, she didn't believe in coincidences. Convinced there must be an important reason for our meeting again in this lifetime, she felt we'd be ignoring our own spiritual callings if we didn't try to find some answers.

As the plane touched down in Salt Lake City, I grew increasingly anxious. Was this a mistake? Would I feel the same vibration I felt in Virginia? Finally, with my heart pounding and my stomach churning, I stepped into the terminal. With open arms and tears in her eyes, Patricia was there to greet me. I breathed a deep and grateful sigh of relief.

The beauty of southern Utah was stunning. Surrounded by gigantic, naturally formed rock statues and canyons, I had never been to a place more spiritual. In awe of its immense, desolate beauty, Patricia and I found the sanctity of the place intoxicating.

We knew our time together would be short. Outside of the workshop, we spent every available minute deep in conversation, learning more about each other's lives and dreams. Our connection deeply spiritual, even though Patricia was still skeptical, I became increasingly intrigued at the possibility of exploring any past lives we might have shared.

For several years I had been investigating numerous forms of consciousness exploration. An important aspect of my research dealt with various modes and applications for hypnotism. Experimenting with a number of possibilities, including past-life regression, I had occasionally enlisted some of my own family and friends to develop a few of my own techniques. At the end of the conference schedule, Patricia and I decided to experiment to see what we could uncover.

As Patricia relaxed on a couch, I guided her through a process of ever-deepening relaxation, leading her into an altered state. The plan was to move back in time, through various stages of her life, until she was able to re-experience herself in the womb. Upon reaching that point, I would then suggest she move even further back, to a time prior to this present life, where she could conceivably recall previous lifetimes. At least that was the plan, but it didn't quite turn out that way.

The session seemed to get off to a good start. Through suggestion, I encouraged Patricia to return in her mind to a happy time when she was 16. Although I hadn't asked her to describe what she was experiencing, from the contented, animated expression on her face, I could tell that she was indeed reliving a happy time. Allowing her to enjoy her memories, I then gave the suggestion that she return to an earlier age, when she was perhaps nine or ten. At this point a change began to take place.

As Patricia settled into the suggestion, her eyelids started to twitch and the expression on her face shifted to sadness. Slowly moving her head from side to side, she looked as if she was trying to block what she was experiencing. I asked her to tell me what was happening.

"It's my puppy," she said in a slow, faltering voice.

"Your puppy?" I repeated.

"Yes, he's just sleeping in the yard."

"How old are you?" I asked.

"I'm nine and a half," she replied. Her voice seemed distant, almost childlike.

"Tell me about your puppy," I said, trying to sound upbeat.

"He's so cute," she responded quickly, her voice a bit brighter. "He's just little, only four months old."

"He sounds like a very nice puppy," I offered. "Was he a good puppy?"

"Yes, he was good," she responded adamantly, almost defensively. And then she became very quiet, seemingly deep in thought. After a few moments she continued, "Well, he was mostly good." Her voice trailed off. . . . She seemed to be struggling with her emotions. Her lips began to quiver. She was trying not to cry. "He didn't mean to be bad. He was just sleeping."

"Did something happen to your puppy?" I asked softly.

"Yes! Something bad," she sobbed. "Something very bad."

With her eyes scrunched up and lips quivering, she now seemed to be fighting for control. Taken aback by the raw power of her emotions, I was unsure how to proceed. I knew that I needed to calm her down.

"It's okay, Patricia," I said, touching her hand to comfort her. "There's nothing to worry about. This is something that happened a long time ago. You don't have to experience it again if you don't want to. Take a deep breath now, and just allow yourself to relax. Let all of your unhappy feelings go."

Within a few minutes, Patricia appeared to be resting comfortably. I wondered if it would be helpful and healing for her to revisit the trauma she had obviously experienced with her puppy. Gently, I broached the subject again.

"There, now that you're relaxed and comfortable again, if you want, we can talk about your puppy. You don't have to be a little girl again. You can just watch what happens as if you're seeing it on television. Any time you want, you can just turn the TV off, or change the channel. Would you like to tell me more about your puppy?"

Almost immediately her body stiffened, her breathing became shallow. "No, please," she whispered pleadingly, "I don't want to see it. It's awful."

Considering the emotional state the mere mention of the puppy elicited, I thought it best to move away from the subject. If it was important for her to relive the experience, she could explore it again another time. Slowly and carefully, I counted her out of her trance. After a few moments of quiet, she stretched her arms and neck, and finally opened her eyes.

I felt bad that she had had a negative experience, and wanted to console her. I told her I was sorry about how the experiment had gone, and hoped that she wouldn't let it deter her from trying again in the future. With a puzzled look on her face, Patricia, however, said she was glad for the experience. She said it must have been previously blocked from her mind, but somehow she could now remember everything. It had been a very sad moment in her life, but she felt the need to share it with me.

Taking a deep breath, Patricia launched into the most compelling and heart-wrenching story I have ever heard.

"It happened the summer that I was about nine years old," she began. "My dad and my little brother and I were living on a small parcel of land on the side of a mountain in Oregon. We had a stallion that we kept in a corral close to the house. Sometimes the horse would get out of the corral and run away. Our closest neighbor was a bit further down the mountain, about a half-mile away. He kept a couple of mares in his pasture. Whenever our horse got away, that's where he would go. It had already happened a number of times and our neighbor was getting really mad about it, and that bothered my dad.

"One Saturday afternoon dad went into town to get some things, and left me to look after my brother. The puppy was just a few months old then. It was a nice warm day, and he just curled up and went to sleep in the middle of the yard. The horse wasn't in the corral. My dad had tethered him to a stake outside the corral so he could eat some grass in the yard. The horse was grazing along when he noticed the puppy. He bent his head down and sniffed at him. It must have startled the puppy, because he jumped up barking. That frightened the horse. He bucked back, yanked the stake out of the ground, and started to run away. I tried to stop him, but I couldn't, and he ran all the way down to our neighbor's property.

"When my dad got home, I told him what happened. He became really angry, and drove down to the neighbor's yard to get the horse. When he got back he was even madder. After he put the horse in the corral, he came across the yard, grabbed the puppy, and tied his leash to a clothesline post. I didn't know what he was going to do. I was sitting on the front step of the house. I told him it wasn't the puppy's fault, but I didn't say anything else because I'd never seen him so angry.

"He walked around the side of the house, and I couldn't see him for a while. I thought he was going somewhere. But a few seconds later he came back around carrying a steel pipe."

At this point Patricia's lips began to quiver. She was struggling to control her emotions. "And, and then," she stuttered, "he started hitting the puppy with the pipe. I screamed, but I couldn't do anything. The puppy was crying, but he just kept hitting him. I didn't know what to do. He was so mad. I ran into the house and hid in my room. But I could still hear the noises. So I just put my hands over my ears and cried and cried."

Tears now flowing down her face, Patricia began to shake. I couldn't believe what I was hearing. I saw only a terrified little girl, traumatized by what she had witnessed. Choking on a burning lump in my throat, I clutched her hand tightly.

"Oh God, please!" I found myself silently begging for the strength to remain in control. At that moment, I couldn't even imagine how awful this would be. But Patricia's horror wasn't over, far from it.

Hyperventilating, with tears streaming down her face, she continued, "And then my dad started yelling at me. He said, 'Patricia, you better get out here right now, and bury this goddamn dog.' I was so scared. I'd never seen him like this. But I had to go outside. I picked up the puppy; he was covered with blood. I didn't want to even look. I took him to an old flower garden behind the house, and I got the shovel. Then I dug a hole and put him in."

Her speech now punctuated with deep uncontrollable sobs, Patricia forced herself to continue. "I started to cover him up. But when I threw the dirt on him, he started to move." Her voice turning to pure horrified anguish, she cried, "Oh God, I'm so sorry! I couldn't stop. I couldn't look at him. I just kept on covering him up. And then I just ran and ran, and I didn't want to ever come back."

Finally, with heart-wrenching sobs, Patricia turned away, buried her head in her arms and wept.

Seconds turned into minutes, and the minutes into eternity.

My heart was breaking. Gasping for breath, I couldn't think what to do. My own tears were now streaming down my face, falling like rain onto my hands. I drew her close, cradling her in my arms. I wanted to pray to God to take away her pain, but instead I found myself silently cursing a humanity that could inflict such devastating pain.

With my own grief and anger slowly boiling into a rage, all of a sudden I was jolted by an internal burst of light. Brief flashes of imagery began to strobe through my mind, piercing my awareness. For a moment I wondered if I was having a stroke. Then in the next instant, my inner vision cleared, and I was rocked by a memory. It was the uncovering of my own horrific trauma. Somehow, I had blocked this memory from my mind.

I was suddenly back in my five-year-old body. It was early on a Saturday morning, and my older sister Josie was shaking me awake. "Come on, Paul, the puppies have been born. Don't you want to see the new puppies?" Half awake, but excited, I scrambled to my feet. Josie pulled a sweater over my head, hurried me through the house, and out the front door.

My excitement mounting with each step, we ran across the farmyard to an old shed behind the workshop. We had two adult German Shepherds on our farm. My sisters had told me that Sheena was pregnant and would be having her babies very soon. I couldn't wait to see them.

Before we even rounded the corner of the shed I could hear little whimpers from the newborn pups. Spotting them immediately, I counted four little balls of fur. In amazement, I sat down beside them as they bumped and bobbed, nosing through their mother's fur. Josie reached into the churning brood, gently withdrew a whimpering, shivering ball of fluff, and placed it in my lap. He was beautiful. I giggled with delight at his closed eyes and clumsy movements. It was a perfect moment.

We had been sitting for several minutes holding and playing with each of the puppies when around the corner of the shed strode our father. "What the hell are you doing back here?" he barked. In instant fear, Josie jumped to her feet. Catching sight of the puppies, he let out a stream of German cuss words. "Jesus Christ, I thought so," he yelled. "Josephine, you're supposed to be helping Mom in the garden."

In a rage, he grabbed the puppy out of my lap. "I told you I don't want any more dogs around here," he screamed. And swiftly raising the puppy over his head, he smashed it to death on the ground in front of us. One by one, he grabbed the rest of the puppies, hurling them to their deaths.

Frozen with shock and fear, I couldn't speak, I couldn't cry. I just sat there shaking. The next thing I knew I was in Josie's arms and she was running as fast as she could towards the house. She put me down on the porch, and through terrified sobs, ordered me back to bed. I couldn't get there fast enough. Racing through the house, I dived under the covers. Mercifully I fell asleep, putting the entire horrible memory forever out of my mind.

Cutting through my thoughts, I felt a hand touching my face, wiping away the tears. I opened my eyes. Patricia was looking up at me, blinking through her own tears, a deeply saddened, concerned expression on her face. "Are you okay?" she whispered.

"I think so," I managed to croak out. "God, Patricia, I'm so sorry you had to go through something like that."

"Shhhh," she hushed me, putting her fingers to my lips. "It's okay now."

Trying to get my wits together, I decided not to tell her about my experience until later. I knew we would have to help each other in our healing.

"What happened when you ran away," I finally asked. "Where did you go?"

Patricia sighed and took a deep breath. "I didn't go very far. I ran up into the mountain where there was a stream about a half-mile away. I used to go there sometimes to just be by myself. But, this time I wanted to die—I wanted to just disappear."

Her lips began to quiver again as she fought to remain in control.

The pained expression on her face ripped into my heart. She seemed so small and vulnerable. It felt like I was looking into the eyes of a little girl. I gently squeezed her hand and, with tears welling up in her eyes, she continued her story.

"At first I was just going to wash the blood off my clothes, but I thought how easy it would be to die. So I walked right into the water. I wanted to drown myself. But I just couldn't make myself do it. Finally, I got out of the water and just sat on the bank for a long time. The sun went down, but I stayed there. I didn't want to ever go home again. It was a few hours later, maybe two in the morning; it got so cold I was shaking. I walked down the mountain to a logging-truck road about a half-mile from our house. I wanted to go all the way down to the highway and run away, but I didn't know where to go. I just couldn't get it out of my mind. It was so horrible. I wanted to die."

Patricia put a hand over her mouth to muffle a sob. After a few moments, with tears freely flowing, she continued. "There was a curve in the road as it came up the hill, so I lay down in the middle of the road, hoping a truck would kill me. But no one came. It was really dark and cold. I couldn't cry anymore and I didn't know what else to do, so after about an hour, I got up and walked home. And that was all." With that, Patricia put her head back, closed her eyes, and lay quietly with her thoughts and tears.

After a few minutes, when she appeared to have settled down somewhat, I broke the silence. "What do you mean, that was all?" I asked. "Wasn't your dad worried and looking for you? Didn't you get into trouble?"

"No, I thought I would. But nothing happened. There were no lights on in the house. Everyone was sleeping. So I just crawled into bed and went to sleep. And that was all. The next morning, life went on like nothing happened. Nobody ever spoke a word about it. You're the only one I've ever told."

I sat quietly, holding her hand. I thought about the unbelievable horror that she had endured. What disturbed me most was that she had spent the greater part of her life carrying a guilt that she had been responsible for her puppy's death when she covered it with dirt.

It occurred to me that just sharing her story was probably a big step in a healing process. And I was grateful for having played a part in that process. I felt fortunate my own similar childhood horror had also been blocked from my memory. It had been strange, recalling an experience that had been erased from my conscious mind.

Feeling that we were both cried-out, I told Patricia about uncovering my own blocked experience with the puppies. By the time I finished the story, we both sat with tears in our eyes and lumps in our throats. We reflected on the similar nature of our experiences, wondering what effect these events had in shaping our lives. We considered that perhaps this was one of the reasons we had been brought together again, to initiate a healing process.

Even though we felt better, it was apparent that we both still carried a deep psychological hurt. The trauma of our experiences had forever changed the way we related to the world. It was as if an innocent, sacred part of our souls had been damaged or lost. The discussion brought to mind the training I had received at The Monroe Institute during the soul retrieval sessions. Some of the participants had talked about retrieving parts of their own souls. They felt that during particularly traumatic events, it was actually possible to lose a part of one's own spiritual energy. They believed that these shadow bits of our soul could be locked into the emotional time-vibration of the event itself. But they also claimed that it was indeed possible for an aware person to find and reintegrate these lost aspects of energy into his or her soul. Doing so often resulted in tremendous healing.

Patricia and I talked about the possibility of trying something of this nature. Although she was dubious, we agreed to experiment. Unsure where it would lead us, we decided on another hypnosis session.

With only a loose idea of the direction we were heading, I guided Patricia through a process of deepening relaxation, and then counted her into a stable hypnotic trance. Allowing her to rest, I closed my eyes and prayed for guidance. Almost immediately, I detected the subtle vibration of my guides.

Thoughts and ideas forming in my mind, I began with the suggestion that whenever she was ready, she could return safely to any time in her life. She could review and re-experience any event or incident, but if she chose to do so, she could also remove herself from the scene and become only an observer. With these final suggestions, we were ready to explore.

Slowly, gently, I guided her back to the awful day her puppy died. I reinforced the concept of retrieving any lost aspects of her energy that may have left her during times of extreme stress or trauma. Allowing that it could very well be that she had no missing aspects, I suggested that if there were, she should locate these lost portions and restore them to her soul.

In anticipation of what was to come, Patricia took a deep breath. I then took her back to the time immediately after the puppy was put into the ground.

"Patricia," I began, "you told me that after the puppy was buried, you ran up into the mountain to a stream. Do you remember how to get there?"

"Yes, I know where it is," she replied, her voice registering a touch of anxiety.

"You'll be just fine, Patricia. Nothing can hurt you." I tried to sound as soothing as I could. "Now, in your mind, return to that place near the stream where you went years ago. I'll just be quiet so you have time to make your way there."

"I'm there." Her immediate response surprised me.

"Very good." I tried to remain calm. "Now, take a few moments to look around and tell me what you see."

Patricia's eyelids began to twitch ever so slightly. There was a pause in her breathing. She seemed to be concentrating on something. "I see a little girl sitting on some dead-fall beside the water." Her voice was slow and absorbed. "There's a nice lady sitting beside her, but I don't think the girl can see her." For a moment, she paused, captivated by what she was seeing. "Her pants and shirt are all wet," she said, coughing slightly, a sound of concern in her voice. "She's shivering, and she's crying." Patricia lay quietly for a couple of moments, and then with quivering lips, she added, "I think she's me."

I could hardly contain my excitement. This was just what we had hoped to accomplish. I searched for the right words to continue the process. "You're doing very well, Patricia. How do you feel now?"

"I feel really sorry for her." Her voice was filled with emotion. "I just want to hug her."

"I think that's a good idea," I encouraged. "I'm sure she could use a hug."

For several moments everything was quiet. The tension in Patricia's face began to soften. Then in a mystified voice, she broke the silence. "She's gone… I was hugging her and then she just disappeared."

"That's wonderful, Patricia," I whispered, struggling to control my emotions. "How do you feel now? Are you okay?"

"Yes, I feel a lot better. I'm really glad I found her."

Tears filled my eyes as I contemplated the power of what I had just witnessed. I knew that regardless of the validity of the experience, whether it was real or imaginary, it must have been healing.

Uncertain what to do next, I suggested that Patricia relax and reflect on all that she had experienced. While she rested, I decided on the next step. I would attempt to guide her back to the dark road where she had lain in the gravel waiting for a truck and then finally to the place where she had buried the puppy.

The process seemed to go well. In the reality of her altered state, Patricia returned easily to the road and then to the puppy's grave. Although she couldn't perceive any further lost aspects of her soul at either site, I encouraged her to go through the process of welcoming any possible stranded energy to reunite with her. When she arrived at the site of the puppy's grave, Patricia began to re-experience some strong emotions, but she was able to maintain control, making it through the difficult final processing.

With the main purpose completed, I suggested that she could instantly travel to any peaceful place she chose. This would give her a few minutes to relax before I brought her out of her trance. Patricia drew in a deep breath, and I watched all signs of tension slowly leave her body. Although curious about where she had gone, I remained quiet. Within minutes her breathing had slowed to a steady relaxed pace. Appearing at rest, her eyelids began to lightly flutter and an expression of peaceful contentment spread across her face. I waited a couple of minutes, and then began the process of returning her to normal consciousness.

Stretching her arms, Patricia opened her eyes. A delighted smile spread across her face. "Wow, that was incredible," she exclaimed. "I don't know where I was, but the most amazing thing happened."

Concerned that she may not have remembered all of the aspects of the session, I asked, "You do remember everything that happened, don't you? You remember finding a lost part of yourself?"

"Oh, yes," she smiled, "that was incredible too. But at the end when you told me to just rest for a few minutes, that's what I'm talking about." Her eyes beamed with excitement. "I don't know where I was, but all of a sudden I felt somebody holding me, and I felt really different. It was like I was a baby again. There were people standing in a circle. For some reason, I couldn't see much of their faces, but they were so happy, just hugging me, and passing me around. It was wonderful. I could feel all of their love, and it was just beautiful. Then they started to fade away and I fell asleep, until you woke me up."

Patricia sat up, a puzzled look spreading across her face. "They seemed so familiar, like I knew them, but just forgot. I think they were from my soul group. What do you think?"

This was completely unexpected. Not knowing what to say, I just sat there, grinning. Frankly, we couldn't have hoped for a better outcome. As I reached out to give her a hug, I silently thanked God and our angels for their help.

The episode had been healing for both of us. Although it was Patricia who had gone through the exercise of uncovering a childhood trauma, her experience was the trigger that allowed me to do the same. Her ordeal had helped in my healing by putting me in touch with my own forgotten past. We had shared a powerfully liberating experience. And we were in awe of the spiritual bond that had brought us together at a time when we needed it most.

Patricia's experience with the rest of her soul group had been particularly gratifying for her. Even though I had shared with her Meldor's insights regarding soul groups, she had remained unconvinced. Now, it seemed, we had crossed another bridge.

Our time together in Utah seemed all too short. Before we knew it, we were at the airport saying goodbye again. With heavy hearts and a few more tears, we hugged each other and headed off on our separate journeys home.

14

The Reading

Throughout this intense period of change, I continued to share everything with my wife. I'm sure there must have been times when Candace simply humored me and only pretended to listen. She seemed happy that I had found such a wonderful friend, and occasionally she and Patricia spoke on the phone. The depth to which Candace supported our friendship was remarkable, and I was grateful for her understanding. Within a few weeks of my return from Utah, however, she had a dream so vivid, it drew her irretrievably into a relationship that may have spanned centuries.

When Candace first told me about the dream, I hadn't offered her more than an amused snicker. It did, however, cause me to worry that beneath the surface, she was more than a little uneasy about my friendship with Patricia. At least, that's what I believed at the time.

Candace recorded the dream in her journal:

> I had a dream last night, and woke up at 2:00 A.M. in a cold sweat. I was feeling really distressed. In my dream, Patricia had

come to our home; I believe it was to help Paul with some project he was working on. I had no idea prior to her arrival that she was coming, and was not introduced when she arrived. We ended up being seated side-by-side at the dinner table, but it was like there was a very dark shadow between her face and mine, which didn't allow us to look at each other. I interpreted this as Paul's reluctance for us to meet.

After the meal, I decided it was time to cut the foolishness, so I shook her hand and introduced myself. The next thing I recall, Paul and I were alone, and I was asking him how long she would be staying. He ignored my question and instead took me to task for being rude to a couple of men who were doing some work around the house. At that point, I held his face in my hands, and said to him over and over again, "When are you going to admit that you don't love me anymore?" He denied it several times, and then finally said, "All right, I don't love you anymore." I felt instantly relieved. I said "Good, now I can get on with my own life." That's when I awoke.

As I woke up, my mind was still in turmoil and I was quite upset. But I had the overwhelming sense that everything was okay. And then I heard these distinct words in my mind, "Don't worry, this was another lifetime."

Candace told me it was the clearest, most powerful dream she had ever had, but admitted she didn't know what to make of it. Never before had she experienced what she felt was direct contact with the spirit world. She joked about the possibility that all three of us could have known each other in previous lives. For my part, I felt strangely uncomfortable with the idea. I swept the notion aside. "It was just a dream," I said. "I wouldn't read too much into it." Dreams, I argued, were mostly symbolic. There could be any number of interpretations for what the subconscious mind is experiencing.

Candace, however, wasn't so quick to write it off. She explained that in the dream, we weren't in any of the homes we had ever lived in. This one was a very large two or three story home similar to those she had seen in movies of the old South. She sensed that we had employed a number of servants in a plantation-type setting. Although she wasn't sure how to interpret it, she felt the dream was too vivid to ignore.

A couple of weeks later, Candace surprised me by announcing that she wanted to attend a program at The Monroe Institute. We had talked about it before. Although she always felt it would be a good experience, she was waiting for the right time. Now she was ready to give it a try.

Delighted with her decision, I knew that she would have a wonderful time. Hopefully, she could experience firsthand some of the things I had shared with her. When the day finally arrived, it was hard to tell who was more excited, Candace or me.

For me, the week seemed to drag on forever, but when she finally got home, Candace's eyes were beaming with wonder and excitement. We spent hours talking about the life-changing insights and revelations she had experienced. But there was something that she particularly wanted to tell me. She had shared the story of the soul mate connection between Patricia and me with a couple of the other participants. One of them had done a lot of past-life work, and seemed to possess a remarkable psychic ability. She told him about her unsettling dream, and asked if it was at all possible that she and Patricia had met in a previous lifetime.

Closing his eyes to contemplate, he replied, "Yes, definitely!" He went on to suggest that the three of us had actually been involved with each other over several lifetimes. His guidance told him that in their most recent connection, Candace and Patricia had in fact been brothers. A serious rift had developed between the two of them, and Candace had supposedly treated Patricia very badly during their last time together.

I'm not sure if I was more surprised or amused by the revelation, but I confess to not giving it any serious consideration. It seemed all too contrived, and I brushed it off as absurd. Although I had visited a few psychics over the years, none of them had impressed me. I surmised that this guy was just blowing smoke. The whole notion was a bit too much of a stretch. "Well, you can think what you want," Candace smiled, "but I think there might be something to it."

My life continued as always: busy, busy, busy. By now, I was becoming accustomed to the strange anomalies and revelations being delivered to me on a regular basis. Sometimes it felt like I was being guided through a specific curriculum. Lessons were laid out for me, but only when I was ready to accept them.

Other than my obsession with reading, the only other pastime I enjoyed was watching movies. I love the big screen and the surround-sound stereo. On one occasion, Candace and I were engrossed in Kevin Costner's movie *Message in a Bottle.* Near the end, there is a particularly dramatic scene in which Costner leaps into the raging sea to save a drowning woman. At the time, I had no idea why it was having such a powerful effect on me, but well before the fateful moment, I found myself becoming emotional. My heart began to pound, and I grew anxious.

Trying to get a grip on my emotions, I closed my eyes. I felt a shift in my perception, and in an instant I was in a small boat caught in the midst of a tremendous storm. In horror I watched as a huge wave slammed over the bow, snatching a young woman off her feet, sweeping her overboard into the dark churning waters. Terrified, I screamed her name, "Yoshi!" and dove into the water after her. The next thing I knew, I was beneath the waves fighting for air. Then as quickly as it had begun, I was transported back to my theatre seat, tears streaming down my face.

The rest of the movie was a blur. Sitting in shock, I knew without doubt that I had been shown yet another scene from a previous lifetime. All of it seemed so real. But what was most surprising was my intuition that the young woman I had tried to save was in this lifetime my daughter, Stacey.

Replaying the scene in my mind, I was puzzled by the questions it raised. Especially unclear was the nature of our relationship in that lifetime. The fact that Stacey is now my daughter only served to confuse the possible scenarios. She could have been my daughter, or maybe even my wife; I didn't have a clear sense of it. I knew only that she had been precious to me. The one detail that was clear, however, was the distinct feeling that we were Asian.

Over the next few days, the past-life episode was often on my mind. Although I tried several times to connect with my spirit guides for clarification, all of my attempts were unsuccessful. Three days later, I awoke from a fleeting dream that involved both Stacey and Patricia. Although I recalled very little detail, it awakened my mind to a new concept. Since Patricia and I were connected through our souls' energy, and Stacey and I had shared previous lives, was it possible that Stacey and Patricia had also shared past lives? I got out of bed with the conviction that this was a very real possibility.

⟨ॐ⟩

By the time winter had tightened its icy grip on the prairies, Candace and I were looking for a break. We had friends in Calgary, Alberta, and we needed a change of scenery. Our friends had told us about an excellent Tarot reader named Janine, encouraging us to see her. Although we knew nothing about Tarot, just for fun, we decided to give it a try.

Janine worked out of a small room in the back of a downtown bookstore. She blew away every doubt or suspicion I harbored about professional psychics. It was the most accurate reading I had ever witnessed. Neither vague nor generalized, she effortlessly nailed down every aspect of my physical and spiritual life.

To give her a good run for my money, I decided to remain tight-lipped throughout the session. As we sat down to begin, I supplied only my first name and date of birth. Janine shuffled the oversized cards, asked me to cut the deck, and then laid them out in an organized spread across the table. A tape recorder captured every word:

Janine: Okay, in Chinese, that's the Year of the Rabbit. So, we can combine that, Gemini, and the rabbit. Those are very similar. It's like being a double Gemini. Do you use a lot of verbalization in your work?

Paul: Yes, I suppose so.

J: And what about writing? Because, I feel that you definitely came here to communicate ideas through writing. It feels like you're full of ideas, and you need to be writing.

P: That's possible.

J: There's something going through a big birthing here, well, like yourself, your own energy. It's very emotional. And it's a spiritual thing . . . can you feel it coming? Like you're really changing?

P: Yes, I think so.

J: Well, it's going to continue. Okay, and there's a huge healing going on around the ego self. There is a sense of healing. Are you headed in the direction of doing some healing yourself, or in healing others?

P: Sometimes healing others, yes, and myself.

J: Are you working in a community right now? Is it a spiritual community or are we talking of a physical world community? There's definitely a sense of bringing people together, being a liaison even. Like you're a politician or diplomat in the work you do. You are a Gemini trying to integrate your male and female parts in this lifetime, and really work with those energies in a combined effort.

I was floored. Could this Tarot reader be intuiting the emotional changes that had been taking place in my life? She had even correctly identified that I was a politician. Could she be picking up on the energy work my angels had initiated to bring me into balance with female energies?

P: That's certainly true. I've been dealt some things recently.

J: It seems like you're really integrating, though, and you end up putting into your work in the world that sense of integration, wherever it works for you.

Okay, I keep getting that this is a real healer card here. It's like the healer in you, mentally, coming up. There's a gift here that you're maybe just beginning to use; are you doing anything like hands-on healing or Reiki or anything?

P: Yes. I'm trained in Reiki. [Several years earlier, I had taken classes in Reiki energy healing.]

J: I get that you have quite a gift and it's necessary to use it more often. This is a healing gift that wants to come out, and it's the more feminine part of you, most certainly. It's like goddess energy, and it's mental and verbal too.

Okay, now I'm getting a victory around a youth. This is a big, positive, trophy card. This could be about childhood issues. Did you just work through a really big childhood issue?

I thought of the repressed childhood memory of the puppies. I could hardly believe what I was hearing.

J: Because I get that you've come to a personal victory with some part of yourself as a young person. There is also a big unconditional love card here, and I'm picking up that you've really come to a place of loving yourself. It's not only about loving yourself, but it's going to help you to also love others. This is really nice.

Now, I get a sense of patience, and deep roots in a relationship that, down the road, will grow great harvest. And the more you do your own personal healing work, the more your relationship with another very specific person will grow because of the work you're doing. I get more independence emotionally, but I'm not getting the ending of a relationship; I'm getting a rebirthing or something. Is there a new relationship, or could this be a rekindling of an old one, because this is so much like roots and birthing.

P: I don't know. Perhaps both.

J: There's beautiful stuff going on there, and I get a fruitful relationship, and it's all because of your personal work, the integration with yourself. Relationships seem to be different, but they're becoming deeper or better.

Okay, here I get a really big restructuring through communication. Have you had a big talk with somebody that first leveled them, and now there's a restructuring going on? Is that in one of your relationships? Almost like something shook up your world and caused you to restructure from the ground level and it's like you're in the process of doing that.

P: Yes, that's very accurate.

J: Only a Gemini could work that fast. You're working very fast at the restructuring. Some people take years and years. It might be a bit intense, though, a shock to the people who know you. Okay, now did you have a really incredible dream or vision recently?

P: Yes, I've had many.

J: Yeah, because it's like your dreams are really challenging you to move through fear-based ideas and really get in touch with what your fears are, so you can release the fear and get on with whatever it is you're doing. I get a lot of dreams or visions here; like you're a dream catcher right now and you're receiving a lot of messages through your dreams. It's karmic that this happens this way right now. It's all predestined. Not everything is; we create a lot of our own destiny, but for some reason there's an overriding energy right now of destiny around you.

And there is also a big sense of vulnerability around you. It's almost in an intimate sense, somehow. There is a sense of you really being open. Are you feeling like you're open in an intimate way around people? It feels like you're opening up like you haven't in a long time. And you're really worried about it.

P: Uh, yes. That's true.

J: It's very healing, but it feels like you are very vulnerable at the same time. Your ego is worried that it's going to completely disappear in this process. But, I'm getting that you really heal through this and that your ego sense actually gets stronger in a more positive way. You will learn how to use it properly.

You need to write. How much do you write now? Ever?

P: No, not a lot. But I know that I should.

J: I get that this could go back lifetimes. I get you bringing this from a place that you developed quite intensely in a past lifetime or something, and you could tap into that. And it could be public speaking, or working with the public in some way. I get like a lot of charisma and you talking to large groups. I don't know where your spiritual path is going, but this is very New Age, very healing, and [involves] working with groups.

You will have, or have already had, a big revelation through dreams or some spiritual process. Now it is time to write or speak about it. It will come from your inner voice. You have quite a lot in store, but you've done this before. This is lifetimes of work. It is like the power of many others; it's like you'll be channeling stuff. It's like there's a whole stored up thing going on here that you can tap into.

Your writing could really heal and shift a lot of that energy. You need more downtime to get that process happening. You will definitely publish something. It might take a whole year to accomplish this, but you will.

Your emotions are sometimes high, and sometimes low, so take some cave time. You will get your shift and messages will come. There's some pure channeling going on here. It's already coming through, and it's going to really move you.

Actually, I get communication on a worldwide scale. It's like an Aquarian card with a Pleiadian knowledge and influence; you are really tapping into it, and will end up being a channel for a very large body of energy that is universal. This is needed in the world, and it's very healing. And you seem to do it through written word, and verbally, or both.

At this point Janine picked up the cards and reshuffled the deck. She had been extremely accurate in identifying so many of the changes taking place in my life. From the emotions of balancing male and female energies to identifying the spirit world's assistance in writing a future book, she was bang on.

She finished shuffling the cards, placed the stack in front of me, and asked if I had any questions. At first I was still too shaken to think of anything, but then I thought of Patricia.

P: This past summer I met a unique person at a seminar, and we seemed to have a very strong connection. Do you have a sense of what this meeting or relationship is all about?

J: Okay, shuffle the cards and separate them into three piles and indicate with your left hand which pile to use.

I pointed to one of the piles. Janine picked up the cards and spread them out.

J: Wow, this is a very powerful feminine card here. I'm assuming it's a woman. She has a powerful energy. There is past life stuff going on here, and it's not bad stuff. She is someone who developed some big esoteric skills in a past life. She could just use them a lot more than she does. This is a very empowered person, with a very sensual energy.

I get that you and she are in a place of healing. There is a sense of finding balance and patience. You are learning to meld and integrate your energies, and you'll be very successful at this healing. This person gives a very strong sense of Scorpio energy. She is very intense and emotional. Has she lived through some hard stuff?

P: Uh, yes. Definitely.

J: Everything she knows she learned the hard way. This is a survivor who has come into herself through a lot of hard work. But there is a sense of sadness or failure.

This is a soul intention; one of you is a messenger to the other, or both to each other. Something is coming out that you both need to hear right now. There is a strong karmic reason why you're pulled together, which is part of your work here.

This is all about integration. It's a very positive influence. This is definitely a soul mate. There is a sense of wholeness when you're together. The challenge, though, is in how to bring it into the world you've created so far.

And this is a surrender card. Surrender to what you're feeling, and also let go of your doubting. But expect the unexpected. What is really going on, and what you both think is going on, may be really different here. I get that it's going to be really surprising and unexpected how this manifests and fits into your life. But it's very good.

I get that this person and you were meant to meet again to help each other quantum leap to where you're supposed to be. So there's a bit of bumping you forward, speeding up your process. I think it has a lot to do with physically manifesting a book. I don't know why, but this is about speaking and putting something down in written form. It's like she speeds up your process. You have definitely done lifetimes together with this person and were one and the same energy. This is definitely soul mate stuff here.

Okay, we have time for another question.

Janine again picked up the cards, shuffled them expertly and placed them in front of me. My mind was reeling. I could hardly think, but finally settled on asking her about the possibility of a previous relationship between Candace and Patricia. I still felt skeptical about a past life involving the two of them and I fully expected that Janine would put the whole thing to rest.

P: Is there a possibility of a relationship in a previous lifetime between the person I recently met and my wife?

With a surprised expression on her face, Janine looked up at me from her cards. Her words almost bowled me over.

J: What about your daughter and this person?

I could hardly believe what I had just heard. How could she know that I even had a daughter, much less my suspicions about a past-life connection between Stacey and Patricia? I finally managed an almost inaudible reply.

P: Uh, quite possibly. I, uh, uh, suspected that there might be.

J: Well, I get that this person certainly has been involved with your daughter. Now usually it's all intertwined, but let's have a look. Okay, now think about your wife and this woman. Cut the cards into three piles and indicate with your left hand, which pile to use.

I quickly made my selection. Janine laid out the cards and began interpreting.

J: Yes. Definitely. Most definitely, and somebody already got this message intuitively. Somebody has had either a dream or an awareness of the other person and what is actually going on. So somebody actually has all the information . . . one of these two people. Have you talked to either one of them about it?

I was shaking. How could she have possibly picked up on Candace's dream? This was too unbelievable. I had to clear my throat before replying.

P: Well, we only joked about it. I wouldn't have believed it.

J: Well, there have definitely been lifetimes between everybody involved here. It's been quite intense, actually. I'm not getting a very pleasant time on some of these lives. There's some sense of a rift somewhere between the two females, but somebody already knows this. It's like one of them has had a dream scenario that relates to that. Somebody has the full information. It feels like your wife might be the one.

There's an awareness of what exactly went on, and they may be in some denial about it. And there's some ego struggle here too. But yeah, there is an awareness and it will heal a lot of things between these two people.

There were some tough times, at least in one lifetime between these two, and it wasn't always pleasant. This is interesting, though; I get that they were both males.

I get that a lot of healing goes on between these two energies that's meant to happen. This is fascinating. But you have to have patience. Over the next six months there seems to be a complete death and rebirth in this whole situation that seems to be quite different than anyone thinks. I get a lot of letting go of guilt and fear. A sense of humor is necessary in this situation, and diplomacy on all sides. And you're right in the middle of it all, *again*.

With those final words, Janine ended the reading. In a dazed state, I thanked her for the session. It was, without doubt, the most remarkable display of psychic intuition I had ever witnessed.

Candace was waiting for me as I opened the door and made my way back into the bookstore. "Are you okay?" she asked. "You look like you've just seen a ghost. How was your reading?"

I managed only a bewildered shrug. "You won't believe it," I whispered. "Wait until you hear the tape."

During our long drive home, we listened to the recording at least three times. Amazed by Janine's accuracy, we talked for hours about the changes taking place in our lives. There was no question about it: we both shared a renewed reverence and respect for the mysteries of life.

15

Affirmation

If there is one thing that I've come to realize over time, it is the more I learn, the more convinced I am how precious little I actually know.

If someone had told me just ten years ago that I would become immersed in a life of spirituality, I would have suggested they go for a drug test. But now I couldn't imagine anything better.

Friends often ask if I have any idea why all of these astonishing things have happened to me. The simple answer is, "I haven't got a clue." It would seem that I must have planned it this way. Or, it could be that—as two different psychics suggested years ago—I had set out a special goal to accomplish in this lifetime, but I was procrastinating, allowing self-doubt and insecurity to defeat my purpose. At the time I had no idea what they were talking about. Perhaps because of my procrastination, my guides and helpers decided to put Plan B into action—the one where they virtually had to hit me over the head to get my attention; the one where I had to be dragged kicking and screaming into territory and beliefs I would not have otherwise accepted. I'm still not sure, but one thing is for certain: I'm forever grateful that they did.

So many inconceivable occurrences have taken place around me that I've come to expect the unexpected. Candace and I often marveled at the steady progression of events and experiences that had been presented to us. There were many times when I couldn't wait for a new day to begin, just to see what would happen next. We were on a remarkable journey, but shortly after we returned from the visit to the Tarot reader, another unexpected piece of the puzzle fell into place.

As winter finally gave way to spring, we looked forward to warmer weather and green grass. While surfing on the Internet we accidentally discovered a place known as the Omega Institute. Located in a beautiful rural area of upstate New York, it was a former boys' camp renovated and updated to provide a large multi-use facility. Advertised as a center for holistic studies, Omega offers a wide variety of spiritual workshops and seminars hosted by many famous authors and teachers.

While Candace and I perused their web site, one particular class caught our attention. Billed as a workshop on soul survival, it was a weekend seminar slated for mid-May. To our delight, one of the main presenters was a favorite author of ours. A prominent psychiatrist, Dr. Brian Weiss had written several best-selling books on the subject of reincarnation and past-life regression. The list included *Many Lives Many Masters, Through Time into Healing, Only Love is Real,* and *Messages from the Masters.* Thinking it would be a wonderful opportunity for a fun weekend, we registered for the workshop and booked our airline tickets.

Omega was everything it promised to be and more. We had a great time listening to the various presentations, but it was Brian Weiss that we had come to see. With his quiet, modest demeanor, Dr. Weiss was every bit the gentle soul we expected him to be. Speaking softly about the importance of love, he radiated genuine caring and trustworthiness. He seemed to practice what he preached.

As part of his presentation, Dr. Weiss announced that he would guide the audience in a group hypnosis session to explore any important past lives that might surface. Even though I had developed a few of my own methods to help others through hypnosis, I personally had very little success in being hypnotized. I'm not sure if I blocked the experience for fear of losing control, but it never seemed to work for me.

The chairs we sat in were comfortable, but I always needed absolute silence to achieve an altered state. With over three hundred people in the room, I expected to be continually distracted by people coughing, clearing their throats, and shuffling about. I didn't give it much chance for success.

Beginning the session with his standard induction into deepening relaxation, Dr. Weiss's soft hypnotic voice lulled the crowd into an eerie expectant silence. I found myself becoming deeply relaxed. Within a short time, I began to notice that his voice was becoming more and more distant, drifting out of my perception. I tried to focus on his fading instructions, but to no avail. Soon there was only silence. My mind awake and alert, I slowly lost all awareness of my body.

Time seemed to stand still. I was lost in my thoughts when I became aware of small jolts of electricity stabbing through my body. My muscles reacted in jerky spasms. Lasting for only seconds, as quickly as the jolts began, they faded away. I started to feel a mounting pressure closing in on me. It was as if my own consciousness was somehow compressing into a small ball. Moments later, I found myself looking down into the top of a bright, golden chalice.

Momentarily bewildered, it took me a few seconds to steady my mind. It seemed as if I was the one holding the chalice. Swirling in the bottom was a small quantity of red wine. It was then that I heard the distinct Latin dialogue of a Catholic Mass. The words echoed around me. I could feel them in my mind and in my mouth—they were my words. *I* was saying them. I seemed to be inside the body of a Catholic priest in the middle of a communion service.

Holding the chalice in my left hand, I watched as my right hand came to rest above the goblet holding a thin, round, white wafer between my index finger and thumb. Who and where was I? I wanted to lift my head to look around the room, but was unable to do so. I saw only what this priest saw as he ceremonially lifted the chalice into the air holding the communion wafer above it. His eyes followed the wafer as he mouthed the memorized words. But his heart and mind wandered, drifting far away—preoccupied.

Focusing more closely on his thoughts and feelings, I became increasingly gripped by an overwhelming crush of hopelessness. I could hardly breathe. It felt like my heart was breaking—and I wanted to know why.

In response to my query, myriad memories instantly downloaded into my conscious mind. For several intense moments I was besieged by an onslaught of emotions. The emotional weight this priest carried was almost unbearable. His heart and, indeed, his very life, lay in the clutches of anguish and despair.

Although this understanding was almost instantly perceived, I'm not sure any words could adequately describe the intensity of the moment. As nearly as I can relate it, this is the story that unfolded in my mind.

Processing his thoughts and memories, I understood the reasons for his, or should I say *my*, desperation. When he/I was a young man, I had fallen helplessly in love with a young woman from a nearby village. We had planned to be married. Our families, however, did not approve of the relationship. I was Catholic and she was Protestant. Finally, due to family pressure, she had broken off the relationship, leaving me in heartbroken desolation. I couldn't imagine how I could possibly live without her. In my grief, I had allowed myself to be talked into leaving the village to join the priesthood.

As these thoughts unraveled, I would catch short intriguing glimpses of a young woman. There seemed to be something familiar about her. Focusing on her energy, a complete image began to form in my mind. The recognition stunned me. It was she! It was the woman I had seen in my dreams, the same woman who had come to me in spirit form while I lay in my bunk at The Monroe Institute.

I followed the chain of events unfolding before me. Several years had passed, and by chance, our paths crossed again. From our first encounter in the streets, our obsession was rekindled. Even though she was now married and I was a priest, we could not resist the temptation of our hearts. We would steal away in secrecy, allowing our passions to carry us to forbidden ecstasy, swearing our undying love.

All of these memories and thoughts flooded into my mind in hardly more than a heartbeat. It was both an instant revelation, and an inner knowing.

Shifting my awareness back to the priest, I felt a numbing despair slowly choking away my life. Continuing mechanically through the ceremony of the Holy Sacrament, I fought for control against the tears of self-pity that burned my eyes, scorching my soul. The guilt of my sin was too much to bear. I had doomed myself to the fires of Hell. As a priest, I found my sin unforgivable. I was trapped between the aching of my heart and the guilt I felt at betraying my church and God. It was all so unfair. Why had I let myself be talked into becoming a priest? Why had she come back into my life?

My dilemma and torment were inescapable. I would be condemned by the church and most certainly by God. In the agony of my guilt, I knew that it would be impossible for us to be together. But I also knew I could no longer live without her.

Suddenly, with a resounding thump, I found myself snapping upright in my chair. The abrupt explosion of another participant coughing directly behind me was all it took to catapult me out of my hypnotic state. Just like that, the vision disappeared.

Frustrated but undeterred I quickly concentrated on reconnecting with this previous life's energy. Within moments I was again floating in a void. Frantically, I tried to home in on the priest's vibration. Minutes ticked by. Then, without warning, I felt my consciousness plummet, and a dizzying burst of energy overtook me. Finally, the darkness evaporated, and I found myself back in the priest's body. Again I felt his crushing desolation and despair.

As my vision opened, I was surprised to find that I was no longer in the middle of the church service. I was outdoors, staring off into distant rolling hills of blue-green grass. My heart was breaking—I seemed to be saying goodbye.

Finally, with tears in my eyes, I spun around. The next thing I knew I was plunging over the edge of a cliff to the rocks and sea below. The shock and sensation of falling was so powerful and frightening, it snapped me out of my trance. In an instant I found myself jerking upright in my chair, my hands clawing the air in front of me.

Opening my eyes, I was thankful the room lay in semidarkness. The session was still underway. No one had seen my flailing arms.

Lost in thought, I sat quietly in my seat waiting for the session to end. The room had been cool, but now I felt sweat trickling down my neck. The powerful scenes played over and over in my mind. I had been a priest who committed suicide. But more importantly, I now knew who the woman was, why I had seen her in my dreams, and why she had come to me in my room at The Monroe Institute.

My sense was that this experience had taken place somewhere in Ireland at least a hundred years ago. Yet, as unbelievable as it seemed, it appeared that my long-lost love was still on the Other Side, apparently still in love, and awaiting my return.

The disturbing episode left me with a jumble of emotions. Torn between the sorrow of this tragic affair and the elation of my discovery, an uneasy melancholy settled over me. There were still too many unresolved issues. Too many questions left unanswered. I realized that it might be some time before I could come to terms with the effects of this revelation.

When the session ended, Candace and I shared our experiences. We marveled at the power of the workshop. Dr. Weiss had truly developed a remarkable technique for uncovering the past to heal the present.

Following our return home from New York, I frequently reflected on the extraordinary events that had taken place, and how they might affect my life. I thought about the young woman I had left behind in another lifetime, and wondered what became of her after my self-inflicted death. One night, about a month later, I had my answer.

As I lay in bed waiting for sleep, fragmentary thoughts about that distant past life in Ireland haunted me. When the hypnagogic images of presleep began to flutter through my mind, I offered a little prayer and again asked my angels to show me what had become of the woman. I had posed the question a number of times before without receiving any kind of response, but this time I seemed more connected.

Within moments of sending out the question, I felt a shift in vibration and in an instant I found myself floating near the ceiling of a rather spacious older home. Wherever it was, the owners must have been fairly well-to-do. Although not overly large, the living room was ornately decorated, containing a large stone fireplace and expensive furnishings. Feeling drawn to the next room, I floated through the wall into an adjacent bedroom. As I came through the other side, my attention was drawn to the body of a woman laid out on top of a bed. I knew instantly that it was the woman I had loved during my life as a priest. A feeling of sadness came over me. I somehow knew that she, too, had taken her own life.

Her long dark hair had been done up in ringlets, meticulously placed on the pillow beneath her to accentuate her ashen but serene face. I contemplated how different she now looked without her normal color, vitality, and beaming eyes.

Laid out on the bed in a beautiful long gown, she still exhibited grace and elegance. Crossed upon her chest, her hands cradled a small golden cross. Her rich, royal blue gown was accented by white and gold lace around the neck and sleeves. Obviously designed for a funeral wake, its long skirt flared out at the bottom, extending past her feet, over the foot of the bed, almost to the floor.

With mixed emotions, I hovered in place, absorbed in the scene, when I became aware of the strangest feelings. Thoughts of Patricia began to permeate my mind. There was no question that the woman on the bed was the one I had loved in that previous lifetime, but I was also receiving strong impressions of Patricia. Their vibrations seemed so much alike. As my confusion grew, I felt a shift in consciousness and I was back in my bed.

Opening my eyes, I lay back, staring at the ceiling, contemplating all that had taken place. Although the journey had given me some answers, it had created just as many questions. Why had I been receiving impressions of Patricia? Was there some sort of connection between the two of them? Could they actually be from the same soul energy? It didn't seem possible. If Patricia was the reincarnated energy of the woman from Ireland, how could she still be on the Other Side in her previous form? The questions hung in the air, but the answers weren't evident. Eventually I fell asleep.

When morning arrived, I awoke with the answers still beyond my grasp. "Someday," I thought, "I'll get to the bottom of it, even if I have to die trying." The irony of this sleepy statement made me chuckle. It occurred to me that it might indeed be the only way I'd uncover the rest of the story.

While the lessons of my life slowly unfolded, time itself was quickly passing. I had a job to do. After months, perhaps years, of procrastination,

I could put it off no longer. I sat down to begin the long task of writing this book.

I wish I could say that writing has been an easy job, that my angels came through as they said they would in the Washington airport. But that might be stretching it a wee bit. To begin with, I wasn't even sure where to begin.

As I started going through my journals containing years of notes, it became not so much a question of whether I had enough material for the book, but rather what would I leave out. The easiest part was the title. I already knew that. But there were so many revelations, incidents, and insights. How could I pick and choose?

After mapping out a chapter outline, I did the next best thing. I lay in bed, opened my consciousness to the Other Side, and asked for help. Within moments, I felt a wave of energy—and the download began. It was like a floodgate had opened. Practically overwhelmed by the flow of information, I realized that if I was already overloading while in an altered state, I had little hope of processing everything during normal consciousness. The angels, however, were probably more aware of what I could handle than I was. As I came out of my meditation, their message was clear. Before each writing session, I was to open myself to guidance, taking it one step at a time.

All of this, however, was easier said than done. In my busy life, it wasn't always easy to find the time to write, and often the circumstances were not ideal. Sometimes the words and information would flow. Other times I might sit and stare at the same paragraph for two hours.

Eventually, I developed a bit of a routine. I found that my most productive sessions came when I first took the time to meditate and offer a prayer for help before I sat down to write. Strangely, I also discovered that my best effort was when I was physically tired or sleepy. I seemed to be able to make a better connection with my more creative side in the quiet of early morning. Consequently, I frequently found myself working through the night until dawn.

The times when I did find myself connected to guidance were wonderful. Concepts and words would form in my mind faster than I could type. I regularly dropped into a deep altered state while sitting at my computer. It was in this profound, focused level of consciousness that my memories returned to life. When this happened, the detail of past events was startlingly clear. Sometimes I became so absorbed that time would simply disappear. Frequently moved to tears, I worked my way through the powerful emotions that accompanied my memories.

Of particular significance, however, were the typing sessions recalling my many visits with Meldor. Often, in a trance, typing while practically unconscious, I would peck away until four or five in the morning before falling exhausted into bed. On my next return to the computer, I was repeatedly amazed at the words that appeared before me. Although I knew the messages well, the diction and words weren't mine; they were Meldor's.

Overall, the experience of writing this book has been an adventure in itself—mystical, gratifying, and very healing.

Now, as I near the end of my account, I am having difficulty finding the right words to convey how thankful I am for the wonderful lessons and blessings I've been given. There have been some tough times, and some great times, but I probably wouldn't change a minute of it. It's been a remarkable journey, an incredible education. But I have still so much to learn, so much more to experience.

As never before, I have learned to love life and everything in it. Hardly a day passes in which I am not reminded of the power of the human spirit, and our relationship to God and to each other. We are not merely the bodies we occupy. We are pure indestructible energy. More powerful than we can even imagine, we—and all the things we experience—live forever. As so many others have discovered, there is but one thing, one essential element that binds everyone and everything together. And that is the power of *love*.

Throughout my life, there has been one main revelation—the single most important message I have ever received—that puts it all into perspective. At the end of our lives, when our bodies finally release us back to the spirit world, it won't matter one little bit who won or who lost, or how rich or famous we became. The only thing that will truly matter is how we treated others along the way. That's the importance of love.

Perhaps the toughest lesson of the human experience, *the reality of love* can sometimes be the most difficult to fully embrace. When we are caught up in the struggle for survival, when seemingly awful things happen to us or others around us, when we are hurt or annoyed by the things other people do, we must strive to see past our biggest fear—the human illusion of separation. There is no real separation. *We are all one!*

We need only to try to remember, to look deeply within ourselves and within others to see the beauty of the unified soul that we all share with God.

If there were any advice that I could offer, it would be this: Don't hold back! Love for all you're worth! That's what hearts are for. Having your heart broken a thousand times is still far better than not having loved at all. That would be the greatest tragedy.

Life is a wonderful gift, so live it to the fullest. Take every single opportunity to hug someone. Take the time to hug your kids, your parents, your brothers and sisters, friends and even strangers. And take the time to look closely into their eyes. Perhaps, when you least expect it, you just might feel a fluttering sensation in your heart and a deep stirring within your soul. You might find yourself looking into the *eyes of an angel.*

As for me, my journey continues with new experiences and revelations almost daily. Where it will take me, and where it will end, I have no idea. I do, however, know one thing for sure. Life is an addictive evolution of steps, lessons, and wonderful mysteries to solve. I can't even imagine how much more I need to learn. But I can hardly wait to find out.

Eyes of an Angel

Through shaded eyes we view the world
Present, past, and future swirl
Only fleeting glimpse there revealed
The mysteries of life concealed

Though evidence in abundance shouts
Thoughts of creation are lined with doubt
Life's grand design in darkness robed
Hints of spirit left unprobed

In days of science and truth unclear
Man and religion fraught with fear
Purpose and destiny remain obscured
Life without meaning long endured

Promises of paradise, and wonders to behold
Man-made dogma, imposed upon the fold
But in frightened hearts there flickers still
Desire for truth that guilt can't kill

So is it still by chance or sad intent
Destruction looms with our consent
While thoughts, the thief within our heads
Leave us fearful in our beds?

Then steadfast courage and honor bequest
The hand of God we'll squarely test
Until lust for battle be lost in the fray
And restless spirit lights the way

Though the stock of angels be divine
Must we yet refuse to see the sign?
Why is it only when troubles abound
He finds us kneeling on the ground?

When horrors plague our daily bread
And grieving thoughts we cannot shed
Is it then we pray our Lord to see?
Shallow promises made in desperate plea

Then comes an angel, eyes ablaze
Heart secure and love unfazed
A glimpse of what was meant to be
Pure light upon reality

And oh what joys will they evoke
When God and angels first uncloak
Life's greatest treasures gleaned at last
Our hearts and souls in light are cast

The message comes from Heaven clear
His wrath was never lent to fear
You see, God has only love to give
It's man distorts the way we live

But in angel eyes love grows complete
While strong hands tremble in defeat
The truth of God is soon revealed
It's through our hearts that we are healed

And now in slumber's sweet delight
Dream angels carry us in flight
When there are no more souls to mend
Who is the angel God will send?

Though late, we find that in the end
Matters not if we break or bend
It wasn't God we were meant to see
For only love can set us free

If it's proof you seek, there's no denying
The truth is only found in dying
But in search of God, and where to begin
You need look no further than within

—Paul Elder

About the Author

A former long-term mayor of a small city, Paul Elder has spent a lifetime studying human nature from a unique perspective. He is a survivor of two near-death experiences: a drowning at the age of 12 and a heart attack while playing hockey at the age of 41. Along with the trauma and subsequent beauty of death came a series of spontaneous spiritual events—events that would rock his world, turning his belief system upside down, leaving him with some profound insights as to the true nature and ultimate purpose of human life.

After spending nearly a decade as a Radio and Television news reporter, he ventured into a career of politics and business spanning more than 20 years. Forever grateful for his near-death experiences, his spiritual insights molded and deeply affected his approach to politics, business, and life.

Now retired, and living on Vancouver Island, British Columbia, Paul spends his time writing, teaching, and speaking throughout the United States and Canada on the phenomenon of near-death and out-of-body experiences.

Thank you for reading *Eyes of an Angel*. Hampton Roads is proud to publish an extensive array of books on the topics discussed in *Eyes of an Angel*, topics such as out-of-body experiences, spiritual guidance, near-death experiences, the exploration of other dimensions, past lives, and more. Please take a look at the following selection or visit us anytime on the web: www.hrpub.com.

Soul Journeys
My Guided Tours through the Afterlife
Rosalind A. McKnight

In *Soul Journeys*, McKnight relates her explorations of the afterlife with a being she calls Radiant Lady. With Radiant Lady as her spiritual guide, McKnight explores and reports on the non-physical energies in the afterlife. *Soul Journeys* reveals the inner workings of the other dimensions including the afterlife and emphasizes that all of us have spirit guides we can work with at any time.

Paperback • 272 pages • ISBN 1-57174-413-4
$14.95

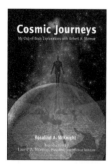

Cosmic Journeys
My Out-of-Body Explorations with Robert A. Monroe
Rosalind A. McKnight
Foreword by Laurie Monroe

McKnight was one of the first and most successful out-of-body research explorers to work with Robert Monroe. In *Cosmic Journeys* she recounts the early days of The Monroe Institute and her sessions in the famed "black box."

Paperback • 304 pages • ISBN 1-57174-123-2
$13.95

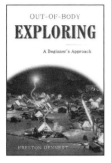

Out-of-Body Exploring
A Beginner's Approach
Preston Dennett

Novice, intermediate, or expert—anyone interested in the spiritual art of astral travel will benefit from Dennett's 20 years of out-of-body traveling. Including his initial forays into expanded consciousness, he shares the many techniques he experimented with, and discusses the people and sights he encountered. Plus, he offers tips on how to go reliably out-of-body, and how to control and maintain this enhanced awareness for extended periods.

Paperback • 200 pages • ISBN 1-57174-409-6 • $13.95

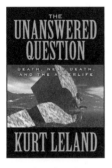

The Unanswered Question
Death, Near-Death, and the Afterlife
Kurt Leland

Seasoned astral traveler Leland explores the deepest reaches of consciousness in an attempt to answer the great question: Is a near-death experience the same as real death? What he finds will fascinate and enlighten you, and more importantly, convince you that everything you think you know about Near-Death may be dead wrong.

Paperback • 496 pages • ISBN 1-57174-299-9 • $16.95

Otherwhere
*A Field Guide to Nonphysical Reality
for the Out-of-Body Traveler*
Kurt Leland

A luminous travelogue of the ethereal world we travel to in dreams, OBEs, and NDEs. Noted psychic Leland guides you to various points of interest in this other-world including alternate realities, the living archives, and offers translation tables that categorize nonphysical energies by function rather than form.

Paperback • 288 pages • ISBN 1-57174-241-7 • $13.95

Ordered to Return
My Life After Dying
George G. Ritchie, Jr., M.D.

In 1943, Army private George Ritchie died of pneumonia. Nine minutes later, he came back profoundly changed. Here, Ritchie recounts one of the most fascinating NDEs ever recorded—and then tells what happened later, including the real miracles that he has seen in his years as a doctor.

Paperback • 184 pages • ISBN 1-57174-096-1
$12.95

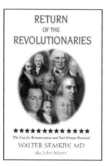

Return of the Revolutionaries
The Case for Reincarnation and Soul Groups Reunited
Walter Semkiw, M.D.

Presenting evidence that facial structure, personalities, and peer groups stay the same lifetime after lifetime, Semkiw shows how America's revolutionary heroes are reemerging today as the force behind America's spiritual rebirth. Semkiw even includes hundreds of startling photos and clues to tracking your own past lives.

Paperback • 464 pages • ISBN 1-57174-342-1
$16.95

Soul Agreements
Dick Sutphen with Tara Sutphen

Your karmic road map was programmed at a soul level before you were born. Soul agreements established how your life's relationships, career directions, and major triumphs and challenges would unfold. Explore your past lives and your destiny and learn how you can create your own reality.

Paperback • 192 pages • ISBN 1-57174-442-8
$14.95

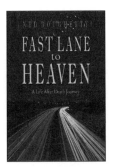

Fast Lane to Heaven
A Life-after-Death Journey
Ned Dougherty

In the midst of a heated argument, Ned Dougherty died—only to be reborn from his self-destructive lifestyle into the divine light of salvation. That unforgettable near-death experience included meeting both the Supreme Being and the Archangel Michael, as well as with an enigmatic Lady of Light, who set Ned on a 15-year mission to communicate her urgent message to the world.

Voted "NDE Book of the Year" by near-death.com

**Paperback • 304 pages • ISBN 1-57174-336-7
$15.95**

Hampton Roads Publishing Company

... for the evolving human spirit

HAMPTON ROADS PUBLISHING COMPANY publishes books on a variety of subjects, including metaphysics, spirituality, health, visionary fiction, and other related topics.

For a copy of our latest trade catalog, call toll-free, 800-766-8009, or send your name and address to:

HAMPTON ROADS PUBLISHING COMPANY, INC.
1125 STONEY RIDGE ROAD • CHARLOTTESVILLE, VA 22902
e-mail: hrpc@hrpub.com • www.hrpub.com